Verbal Learning Research and the Technology of Written Instruction

Verbal Learning Research and the Technology of Written Instruction

Edited by

Ernst Z. Rothkopf and Paul E. Johnson

TEACHERS COLLEGE PRESS

Teachers College, Columbia University

Figures in the paper by Lawrence M. Stolurow originally appeared in *Air Force human engineering, personnel, and training research,* Publication 516, Committee on Military Psychology, National Academy of Sciences–National Research Council, Washington, D.C., 1958.

MANUFACTURED IN THE UNITED STATES OF AMERICA

Contents

v

Preface

For three days during May 1966, a small group of scientists lived, ate, and drank together in a comfortable house high on a bluff above the Hudson River, in Riverside, New York. The participants were about equally divided between researchers in verbal learning and educational psychologists concerned with instructional technology. The meeting was a very literal step toward establishing a dialogue between the verbal learning laboratory and the world of instructional research. The present book is one result of this dialogue.

The symposium was made possible through financial support from the Office of Naval Research under Grant No. Nonr N00014-66-C0038. Special thanks are due to Dr. Glenn L. Bryan for his help and encouragement.

The conference site, the stately Greyston House, was provided by Teachers College, Columbia University, through the good offices of Dr. Edward J. Green and Dean Arthur W. Foshay.

Miss Lois C. Schwartz made most of the physical arrangements for the symposium, and Mrs. Ernst Z. Rothkopf gave very generously of her time toward editing the manuscripts. Their valuable assistance is hereby gratefully acknowledged.

For various reasons a number of papers presented at the symposium were not included in this book. In some cases the authors did not wish to wait for a manuscript of all the papers to be prepared, and so they published elsewhere. Others, whose ideas were in a state of flux, preferred not to publish their papers without further data and study. Each participant, however, through discussion and debate, contributed to the success of the symposium.

PARTICIPANTS IN THE 1966 SYMPOSIUM ON VERBAL LEARNING RESEARCH AND THE TECHNOLOGY OF WRITTEN INSTRUCTION

Richard Anderson, University of Illinois
John R. Bormuth, University of Chicago
Vincent N. Campbell, American Institutes for Research, Palo Alto
Burton H. Cohen, Lafayette College
Edmund B. Coleman, University of Texas, El Paso
Murray Glanzer, New York University
Robert Glaser, University of Pittsburgh
Albert E. Goss, Douglass College, Rutgers — The State University
Edward Green, Columbia University
H. W. Gustafson, Bell Telephone Laboratories
James G. Holland, University of Pittsburgh
Neal F. Johnson, Ohio State University
Paul E. Johnson, University of Minnesota
George R. Klare, Ohio University
Arthur A. Lumsdaine, University of Washington
Walter H. MacGinitie, Teachers College, Columbia University
Edwin Martin, University of Michigan
Max V. Mathews, Bell Telephone Laboratories
Barbara S. Musgrave, Smith College
Slater E. Newman, North Carolina State University
Joan L. Prentice, Indiana University
Sheldon Rosenberg, University of Illinois, Chicago
Ernst Z. Rothkopf, Bell Telephone Laboratories
Lawrence M. Stolurow, Harvard University
William S. Verplanck, University of Tennessee
Wendell W. Weaver, Campbell College

Introduction

The symposium on which this report is based was motivated by the belief that scientific understanding of how man learns through language will some day help in the development and use of written instructional materials. The main purpose of the symposium was to take stock of the more promising findings and concepts about verbal learning processes in order to see whether they had any practical implications that should be pursued. A second purpose was to encourage a dialogue between the verbal learning laboratory and the world of instructional research.

There appears to have been relatively little interaction in the past between those doing research on verbal learning processes and those concerned with instruction. This is best illustrated in the rhetoric of programmed instruction, which has been drawn to a remarkable degree from the work on operant conditioning rather than verbal learning, despite the fact that many self-instructional programs are largely composed of verbal materials.

One reason for the lack of interactions between the two areas may be that verbal learning studies have during the past two decades been a fairly parochial enterprise. They have been marked by the standardization of techniques from which a very substantial literature has grown that deals largely with problems peculiarly associated with these techniques. This "inward turning" of research appears to have been accompanied by a decided weakening of the virile intellectual imperialism that is usually associated with growing fields of knowledge.

It would be superfluous to detail the general intellectual and economic importance of written instruction in American education. In the present context, instructional material refers to the development and use of a great variety of written materials. Among these are textbooks, certain self-instructional programs, magazines, and pamphlets, the alphabetic outputs of computers whether printed on paper or displayed on a cathode ray tube, microfilm, writing in films and on film strips, and slides. All such materials share the characteristic that they use an alphabetic code for something that resembles language.

Written instruction serves as an excellent source for concrete illustrations of unsolved problems in instructional research. Another reason for the choice of this emphasis is the belief that written materials have characteristics that make them peculiarly responsive to rational methods for their production and use. Most important among these is that they are documents; i.e., they have tangible form. As a consequence, principles of instruction can be incorporated into them in a concrete manner.

Written materials are important to the psychologist and educational psychologist because assertions about learning cannot be tested in instructional systems that are not stable, i.e., those that are subject to change from undefined variables. Nor can principles for effective instruction be easily implemented in systems that do not respond faithfully to the intent of the instructional designer. The characteristic of an instructional system that makes it useful for systematic experimentation is the consistency with which it delivers the instructional communication. Teachers, speaking extemporaneously or from notes to a class, are not a consistent system in the present sense, nor are they stable with regard to the prediction of instructional outcomes. Written materials, on the other hand, provide a reasonably stable instructional configuration.

Written materials have another property that is conducive to rational development and systematic experimentation; namely, changes can be incorporated into them by an iterative process, i.e., editing. Moreover, modifications by the editor are simpler with written material than other media such as videotape or film. The reason is that these modifications involve writing. Most instructional editors know how to do this. Editorial amendments to films or videotape, on the other hand, sometimes require complex instrumentation or camera work.

Another important attribute of written instructional materials is that they can be centrally developed and produced. This characteristic has, in other instances, favored the manufacture of inexpensive, good quality materials and has provided good prospects for technological inputs. At the same time, however, the book publishing industry has little or no tradition for the systematic development of such materials. Rather, its chief concern has been selection, printing, packaging, and distribution. The hope that the publishing industry would adopt technological approaches to the production of instructional materials was one of the stimuli that prompted the organization of this symposium.

The collection of papers comprising the book is divided into four main sections. The first section, entitled "Verbal Learning and Connected Discourse," contains three papers that describe acquisition processes in terms of concepts derived from the laboratory study of learning. The second section, "Stimulus Measures and Characterizations of Performance," deals mainly with empirical efforts to characterize the difficulty of prose materials and the quality of performance that results from the exposure to such materials. The third section, entitled "Motivational and Attention-Like Factors," includes three papers concerned with the role of learner variables. The final section, "An Addendum from Computer Technology," deals with the role of the computer in written technology.

All papers except three are followed by remarks from one or two other participants in the symposium. The lively disputes that invariably followed each paper proved very illuminating. They have not been included in this volume because the editors felt that they were not sufficiently well organized to warrant the required extra space. Instead, general discussions by three distinguished scientists have been appended to the end of the book.

PART I

VERBAL LEARNING
AND CONNECTED DISCOURSE

Paired Associates and Connected Discourse in the Acquisition of Knowledge [1]

ALBERT E. GOSS

Douglass College, Rutgers — The State University

The nature and origin of knowledge can be considered the major concern of many of those philosophers, philosopher-psychologists, and psychologist-philosophers from Hobbes and Descartes to Lotze and Bain, who are considered the "modern" ancestors of near-contemporary and contemporary psychology and psychologists. However, beginning with Wundt, accelerated by Watson, formalized by Hull, and perpetuated by various contemporary "S–R" psychologists (i.e., neobehaviorists), so the charge goes, the psychology these systematists proposed, and many of the psychologists they trained and influenced, have increasingly ignored, even denied issues of the nature and origin of knowledge. Many have made this charge, in various guises. Beginning before World War I, and extending to the recent past, the "original" Gestalt psychologists — Wertheimer (1924), Koffka (1935, pp. 3–105), and Kohler (1929) — were persistent and sharp critics. Among other prominent critics of these decades were Bartlett (1932), Lewin (1935, pp. 1–65), and Tolman (1932, pp. 3–22, 319–370).

Among the more prominent critics of the last few years are Miller, Galanter, and Pribram (1960), Bruner (1965), Chomsky (1965), and Deese (1965). The particular contemporary S–R

3

psychologists named or referred to indirectly by these critics range from Spence and Skinner to Postman and Underwood. However, homogeneous as S–R psychologists may sometimes appear to their critics, Skinner (1968) has been among the most severe critics of the utility of most research on verbal learning.

The interests of the early behaviorists in those phenomena typically subsumed under "knowledge," and the general nature of their analyses of those phenomena, are described elsewhere (Goss, 1961a). Noted there also are the general nature and intent of Hull's (1930, 1931) analyses of phenomena of knowledge and purpose. During the 1930s and 1940s, Hull did temporarily set aside his interests in and analyses of these phenomena. He did so in order to formulate better theoretical analyses of acquisition, extinction, and other phenomena that occur in what he considered simple or elementary situations. However, the existence of phenomena of knowledge was neither denied nor ignored in Hull's overall plan of theorizing and research. Once the principles required to explain phenomena obtained in elementary situations had reached reasonably satisfactory form, Hull then extended them (1953) in some measure to more complex situations and phenomena. Furthermore, several of Hull's students and collaborators, such as Gibson (1940), Miller and Dollard (1941, pp. 69–90), Dollard and Miller (1950, pp. 97–124, 281–328), Osgood (1953, pp. 392–412, 610–727), Sears (1936), and Spence (1936, 1937, 1950, 1958), either proposed extensions to more complex situations and phenomena, or dealt with knowledge and related phenomena directly. Some did both.

Skinner's (1953, 1957) exercises in the analysis of the nature and origin of various phenomena often subsumed under "knowledge" are well known. If the contributions of Hull and his students and collaborators — Osgood excepted — were ignored, Skinner's contributions were probably overemphasized (e.g., Carroll, 1962; Staats and Staats, 1963) and overcriticized (e.g., Chomsky, 1959).

Neither Hull and those influenced by him, nor Skinner, may prove to have been substantially or even slightly correct in their analyses of the nature and origin of knowledge. That is not the thesis here. The thesis is instead that they denied neither the existence nor the importance of these phenomena. Nor did they neglect them. The relatively simple classical conditioning, instrumental conditioning, and two-choice spatial and nonspatial discrimination situations favored by Hull, Spence, Miller, Skinner, and others differ markedly from those situations used to teach students substantive knowledge of various areas. The differences are in characteristics of stimuli and responses, in their number and interrelationships, and in ways of presenting stimuli and of recording responses. These differences in appearance, content, complexity, and method give a surface plausibility to the erroneous charge of denial or neglect of phenomena of knowledge by these theorists, and by many of their students and collaborators.

But the same charge of denial or neglect of phenomena of knowledge is directed frequently at those who employ stimuli and responses whose characteristics, numbers, interrelationships, and manner of presentation and of recording do not differ so markedly from those of the situations or tasks typically employed to teach students knowledge of substantive areas. A refutation of this charge was developed (Goss, 1965b) in detail elsewhere for one almost universal kind of knowledge, which is labeled here "classificatory knowledge." The basis of this refutation was that diverse homologies exist between component structures of classificatory knowledge and the structures of typical paired-associates situations.

In the present paper, the more important features of those homologies are repeated. Also mentioned again are some of the factors that probably underlie the charge that theory and data on paired-associates learning have little or no pertinence for acquiring knowledge about any substantive area. The first general objective of this paper, however, is the specification of the general nature of scientific and other systematic knowledge and how the general nature of such knowledge relates to conventional formats of presentation for written instruction and to common or possible laboratory situations. Within this general objective, the subsidiary objectives are description of relationships among the several formats of presentation for written instruction, and description of relationships between each of these formats and common or possible laboratory situations.

Description of relationships between formats of presentation for written instruction and common or possible laboratory situations is a means to the second general objective of the present paper. This objective is detailed consideration of similarities in the structures or patterns of component relationships of those laboratory situations labeled "paired associates" and those labeled "connected discourse" or "discourse." Once similarities in structures of relationships are delineated, the two kinds of situations can be compared with respect to other classes of variables. In turn, paradigms for conceptualizing and for investigating transfer from one kind of situation to the other can be considered.

When structural and other ties between paired-associates situations and connected discourse situations have been described, various ways of applying explanatory concepts and principles discovered and organized by means of these laboratory situations to "production and use of instructional materials" can be examined. As these three general objectives are explored, hopefully a fourth general objective is also achieved. This objective is demonstration that, indirectly or directly, many of the concepts and principles discovered and organized by so-called S–R psychologists are pertinent to an understanding of the nature and origin of knowledge.

NATURE OF KNOWLEDGE AND ITS REPRESENTATION

One kind of knowledge of particular concern herein comprises scientific or systematic classificatory arrangements or the coexistence of properties. Another kind of knowledge is observed or assumed functional relationships between and among variables and categories with empirical reference. A distinction between classificatory arrangements and functional relationships involving empirical reference is somewhat forced. But the distinction is convenient and has the sanction of convention. Although mathematics and logic also appear under functional relationships, such knowledge is substantially ignored here.

Knowledge does not appear as an epiphenomenal shadow. Typically it is presented in "written" (printed, typed, hand-printed, handwritten, etc.) form. There are several conventional formats for written presentation. Among these are laboratory situations or tasks that have been or might be used to investigate the learning of patterns of stimulus-response relationships that are homologous with the patterns of relationships of some kinds of knowledge. Learning is employed here as subsuming more specific phenomena of acquisition, extinction and spontaneous recovery, retention, and transfer, including proaction and retro-action. Of particular concern are the relationships among the several formats of presentation for written instruction, and description of the relationships between each of these formats and each of the common or possible laboratory situations.

Relationships Among Formats for Written Instruction

The most common format of presentation of knowledge in written instruction might be labeled textual exposition. Loosely, textual exposition involves words and sometimes symbols arranged in sentences, paragraphs, sections, and chapters. There may be headings of varying degrees of generality and explicitness. Conventional textbooks and workbooks, programmed textbooks, and programs for teaching machines are more specific variations on textual exposition. In addition to presenting the knowledge of a specific substantive area that is to be learned, each format might include provisions for testing extent of acquisition of that knowledge. The tests might also be separate.

Often, tables, graphs, diagrams, and mathematical, logical expressions parallel each other, or are interposed between successive parts of textual expositions. Occasionally, as in handbooks, these formats are used with little or no accompanying text. Unlike textual exposition, these formats involve little or nothing that could be considered words arranged in sentences, paragraphs, sections, and chapters. Words are often replaced by lines and other symbols. Some words, particularly logical terms such as "and" and "or" may even be replaced by arrangement into headings and subheadings, columns and rows. Ideally, of course, elements of tables, graphs, diagrams, and mathe-

matical, logical expressions with empirical reference, and relationships among these elements, correspond with the words,
phrases, sentences, paragraphs, and perhaps larger units of text.
These actual or possible correspondences are indicated by the
double-headed arrows. Similarly, there may be correspondence
between elements of tables and their interrelationships and elements and relationships of graphs, diagrams, and mathematical,
logical expressions. Such correspondence may hold for elements
and relationships of each of the latter three formats with respect
to each other. For brevity here, these correspondences, as indicated by the double-headed arrows in figure 1 (page 10), are
taken for granted.

Tables, graphs, diagrams, and mathematical, logical expressions might have several advantages over textual exposition.
One advantage is elimination of distracting trivial words, phrases,
and sentences that waste both space and time. Another advantage
is a reduction in time and effort to meet often ambiguous criteria of adequacy of style in terms of novelty and vividness of
words and of variations in length and form of sentences. A
third advantage is greater assurance of close proximity in space
and time of those elements that should be together. In diagrams,
for example, reasonable spatial and temporal congruence may
be achieved between elements and relationships of the diagrams
on the one hand and elements and relationships of the object
or situation referred to by the diagram on the other.

Column and row headings and subheadings of tables permit
systematic search and systematic synthesis or analysis more
rapidly than do most textual expositions. Often, the same advantage may be obtained from graphs, diagrams, and mathematical, logical expressions. Often, too, column and row headings
and subheadings of tables constitute "conceptual schemes" that
should facilitate acquisition and retention of more specific relationships through one or more of the means suggested elsewhere (Goss, 1961c, p. 52).

Tables, graphs, diagrams, and mathematical, logical expressions, however, may have disadvantages of unfamiliarity and of
omission of critical elements and relationships or considerations.

For the novice especially they may seem artificial. For the particular item(s) of knowledge to be presented, they may not be as simple and clear as possible.

Table 1

"Structure" of Classificatory or Coexistential Knowledge in an Incomplete Tabular Summary of Information About Insects

Name		Order
Common	Scientific (Family)	
Long-Horned Grasshoppers	Tettigoniidae	Orthoptera (Straight-wings)
Short-Horned Grasshoppers	Acrididae	
Click Beetles	Elateridae	Coleoptera (Sheath-wings)
Blister Beetles	Meloidae	

Table 1 illustrates the presentation of classificatory or coexistential knowledge in a tabular format. The particular substantive area is classification of insects. The column headings (name, order) and subheadings (common, scientific) of this table can be regarded as a conceptual scheme or structure within which many important aspects of knowledge about members of particular classes of insects can be organized. The table could be elaborated to include physical characteristics or "dimensions" (form, color, size, etc.) of whole insects or parts thereof and the nature of relationships among the parts. The table could be elaborated further to include features of life cycles, reproduction, and other physiological and behavioral phenomena. The same conceptual scheme and specific information about insects of particular orders could be and often are presented by means of textual exposition.

Figure 1 illustrates the presentation of knowledge considered here as functional relationships with empirical reference in a diagram format or, more precisely, in a format that combines a diagram and mathematical expressions.

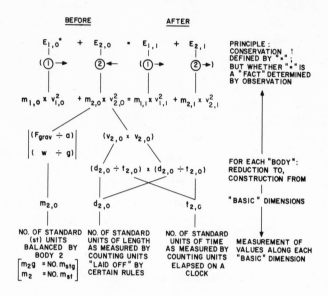

Fig. 1. "Functional relationships" illustrated by the concepts and relationships (conceptual structure) of the principle of the conservation of energy.

Formats for Written Instruction and Laboratory Situations

The kinds of laboratory situations of immediate concern here are those commonly labeled "paired associates." The emphasis on paired-associates situations reflects several considerations. First, they are of greater current interest and have provided data on learning phenomena of greater range and depth than any other kind of verbal learning situation. Second, there is more explicit and complete development of paradigms for transfer with paired-associates situations than with any other kind of verbal learning situations. Third, there is the seeming superiority of paired-associates situations as a starting point for understanding acquisition and other phenomena with an experimental, analytical unit whose elements approximate a manipulatively separable "single" stimulus (stimulus member, item, term) and a "single" (stimulus for) response (response member, item, term). A fourth consideration is the possibility of substantially eliminating the influence on learning of rules of some grammar, scientific or otherwise. However, paired-associates situations can be contrived whose stimulus-response relationships presumably reflect the rules of some grammar, scientific or otherwise (see, e.g., Martin and Jones, 1965; and Martin, Davidson, and Williams, 1965). A fifth, and perhaps the most important, consideration is the possibility of elaboration from the more elementary and the manipulatively more flexible paired-associates situations to increasingly close approximations of other laboratory situations.[2]

Basic and Derived Paired-Associates Situations. As shown in table 2, four basic or general paired-associates situations can

Table 2

Stimulus-Response Elements and Relationships of Initial and Terminal Trial(s) of Four Basic Patterns of Pairing of Stimulus Members and Response Members of Paired-Associates Units Presented Under an Anticipation Format

Pattern of Pairing	Initial Relationships		Terminal Relationships	
	Stimulus Members	Response Members and Recognition Responses	Stimulus Members and Anticipations	Response Members and Recognition Responses
1:1 (Conventional, Identification)	S_{11}	$S_{12}-R_{12}$	$S_{11}-R'_{12}$	$S_{12}-R_{12}$
	S_{21}	$S_{22}-R_{22}$	$S_{21}-R'_{22}$	$S_{22}-R_{22}$
n:1 (Convergent, Concept Formation, Stimulus Equivalence)	S_{11}	$S_{12}-R_{12}$	$S_{11}-R'_{12}$	$S_{12}-R_{12}$
	S_{21}	$S_{12}-R_{12}$	$S_{21}-R'_{12}$	$S_{12}-R_{12}$
1:n (Divergent, Conflict, Response Hierarchy, Response Equivalence, Meaning and Meaningfulness)	S_{11}	$S_{12}-R_{12}$	$S_{11}-R'_{22}$	$S_{12}-R_{12}$
	S_{11}	$S_{22}-R_{22}$	$S_{11}-R'_{12}$	$S_{22}-R_{22}$
n:n (Simple Structure, Net)	S_{11}	$S_{12}-R_{12}$	$S_{11}-R'_{22}$	$S_{12}-R_{12}$
	S_{21}	$S_{12}-R_{12}$	$S_{21}-R'_{22}$	$S_{12}-R_{12}$
	S_{11}	$S_{22}-R_{22}$	$S_{11}-R'_{12}$	$S_{22}-R_{22}$
	S_{21}	$S_{22}-R_{22}$	$S_{21}-R'_{12}$	$S_{22}-R_{22}$

be distinguished. These situations differ with respect to the pattern of pairing of stimulus and response members. Both are indicated by S with R for recognition responses to response members and R' for anticipation of these responses. The first subscript indicates the particular stimulus member, response member, recognition response, or anticipation response. The second subscript indicates the function with 1 for stimulus members and 2 for response members. When the numbers differ, the stimuli are different; when the numbers are the same, the stimuli are identical. For each pattern both initial and terminal or criterial stimulus-response relationships are shown.

With the 1:1 pattern of pairing, each different stimulus is accompanied by a different stimulus for responses. The 1:1 pattern, conventional for paired-associates learning, is also called "identification learning." To limit paired-associates situations to the 1:1 pattern is unduly restrictive and without historical sanction. The apparent first, or co-first, use of paired associates in the laboratory (Calkins, 1894, 1896) was with lists whose units exemplified both 1:1 and 1:2 patterns. The latter pattern is a special case of the 1:n pattern in which each unit consists of a single stimulus member and two or more response members. The 1:n pattern might also be labeled divergent, conflict, response hierarchy, response equivalence, or meaning and meaningfulness. It has also been labeled S–R$_1$ and S–R$_2$, or probabilistic (Voss, Thompson, and Keegan, 1959).

Two or more stimulus members may be paired with one response member. Labeled n:1 in table 2, this third pattern is the critical feature of concept-formation situations (Goss, 1961b). Other labels are convergent, stimulus equivalence, or S$_1$–R, S$_2$–R (Wittlinger and Voss, 1964). A fourth pattern, labeled n:n, involves units in which two or more stimulus members are each paired with two or more response members. It might be called a "structure" or "net."

Specific paired-associates situations can be constructed that include two or more of these patterns of pairing simultaneously. Also, 1:1 and 1:n patterns can be combined in relationships of stimulus members that are compounds of two elements and response members that are elements (L. R. Peterson, 1956). These patterns can be separated for test trials with elements of the stimulus members alone. By the use of stimulus members that are compounds of two or more elements and of response members that are elements of compounds of elements, many different superimposed or derived patterns can be generated. The component patterns can be separated for test trials with elements alone or with compounds of fewer elements (Goss, 1962, 1964b).

Homologies Between Paired-Associates Situations and the Tabular Format. As noted previously, table 1 illustrates the presentation of classificatory or coexistential knowledge in a tabular format. The relationships of the elements of table 1 *as a whole* do not correspond exactly either with the relationships of the four basic paired-associates situations in table 2, or with those of any relatively simple combination of these basic situations. But to deal with table 1 as a whole is both unprofitable and unrealistic. It is unprofitable because component patterns are overlooked. It is unrealistic because it is doubtful that the relationships of table 1 are either ordinarily acquired or ordinarily used as a whole.

Among the stimuli in the three columns of table 1 that are designated "name, common," "name, scientific," and "order," it is possible to distinguish $1:1$, $1:n$ and $n:1$ patterns of pairings of terms in one column with terms in another column. Specifically, the terms in the columns headed "Name, Common" and "Name, Scientific" are paired $1:1$; the terms in each of these columns are paired $2:1$ (or $n:1$, $n=2$) with the terms in the column headed "Order"; and the terms in the latter column are paired $1:2$ (or $1:n$, $n=2$) with the terms in each of the former two columns.

As noted above, the column headings and subheadings of table 1 can be regarded as a conceptual scheme or structure within which values with respect to characteristics of individual objects or events are located, arranged, represented, or organized. More generally, either column headings and subheadings or row headings and subheadings or both can be regarded as conceptual schemes.

Proceeding from the top row of the column headings and subheadings downward, the patterns of relationships between the terms of each row and of the row just below approximate the $1:n$ pattern. Proceeding upward, they approximate the $n:1$ pattern.

These homologies between the patterns of pairings or structures of paired-associates situations and the patterns of pairings or structures of "parts" of tabular presentations of knowledge serve two purposes. First, they show how principles obtained with paired-associates situations could be applied to production and use of written instructional materials in a tabular format. Various specific limitations on the pertinence of available data are mentioned. Second, they show some important general limitations on the pertinence of available data on learning as obtained with paired-associates situations.

APPLICATION OF PRINCIPLES OF PAIRED-ASSOCIATES LEARNING. Homologies in structure is the first basis for application of principles of paired-associates learning to production and use of written instructional materials. The second basis is actual or prospective commonality of many other classes of characteristics and variables. These bases we shall consider with respect to acquisition, possible "extinction," retention, and transfer.

A. Acquisition. For acquisition with lists of verbal stimuli conforming to the $1:1$ pattern of pairings, relatively extensive data are now available on the influence of meaningfulness and related attributes of stimulus members and response members; of similarity among stimulus members, among response members, and between stimulus and response members; of familiarization of stimulus members and response members; and of number of and associations between or among elements of stimulus members and response members. Some data are also available for acquisition with lists with nonverbal stimulus members and verbal or nonverbal response members (Goss and Nodine, 1965). Moreover, these relationships have been interpreted within the framework of more general concepts and principles, such as contiguity, similarity, and frequency (Goss, 1963; Goss and Nodine, 1965, pp. 111–124; Underwood, Ekstrand, and Keppel, 1965). Other factors being equal, the findings with lists of verbal stimuli suggest that when synonymous terms are available for inclusion in written instructional materials, at least in a tabular format, the specific word selected should be the most meaningful, familiar, easily pronounced, concrete, and specific one possible, and of high imagery, too. The specific word should be the least similar to the other words, and the least complex in terms of number of elements. A difficulty is that in order to so select words, normative values must be established for the meaningfulness and related attributes of very large numbers of words.

Reasonably systematic data are accumulating on the influence on acquisition of strengths and patterns of initial associations among and between stimulus and response members (Goss, 1966; Goss and Nodine, 1965, pp. 101–110; McCullers, 1963, 1965; Shapiro, 1965). Reasonably systematic data are also accumulating on the influence on acquisition of percentage of occurrences of stimuli for response members (% ORM) and, more recently, of percentage of occurrence of stimulus members (% OSM) (Cobb, Farrick, Goss, and Gregory, 1964; Goss and Nodine, 1965, pp. 317–322; Schulz, 1965). Two additional areas of the accumulation of reasonably systematic data are acquisition as influenced by format of presentation such as anticipation vs. recall, confirmation vs. prompting (Goss and Nodine, 1965, pp. 283–317), and as influenced by temporal aspects of presentation (Nodine, 1965; Nodine and Goss, unpublished manuscript). Some data are now available on acquisition under whole and under part or, more accurately, part-whole arrangements for presentation (Goss and Nodine, 1965, pp. 294–310).

In many of these investigations, variables from two or more of the preceding classes of variables have been combined. At present, data on the effects of these and other classes of variables and some of the related theory do not permit specification of the exact combinations of values necessary to achieve an optimal rate of acquisition. But these data can often serve as the basis for elimination of some combinations of conditions as clearly less than optimal.

For acquisition with lists exemplifying the $n:1$ pattern with words as stimuli, both nonmediational and mediational analyses have been proposed (Goss, 1961b, 1964a). Some data are available from earlier investigations by Reed (1946). More recently, parametric data have been reported, particularly on the influence of strengths and patterns of initial associations between stimulus and recognition responses to response members (Goss and Nodine, 1965, p. 110). Goss (1964a) describes the methods and results of an experiment in which relationships between stimulus members and mediating responses and between mediating responses and terminating responses were established experimentally. In these experiments, the stimuli were single words. But Duncan (1965) and Musgrave and Cohen (1966) have employed stimuli that are compounds of two words. Such data are requisite to understanding acquisition of different and of common responses to stimuli that are compounds of the same and different words.

More often than words, the stimuli of lists exemplifying $n:1$ pairings have been different combinations of values along two or more physical dimensions. Those dimensions are frequently form and color. In addition or alternatively, size, number, and other dimensions have often been used. To explain acquisition with these lists or what is conventionally labeled concept identification, attainment, formation, or discovery, both nonmediational and mediational analyses have been proposed (Goss, 1961b). The latter analyses serve as a means of proceeding from values along physical dimensions to mediating verbal responses that label those values to terminating responses.

Approximations to actual physical characteristics in the form of photographs, drawings, or both might be incorporated into table 1, with or without names for the dimensions of interest and for the appropriate values along those dimensions. An extensive analysis of acquisition with $n:1$ pairings or of conceptual behavior thus conceived has been proposed previously (Goss, 1961b). The principles and derivations therein provide a rough guide to the development and use of written instructional materials presented in a tabular format. Some pertinent data are summarized in Goss (1961b), Hunt (1962), Pikas (1965), and Bourne (1966). They suggest the significance of similarity among the stimuli and of strengths of associations between stimuli and mediating responses. They also suggest the significance of number of relevant and of irrelevant dimensions, of time between an informing stimulus and presentation of the next stimulus, and of other variables (see Bourne, Guy, Dodd, and Justesen, 1965).

On occasion, stimuli might be distinguished further or, perhaps, entirely by differences among each other in form or in some other dimension. Both nonmediational and mediational analyses of conceptual behavior with such sets of stimuli have been proposed (Goss, 1961b). But available data are too limited to warrant more than tentative application to problems of development and use of written instructional materials in tabular format or in any other format.

The data available on acquisition with $1:n$ pairings are of relatively recent origin and are still of limited scope. One conclusion that seems warranted is a direct relationship between actual percentages of occurrence of alternative response members and percentages of anticipation or recall of these responses. The direct relationship also holds when response members are absent in the context of acquisition and in a changed context (Goss and Cobb, 1966).

When alternative response members are (a) both of high meaningfulness, (b) one of high meaningfulness and the other of low meaningfulness, or (c) both of low meaningfulness, learning is most rapid under condition (a) and slowest under condition (c). Moreover, when response members of high and low meaningfulness occur with equal frequency, the member of high meaningfulness is anticipated and recalled more frequently than the member of low meaningfulness (Goss and Cobb, 1967). As additional data becomes available, it seems likely that the resultant concepts and principles will be applicable to development and use of written instructional materials.

Data on acquisition of lists exemplifying $n:n$ patterns of pairings are virtually nonexistent, as are data on other phenomena with such lists. For the present, therefore, this pattern is ignored.

B. Extinction. With respect to possible decrements in response frequencies or "extinction" as a consequence of removal of response members, data for lists conforming to the $1:1$ pattern (see, e.g., Goss, 1965a; Goss and Nodine, 1965; Goss, Nodine, Gregory, Taub, and Kennedy, 1962), $n:1$ pattern (Richardson, 1958), or the $1:n$ pattern (Goss and Cobb, 1964, 1966) are reasonably consistent in indicating that, with stimuli of low similarity and high meaningfulness in relatively well-learned stimulus-response relationships, little or no extinction occurs. With stimuli of high similarity and low meaningfulness in lists acquired to different levels of strength, some extinction may occur (Goss, 1965a).

C. Retention. Responses or stimulus-response relationships acquired with lists exemplifying $1:1$, $n:1$, and $1:n$ patterns may decrease in strength over intervals of no practice. Available data on retention, particularly with $n:1$ and $1:n$ patterns, are still relatively limited in terms of effects of variables such as strength and patterns of initial associations, and of effects of percentage of trials on which the stimulus or response member occurs, or relative percentages of occurrence of alternative response members. Available data are also limited with respect to the influence of meaningfulness, similarity, familiarization, and other classes of variables except, perhaps, for the temporal parameter of the inter-trial interval (Underwood, 1961). But as more complete data become available, they may serve to guide development and use of written instructional materials to provide for maximum possible retention.

D. Transfer. At present, data and theory on transfer are conveniently divided into those for paradigms and conditions that are not mediational, at least in intent, and that those are mediational, at least in intent. Data and theory for the former paradigms and conditions are considered first. With the $1:1$ pattern, almost all available data are for two different lists. In simple transfer, each list is used once. Alternatively, the first list is repeated (retroaction) or the second list is repeated (proaction). The relationships of the two different lists are typically schematized as A–B for one list and A–C, A–B$_r$, D–B, D–C for the other list. The C indicates substitution of new response members in the second list; the B$_r$ indicates reversal of the original response member; and the D indicates substitution of new stimulus members.

Most of the available data are for experiments in which effects on simple transfer, proaction, and retroaction of different relationships between the two lists are compared. On occasion these relationships are given more general form in terms of similarity of stimulus members of the two lists, similarity of their response members, or both (Dallett, 1965; Ellis, 1965; Martin, 1965; Postman, 1961; Underwood, 1961; Wimer, 1964). Some data are available on the influence on transfer phenomena of additional classes of variables such as meaningfulness and similarity (Goulet, 1965; Houston, 1965; Saravo and Price, 1967). But these data are still too limited to serve as bases for development and use of written instructional materials.

Moreover, the conditions and terminal requirements of almost all of these investigations of simple transfer, proaction, and retroaction have been such as to preclude or minimize acquisition of structure for which the criteria are filling in several columns of a table in different ways. With several columns, for example, only terms in one column might be given with the requirement of responding with the terms in two or more other columns to the right, to the left, or to the left and right. Column headings might or might not be provided. However, recent experiments, such as that of Postman (1965), in which responses of both the original (A–B) and interpolated task (A–C) were obtained in modified free recall provide an exception to this stricture.

Data on simple transfer, proaction, and retroaction with $n:1$ and $1:n$ patterns are also virtually nonexistent. At present no empirically based principles established directly with such patterns are available to guide development and use of written instructional materials.

Data and theory on transfer with paradigms that are mediational, at least in intent, have been with $1:1$ patterns for two or three different lists; with $n:1$ patterns for two or three different lists, and with other combinations of patterns for two different lists (Lacey, 1961). As shown in table 3, which represents a slight modification of an earlier classification (Goss and Nodine, 1965, p. 180), sixteen different paradigms or structures can be generated for criterion tasks involving the following binary characteristics: (*a*) similar or dissimilar stimulus members; (*b*) similar or dissimilar mediating responses and stimuli; (*c*) similar or dissimilar response members and recognition responses; and

Table 3

Paradigms Generated by Binary Values for Similarity Among Stimulus Members, Similarity Among Mediating Responses and Stimuli, Similarity Among Response Members and Recognition Responses Thereto, and Strengths of Initial Relationships Between Mediating Stimuli and Recognition Responses

Conventional Label for Paradigm	Stimulus Members	Mediating Responses-Stimuli	Response Members	Strength of Initial Relationship
	Similar	Similar [a]	Similar [b]	0
	Similar	Similar	Dissimilar	0
	Similar	Similar	Similar	>0
	Similar	Similar	Dissimilar	>0
Acquired distinctiveness; response-mediated dissimilarity	Similar	Dissimilar	Similar	0
	Similar	Dissimilar	Dissimilar	0
Response-mediated discrimination	Similar	Dissimilar	Similar	>0
Response-mediated discrimination	Similar	Dissimilar	Dissimilar	>0
Acquired equivalence; response-mediated similarity	Dissimilar	Similar	Similar	0
	Dissimilar	Similar	Dissimilar	0
Response-mediated generalization	Dissimilar	Similar	Similar	>0
Response-mediated generalization	Dissimilar	Similar	Dissimilar	>0
	Dissimilar	Dissimilar	Similar	0
	Dissimilar	Dissimilar	Dissimilar	0
	Dissimilar	Dissimilar	Similar	>0
Response-mediated association	Dissimilar	Dissimilar	Dissimilar	>0

[a] The limiting case for similar mediating responses is the same response to two or more similar or dissimilar stimuli.
[b] Evocation of similar responses by similar stimuli is assumed, but this is not a necessary relationship.

(d) zero or greater than zero strengths of initial association between mediating stimuli and recognition responses to response members. These particular paradigms are reached by means of different kinds and sequences of experiences in acquiring prior lists that exemplify $1:1$, $n:1$, or $1:n$ pairings. A number of different arrangements of pairs of prior lists have been distinguished as bases for bringing about the particular paradigm labeled "response-mediated association" (see Goss, 1964c, unpublished manuscript; Jenkins, 1963). Such arrangements have also been distinguished as bases for bringing about the other paradigms of table 2 (Goss, 1964b).

Theory and data for various paradigms of table 3 are reviewed in Arnoult (1957), Earhard and Mandler (1965), Goss and Greenfeld (1958), Goss and Nodine (1965, pp. 179–195), Jenkins (1963), and Spiker (1956). Except for data obtained in experiments with the paradigm designated response-mediated association, and perhaps in a few other experiments (see Duncan, 1965; James and Hakes, 1965; Lacey, 1961; Richardson, 1963), available data are of limited significance. The reason is the use of motor terminating responses in most of the other experiments rather than verbal terminating responses. The data obtained in even those experiments with verbal terminating responses, while of slightly greater significance, are still not as pertinent as might be desired. In general, in the presumed sequences of stimulus, verbal mediating response and stimulus, and verbal terminating response, the mediating responses and stimuli have not been overt or explicit as they would be in reproduction of stimuli and their relationships in a tabular format. Moreover, virtually no data are available on the circumstances under which the mediating responses and stimuli occur essentially *in toto* or not at all, whether covertly or overtly. One factor is probably the relatively strong relationships between stimuli and mediating responses and between mediating stimuli and terminating responses. Another factor may be experimenter-induced or subject-induced instructions to use the mediating responses and stimuli (Dallett and D'Andrea, 1965). Almost certainly, still another factor is sufficient time for the occurrence of mediating responses and terminating responses (Schulz and Lovelace, 1964).

Without data on formation of structures by means of successive acquisition of different lists such as those designated A–B, B–C, A–C, even the relatively primitive principles derived from experiments on response-mediated association cannot be applied readily to development and use of written instructional materials.

In summary, when the relationships between and among

columns of table 1 or between and among the rows of headings
and subheadings are approached more analytically, homologies
in structure can be identified between those relationships and
patterns of pairings of paired-associates situations. Because of
these homologies and because of actual or potential commonality of many other classes of characteristics and variables,
principles derived from experiments on paired-associates learning seem prospectively, if not immediately, applicable to development and use of written instructional materials in a tabular
format. Available principles are progressively less satisfactory
as one proceeds from acquisition with lists exemplifying the $1:1$
pattern to transfer in mediational paradigms with lists exemplifying $n:1$, $1:n$, and $n:n$ patterns.

As noted before, despite these homologies and commonalities,
a common charge is that data and theory on verbal learning
obtained through conventional laboratory situations have little,
even nothing, to do with understanding the acquisition and use
of knowledge (see, e.g., Miller, Galanter, and Pribram, 1960), or
of those patterns of stimulus-response relationships conventionally called language (see, e.g., Chomsky, 1965; Johnson, 1965,
p. 30).

A number of factors may underlie these charges. One might
be explicit or implicit restriction of the paired-associates situations to the $1:1$ pattern of pairing. A second factor might be the
predominant use of nonsense syllables and other nonwords as
stimuli. Such use is entirely legitimate, even highly desirable, but
it is not essential. Both what is learned and the "content" of the
task can be separated from the pattern of stimulus-response
relationships of the task. A third, related factor might be the use
of verbal stimuli to the substantial neglect of nonverbal stimuli.
Clearly, nonverbal stimuli can be and have been used.

A fourth factor might be restriction of arrangements for
paired-associates learning to those for which the experimenter
supplies the responses by means of response members. Although
conventional, this arrangement is not necessary. Subjects can
be required to supply responses, one or more of which are
presumably followed by strengthening events, such as the experimenter saying "good" or "right," the sound of a buzzer, or

the presentation of the next stimulus member (see, e.g., Goss and Greenfeld, 1958; M. J. Peterson, 1956).

A fifth factor might be the predominant use of stimuli that are treated as elements. Thus, the manifold possibilities of transfer from elements to compounds, compounds to elements, and compounds to compounds have not been explored extensively (Goss, 1962, 1964b; Goss and Nodine, 1965, pp. 195–214; Musgrave, 1962; Musgrave and Cohen, 1965).

A sixth factor may be the relative neglect of transfer from the paired-associates situation to other situations, and the converse. Excluding familiarization-satiation experiences, only transfer from paired associates exemplifying the 1:1 pairing to serial anticipation and the converse has received any serious empirical and theoretical attention (Jensen and Rohwer, 1965).

A seventh factor might be the failure to separate knowledge and a particular situation used to present and transmit knowledge. Specifically, the presentation and transmission of knowledge is often treated as exclusively a matter of the connected discourse situation. As shown in figure 1 and table 1, this need not be the case. Indeed, as suggested above, instead of being "revealed," the structure of knowledge may be concealed by the typical redundancy of connected discourse, the presence of function words and punctuation, and the frequent lack of an orderly presentation of information and of headings and sub-headings.

An eighth factor might be the emphasis on the pertinence or, conversely, the lack of pertinence of the operant conditioning situation for understanding the acquisition and use of knowledge, language, or both, by some psychologists (e.g., Carroll, 1962; Skinner, 1957; Staats and Staats, 1963) and linguists (e.g., Chomsky, 1959). The operant conditioning situation, even when extended to the discriminative operant situation, is very likely the least pertinent of the several possibly pertinent simple learning situations as a source of concepts and principles for understanding the acquisition and use of knowledge. Moreover, various limitations of the operant situation such as relative lack of control of trial onset and of initial elicitation of desired responses apply to many verbal learning situations.

A ninth factor might be the insistence of some psychologists that the best, possibly the only, course for studying language behavior and sometimes — by implication — knowledge is through the rules of some "scientific" grammar. Lexical rules or the "referential process" may be included, but these rules are often minimized, as are attempts to account for the development of meaning by means of principles arrived at in various simple and complex learning situations (e.g., Miller, 1962, p. 748).

With respect to this thesis, an important consideration for psychologists is that various attempts to formulate "scientific" grammars are probably as little relevant to explanation of verbal behavior and verbal learning as various "logics" are to the explanation of phenomena labeled thinking. The nature and extent of the relevance of the rules that constitute various "scientific" grammars is, immediately, a heuristic matter and, ultimately, an empirical matter. Instructive with respect to the pertinence of "scientific" grammars is the abandonment of what were conceived as "functional requirements" derived by a linguistic theory for a "characterization" involving but "two psychological issues" (i.e., unit formation and unit manipulation) (Johnson, 1965, pp. 41–47). It is not clear how these "psychological issues" differ in any significant fashion from analyses proposed within the conventional concepts and principles of verbal behavior and verbal learning (Goss, 1961c; Underwood, 1965).

Some psychologists who are aware of the situation with respect to various "logics" and thinking caution that "this distinction [between the theory of logic and the theory of logic users] is just as valid and as valuable in the study of natural languages" (Miller, 1964, p. 93), and warn that "a description of a language and a description of a language user must be kept distinct" (Miller, 1965, p. 18). There may be ambivalence here because the implication drawn from the latter expression is that "psycholinguists should try to formulate performance models that will incorporate in addition to a generative knowledge of the rules, hypothetical information-storage and information processing components that can simulate the actual behavior of language users" (ibid.). The nature and source of the rules is not specified explicitly or exactly. From another context (Miller, 1962), it seems likely that they include the rules of "scientific" grammar(s). Should this be the case, the distinction between description of a language and description of a language user is not between the "rules" involved in description of a language and the "rules" used by the language user. The "rules" are presumably the same, but something more, i.e., hypothetical information-storage and information-processing components, had to be added. The distinction, therefore, is not in the "rules" but in the "something more."

Not apparent on the part of those psychologists and linguists prominent in their insistence on the primacy of "rules" is any acceptance of the possibility that acquisition and use of "rules," whatever their nature, might be explained wholly or in part by concepts and principles derived from investigations involving both simple (e.g., classical conditioning) and relatively more complex (e.g., paired-associates) situations. Few, if any, psychologists question that some aspects of human behavior can be *described* as rule acquisition and rule using, just as few question that some aspects of human behavior are purposive. But these labels do not, unfortunately, explain. Instead, they identify phenomena requiring explanation.

A tenth related factor might be the casual and misleading use of the term "rule." Thus, McNeill (1966) supposes children's competence to include "the rule: $S \rightarrow (P) + O$" (p. 23), where S = sentence, P = pivotal, and O = open word class. The "rule" is casual because it offers no probability of occurrence of sentences exemplifying this rule among all one-word and two-word sentences within the corpus for even a single child, and because it offers no marginal and joint probabilities of occurrence of "P" and "O" words. The "rule" is misleading because it is actually a crude empirical generalization based ultimately on marginal and joint probabilities of occurrence of words in sequences of one and two words. The manner of arriving at the generalization is as debatable as it is obscure in that allegedly "the grammarian necessarily imposes his knowledge of English on the child's corpus if he wants to use the material at all" (p. 23).

By calling this empirical generalization a "rule," through the connotation of "rule" it is possible to transmute a degraded contingency table into an apparently profound statement about the nature of young children's verbal behavior. However, the "rule" is clearly of limited value as a description of one-word and two-word sequences in the speech of children of a given age. Moreover, the "rule" is clearly not an explanation of the origin of the marginal and particularly of the joint probabilities of the original contingency tables.

Instead, the "rule" is a description of consequences. It says nothing of the immediate stimulus conditions and of the more remote stimulus-response sequences that are required as the beginnings of explanation of the origin of the probabilities of the original contingency tables.

In contrast, paired-associates situations, particularly those exemplifying $1:n$, $n:1$, and $n:n$ patterns of pairing, provide a means for achieving relationships among stimuli and responses that might lead to those of contingency tables for words of one-word and two-word sequences. Also, despite their inadequacy, available concepts and principles of paired-associates learning for these patterns of pairing per se or as extrapolated from the $1:1$ pattern provide the beginning of an explanation of the origins of the relationships in the contingency tables. Certainly no evidence exists that these concepts and principles are not relevant. And there is substantially greater empirical justification of their relevance than there is for an explanation such as one that appeals to an unknown "box" of "unknown content" (McNeill, 1966, pp. 38–39). "Linguistic universals" arrived at by analyses of other data for other kinds of subjects are hardly specific "stuffing" for the "box."

An eleventh factor, the last noted here, might be described as misunderstanding about understanding. Understanding is one of those apparently profound words of the lay vocabulary that some psychologists and professionals in other disciplines use either to score for or against some particular view by connotation or to advance an all-encompassing but substantially empty proposition. Illustrative of the former use is dismissal of data and theory for paired-associates situations as unimportant for explaining the acquisition of knowledge because acquisition and other phenomena with these situations are by "rote" rather than with "understanding." Illustrative of the latter use is the assertion "that knowledge of a language involves the implicit ability to understand indefinitely many sentences" (Chomsky, 1965, p. 15).

In both cases, "understanding" is typically undefined or defined by example rather than by general criteria. In both cases, unless "understanding" is defined, the notions expressed are empty. Finally, in both cases, when definition is attempted, there are several possible meanings. Some of the definitions that are pertinent to verbal behavior and verbal learning are listed here, though the list is neither exhaustive nor systematic. It suffices, however, to illustrate the need for care when words from the vernacular are used in an apparently technical fashion.

One definition of "understanding," perhaps the simplest, is the ability to recognize whether or not words alone or in sequences, including "sentences," are in a particular language. A second definition is the ability to judge whether words, usually in sequence, are or are not "acceptable" or "grammatical" sentences in a particular language.

A third definition of "understanding" is the ability to recognize (repeat, echo, imitate) words alone of some language, or sequences of those words including sentences, in correct order and sequence, with what is judged as appropriate pronunciation under both good and degraded conditions of hearing and/or viewing the stimuli. Such repetition might be as the words or word sequences occur ("listening, reading"), immediately thereafter (immediate memory span), or after some delay ("retention").

A fourth definition is the ability to spell and to write words of lists and sequences. A special case of this is the ability to "spell" in special "alphabets," such as the International Morse Code or the International Phonetic Alphabet.

A fifth definition is the ability to put words in lists or initial sequences in new sequences that are "acceptable" or "grammatical" sentences in the particular language, and to carry out various transformations on these sentences such as negation. A sixth definition is the ability to carry out analyses designed to specify the grammatical or syntactic "structures" of sentences at or to one or more levels of "deepness," "generality," or whatever other descriptive label for "organization of the generative grammar" might be current. A seventh definition, one related to analysis into syntactic structures, is the transformation of complex sentences "by a set of rules into an exhaustive set of 'kernel assertions,' all of the subject-copula-object form and together being semantically equivalent to the original sentence" (Osgood, 1963, pp. 748–749).

An eighth definition of "understanding" is the ability to define each word of a list of words alone or in sequence. A ninth definition is the ability to paraphrase words alone or in sequences including sentences, both in the vernacular and in one or more "special" or "technical" languages. A tenth is the ability to express or represent words alone or in sequences in other modes such as pictures, diagrams, and logical or mathematical formulas. An eleventh is "free" associations to words alone or in sequence.

A twelfth definition is the ability to develop the "significance" of words alone or word sequences, i.e., to relate the words or word sequence to other words or word sequences. A thirteenth is the ability to organize or recognize words alone or in sequences into hierarchic structures such as outlines. A fourteenth is the ability to translate words alone or word sequences to and from one or more other natural languages.

All the preceding definitions of "understanding" involve verbal stimuli and verbal responses. Others that do not are the ability to: match words of sentences with stimuli that are primarily but not exclusively external; make locomotor-manipulative responses called for either in response to the verbal stimuli alone or in response to such stimuli and other stimuli, again primarily but not exclusively external; and "construct" or otherwise modify the environment in ways called for in sentences.

Acquisition and other phenomena with paired-associates situations can be viewed as involving or as being readily extended to accommodate essentially all of these definitions of "understanding." Definition-by-definition development of this claim for paired-associates learning is ignored here. However, without specification of correspondence with a specific definition, much of the present paper constitutes an elaboration of this claim.

In addition to some of the above definitions, when the term "understanding" is used in contrast with "rote" learning, understanding very likely also includes the notion of complexity of initial stimulus-response relationships and of changes in those relationships during acquisition and other phenomena of verbal learning. With understanding equated with relative complexity, initial and subsequent stimulus-response relationships of phenomena of paired-associates learning are sufficiently complex to render use of "rote" questionable even as a loose descriptive label. Perhaps they are sufficiently complex to warrant use of "understanding," at least under some conditions.

GENERAL LIMITATIONS ON AVAILABLE DATA WITH PAIRED-ASSOCIATES SITUATIONS. Various relatively specific limitations on available data based on learning in the paired-associates situations have already been mentioned. Also mentioned was the more general limitation that little or none of the data on transfer with paired-associates situations for different mediational paradigms can be considered satisfactory for the explanation of acquisition of relationships or structures that involve several stimuli, each of which evokes several successive responses as a chain. Such relationships or structures might be acquired in one stage as one complete list or task, or in two or more successive stages. The first of these might involve parts of the stimulus-response relationships of the more complex terminal list or task. In acquisition of the terminal task, the part or parts would be extended, combined, or both. The two or more successive stages might be to add more responses to hierarchies or chains initiated by each of a large number of stimuli. They might be to add more units, each of which consists of a stimulus and a complete hierarchy, or a chain of responses. Several such expansions of the stimulus-response relationships might be carried out simultaneously. Development of response hierarchies and chains might proceed undirectionally from each member of a set of stimuli. Development of response hierarchies and chains, by intent and by arrangement, might also be bidirectional both from and to each member. Arrangements for development of bidirectional chains might be successive or simultaneous.

Typically, paired-associates learning has been with but one list or two different lists. The stimulus members of these lists have been single syllables or words, or compounds of two or perhaps three of these elements. Similarly, the response members have been single syllables or words, or compounds usually of but a few of those elements. Typically also, when two different lists have been employed, the interest is in simple transfer, proaction, or retroaction with respect to a relationship between single stimuli and single responses rather than between single stimuli and hierarchies or chains of responses, or compound stimuli and hierarchies or chains of responses.

In their contribution to this volume, Barbara S. Musgrave and Jean Carl Cohen show in considerable detail the manners of construction of paired-associates lists that permit close approximations to stimulus-response relationships or structures of knowledge as presented in a tabular format. Accordingly, such elaboration of paired-associates situations need not be discussed here.

A related general limitation of typical paired-associates learning is the absence of explicit labeling of the referential class of the stimulus and response members. With nonsense syllables and words of heterogeneous reference, such labeling might be of no significance or even misleading. But with sets of words from given referential classes, such labeling might facilitate differentiation of the word "stimuli" into groups such as initiating stimuli, stimuli for mediating responses, and stimuli for terminating responses. For these sets of words, such labeling might also facilitate differentiation between lists, as well as orderly progression through successive lists in which, for example, the response members of one list become the stimulus members of the next list. Barbara S. Musgrave and Jean Carl Cohen also show the manner in which such labels or column and row headings and subheadings might be incorporated in derived paired-associates lists.

As suggested earlier, column headings and subheadings such as those of table 1 illustrate a conceptual scheme or structure that can be expected to influence acquisition, retention, and transfer of relationships among stimuli of lists such as those embodied in table 1 (Goss, 1961c, p. 58). On some occasions responses might progress across columns from left to right along each row. On other occasions the progression might be both across columns and between rows in a zig-zag pattern. Specifically, it might begin with the column heading "Name, Common," go to the column heading "Name, Scientific" as a mediating response-stimulus to a specific "scientific name" in a row as a desired response. From the specific "scientific name" of a row, the progression might be to the column heading "Order" as a mediating response-stimulus and then to a specific "order" name as a response. Response sequences in the pattern of the words of the column heading on the extreme left, to a specific name in that column, to the words of the next column heading, to a specific name in that column might continue through successive rows of specific names until all such names had been exhausted.

On still other occasions, responses might proceed downward from a particular column heading through successive rows of that column, or the converse. Such sequences might occur through successive columns. Learning the contents of a table in this pattern is related to learning with lists, particularly those consisting of several subsets of stimuli, each with a presumed common implicit response. However, there is an important difference in that tables may have the column heading as an initiating stimulus. The pattern might be described as $1:n$ with the order of occurrence of the n responses open to variation from a random, variable order to some fixed order.

A third general limitation on data available on learning in paired-associates situations is the relative elimination of the factor of attention, that is, of orienting toward one stimulus, making a recognition response to that stimulus, then orienting toward another stimulus and making a recognition response to that stimulus, and so on. Presenting the stimuli as pairs, with one stimulus consistently on the right and the other consistently on the left, and randomizing the order of the occurrence of these pairs assures spatio-temporal contiguity of the stimuli of each pair, and stimuli within each occur with each other far more frequently than with any other stimuli. Data on learning to respond to more discriminable features of stimuli or cue-selection during acquisition of paired associates are of some pertinence (Goss and Nodine, 1965, pp. 210–214). However, more data are desirable, particularly when headings and subheadings are supplied as means of facilitating subjects' responses to a particular stimulus within a set of stimuli. Headings and subheadings could be added as means of facilitating subjects' selection of elements of compound stimulus members, of elements of compound response members, or both. The headings and subheadings of tabular formats, and the regular spatial arrangements of terms, should facilitate subjects' responses to the stimuli of just one column or the more particular columns. Thus, tables might be regarded as a means of reducing time and effort in responding to particular stimuli.

Homologies Between Other Laboratory Situations and Other Formats of Presentation. Lists are another laboratory situation for which some theory and a reasonable amount of data are available. Connected discourse in the form of standard or acceptable sentences and in the form of approximations to connected discourse is another situation that has been persistently and, perhaps, increasingly of theoretical and empirical concern.

Except for theory and experimentation concerned with the "memory trace" for forms (Gomulicki, 1953; Riley, 1961), acquisition and other phenomena of learning with graph and diagram situations have been almost completely neglected. Until recently, acquisition and other phenomena of learning mathematical, logical expressions or approximations to such expressions were almost completely neglected. Gagné and his collaborators (Gagné, 1962; Gagné, Mayor, Garstens, and Paradise, 1962) have outlined a theoretical analysis of acquisition of mathematical expressions that embodies more general concepts and principles of learning, and have reported pertinent data. Frase's (1966) experiment on the use of syllogisms, and his theoretical interpretation of the observed phenomena in terms of response-mediated association, represents the beginning of a parallel contribution on the acquisition and use of logical expressions. Despite these interesting initial efforts, the data presently available on acquisition and other phenomena with mathematical and logical expressions are primarily demonstrative rather than parametric. Therefore, homologies between laboratory situations involving graphs, diagrams, and mathematical, logical expressions, and corresponding formats for the presentation of knowledge, are not considered here.

In considering homologies involving list and connected discourse situations, it is necessary to examine the observed and presumed stimulus-response elements and relationships of these kinds of situations. Such examination is also preliminary to subsequent consideration of relationships between paired-associates situations and connected discourse situations. As shown in figure 1, the list situation is conceived as, loosely, a transition from paired associates to connected discourse or the converse. Once the structures of list and connected discourse situations have been examined, homologies with respect to conventional formats of presentation for instruction can be considered, particularly with respect to the formats of textual exposition and tables.

STIMULUS-RESPONSE RELATIONSHIPS OR STRUCTURES OF LIST AND CONNECTED DISCOURSE SITUATIONS. Lists and connected discourse (e.g., Slamecka, 1962) have been presented by means of a serial anticipation arrangement. Despite the traditional importance of the serial anticipation arrangement and the considerable theory and data on serial anticipation learning, such theory and data are ignored here. The reason for doing so is that other arrangements for presenting lists and connected discourse permit easier and clearer development of homologies between these situations and formats for the presentation of knowledge. Those other arrangements involve presenting the lists or connected materials one to several times and then testing to determine the number of stimuli that can be reproduced or are recognized. These are the study and test phases of a trial, respectively. Reproduction or recognition of the stimuli in the same order as they occurred may be a criterial requirement; reproduction or recognition in any specified order may be a criterial requirement. Reproduction or recognition of the specific stimuli that occurred may also be a criterial requirement; however, this requirement may be liberalized to equivalent stimuli or "ideas." In the experimentation with lists of the past decade and a half, exact or verbatim reproduction of the stimuli in any order has been the typical criterial requirement. In experimentation with connected discourse, reproduction in order of occurrence has typically been required, but frequently both exact reproduction and reproduction that permits equivalent stimuli or "ideas" have been allowed.

Lists and connected discourse situations can be regarded as two extremes of continua of form, grammatical function, and patterning of the order of stimuli by rules. Typically, lists are constituted of nonword or word stimuli of homogeneous form, such as, for example, consonant-vowel-consonant syllables; words of a single grammatical class, such as all nouns; words with common denotative reference, such as the names of dogs. Typically, too, function words do not appear. Thus, lists do not form sequences that resemble the patterns of phrases and sentences, lines and stanzas of connected discourse. Typically, connected discourse is constituted of word stimuli of heterogeneous form. By definition, the stimuli are heterogeneous with respect to grammatical function and denotative reference. Included are content words with denotative reference and function words with (e.g., prepositions) and without (e.g., conjunctions) specific denotative reference. Miller and Selfridge (1950) initiated interest in the development of techniques for constructing sets of stimuli that represent multivalue transitions from lists to connected discourse. Among other techniques designed to realize such transitions is one developed by Cofer (1961). Recall of stimuli presented in sentences can be compared to those presented in other forms.

Figure 2 shows observed and presumed stimulus-response elements and relationships of a typical list situation. During the study phase of each trial, the stimuli are presented sequentially at a uniform rate (e.g., one every two seconds). Each stimulus is shown as eliciting a recognition response, ordinarily a repetition of the stimulus. In addition, each stimulus is shown as a possible source of (extra-list) association responses that might be unique to the stimulus or common to two or more stimuli. Relationships involving association responses can vary in strength from low to very high. The relationships among the stimuli or, as shown, among the recognition responses to the stimuli can also vary from zero to very high initial strength. The strength and pattern of these relationships constitute an important class of variables (Deese, 1959).

A special criterion for making up subsets of stimuli is classification in terms of an observed or presumed common function or common property of the objects referred to by the stimuli. Subsets thus constituted have been called taxonomic categories (Bousfield and Cohen, 1956). The names for such categories might often be the association responses common to two or more stimuli. Whether or not such association responses occur probably depends on the strength of the relationships between and

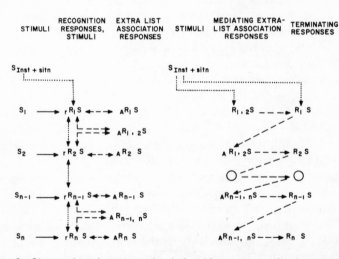

Fig. 2. Observed and presumed relationships among stimulus-response elements in the study phase of the first trial of learning and the test phase of the criterion trial. Subjects may be instructed to reproduce the stimuli in order of their occurrence or to disregard order of occurrence. (Solid lines refer to pre-experimentally established relationships between stimuli and recognition responses; dashed lines refer to pre-experimentally established relationships between response-produced stimuli and extra-list responses; dotted lines refer to relationships among recognition responses.)

among recognition responses, that strength involving association responses, rate of presentation, instructions regarding the
occurrence of association responses either induced by the experimenter or by the subject, and other factors. Conceivably,
taxonomic categories function primarily to specify subsets of
stimuli whose recognition responses are related by greater-than-
zero average initial strengths.

During the test phase of a criterion trial specified as perfect
reproduction of the stimuli of the list, the order of reproduction
shown in figure 2 is the order of occurrence of the stimuli during
the study phase of the first trial. For so-called free recall this
need not, usually does not, hold. The evidence for clustering of
terms during free recall on the basis of observed or presumed
membership in particular taxonomic categories is reasonably
compelling, as is the evidence for clustering on the basis of
associations among stimuli or among recognition responses to
the stimuli (Cofer, 1965). Whether or not common association
responses function during test trials as mediating responses and
stimuli to bring about clustering of those stimuli that have some
particular common association, may also depend on the strength
of those associations, time allowed and taken for responses,
instructions, and other factors.

Figure 2 could be elaborated to show possible interference
from extra-list associations. Also, it could be elaborated to show
the possible influence of instructions to use category names as
induced by the experimenter or by the subject.

Figure 3 shows observed and presumed stimulus-response
elements and relationships of a connected discourse situation.
Except for the small number of stimuli, the situation is typical
of those requiring reproduction of a sentence, or of each of
several sentences verbatim. During the study phase of each trial,
the sentence might be spoken or shown sequentially, or it might
be presented all at once for subjects to read from left to right.
Each stimulus is shown as eliciting a recognition response,
ordinarily repetition of the stimulus. In addition, each stimulus
is shown as a possible source of extra-list association responses
that might be other ideas, names for grammatical categories,
or both.

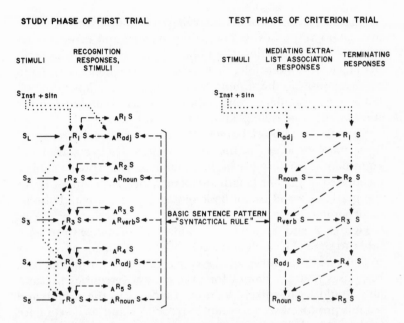

Fig. 3. Stimulus-response elements and relationships of the study phase of the first trial of learning and of the test phase of the criterion trial; subjects are instructed to reproduce the stimuli in order of their occurrence. (Solid lines refer to pre-experimentally established relationships between response-produced stimuli and extra-list responses that are both other "ideas" and names for grammatical categories; dotted lines refer to relationships among recognition responses.)

Relationships among the stimuli or recognition responses to the stimuli may vary from zero to very high initial strength. Relationships that involve other ideas or names for grammatical categories may also vary in the same degrees. With sophisticated subjects, relationships might be expected among the association responses that are names for grammatical categories. A stable sequence of such responses can be considered a basic sentence pattern or a somewhat derived "syntactical rule."[3]

During the test phase of a criterion trial, specified as verbatim reproduction of the sentence, the names for grammatical categories might or might not function in a mediating relationship that, in part, determines order of occurrence of the stimuli.

Strengths of relationships involving recognition responses or association responses or both, time allowed and taken for responses, and instructions could prove among some of the pertinent factors. Conceivably, all that occurs is a sequence of recognition responses to the stimuli. Such a sequence, independent of, but in correspondence with, "the world" as exemplified in the stimuli, might be called "knowledge" (Hull, 1930).

Figure 3 could be elaborated to show possible occurrences of association responses in the form of ideas that are considered equivalent to two or more of the stimulus words. Also, it could be elaborated to greater length and complexity. Instructions about the pertinence and use of basic sentence patterns could also be incorporated.

Figures 2 and 3 could be modified in relationship to each other to show the changes in each with transformation from lists to connected discourse, or the converse. With transitional lists, responses that are names for grammatical categories presumably would be less likely both as responses to the stimuli and stimuli produced by recognition responses and as a sequence in the form of a basic sentence pattern.

HOMOLOGIES INVOLVING LISTS AND CONNECTED DISCOURSE. List situations can be considered reasonably homologous with parts of the tabular format. They can also be considered reasonably homologous with at least one kind of textual exposition. The parts of the tabular format are the stimuli of each column or of several columns, as in table 1. The stimuli of each column are likely to have the same grammatical function. Moreover, they often have been placed in a particular column because of a common function or a common property of the object referred to by the stimuli. Thus, acquisition and other phenomena with lists constituted of several subsets of stimuli, with each subset representing a different taxonomic category, can be considered to approximate such phenomena with several columns of a table.

But there are important differences. One is between the explicit immediate subheadings of each column of a table and the typically implicit actual or possible occurrences of the names of the category represented by each subset of stimuli of a list.

A further difference is between the explicit superordinate sub-headings and headings of the tabular format and the typically implicit actual or possible occurrence of names for combinations of categories represented by subsets of stimuli of a list. Stimuli of each column of a table have to be reproduced in an order isomorphic with the orders of the stimuli of each of the other columns. In contrast, although not a necessary requirement, reproduction of the stimuli of lists typically has been in any order.

As suggested above, initial strengths of relationships among stimuli and among recognition responses has been an important consideration in the construction of lists, as has inclusion of the stimuli in different taxonomic categories (Cofer, 1965; Wicklund, Palermo, and Jenkins, 1965). Both classes of variable influence clustering, which in turn might be regarded as a first approximation both to placing stimuli in columns and in assuring isomorphism of orders of stimuli in the columns.

The presence or absence of words of lists in categories and the exhaustiveness or nonexhaustiveness of those categories influences acquisition of words and "chunks" (occurrence of any one or more words of a category) in lists of different numbers of words or "chunks" (Cohen, 1963). The strength of initial relationships among stimuli is considerably higher for exhaustive than for nonexhaustive categories. In part for this reason, whether the stimuli of columns are exhaustive or nonexhaustive of instances under the column subheading may predict the rate of acquisition of stimuli in columns of a table. Number of stimuli in the column — or number of "chunks" when stimuli in columns of tables can be divided into further categories by, perhaps, row subheadings and headings — may also predict column recall.

Formal similarity among the stimuli (Battig, Allen, and Jensen, 1965) and a variation on such similarity, called "internal structure" (Garner and Whitman, 1965), seemingly influence acquisition of lists. Counted frequency of occurrence of members of pairs of words and strengths of associations between members of each of the pairs of letters that were used as lists (Ekstrand and Underwood, 1965) are additional determinants of the rate of acquisition. Whether lists are learned by whole, part, or progressive part arrangements apparently influences rate of acquisition (Garner and Whitman, 1965), as does requirement or nonrequirement of recall in serial order (Jahnke, 1965). Because of the approximate homology of lists and parts of tabular formats, each of these variables and other variables could be expected to influence acquisition of at least comparable parts of tabular formats and, perhaps, of those parts combined into complete tables.

Unfortunately, data on possible extinction of terminating responses of lists and on transfer are virtually nonexistent. Even recent parametric data on retention are too limited to warrant their application to development and use of written instructional materials.

Some textual exposition is not markedly different from presentation in tabular format. Thus, each of several successive sentences may consist of a "subject" that is a heading or subheading and a "predicate" that is a list of the stimuli in the particular column, each separated by a comma or an "and." Data on acquisition of lists should be reasonably pertinent to explanation of acquisition of at least the "predicate" of each of such sentences.

The sentences employed in many experiments on connected discourse (e.g., King, 1966, unpublished manuscript) are not as homologous to classificatory knowledge presented by textual exposition as might be expected and as is desirable. The reason is that each component sentence has markedly different content, whereas textual exposition of classificatory knowledge is likely to involve several sentences, each with some shared content.

The sentence or sentences typically employed in connected-discourse situations can be regarded as somewhat homologous to rows of tabular formats such as table 1. Essentially, those sentences name some object and describe the properties of that object, its relationships to other objects, or both. Their content is heterogeneous. The same heterogeneous information appears in each row of table 1, but without function words, punctuation, and other features of sentences.

Parametric data on acquisition of connected discourse and

on possible extinction, retention, and transfer are relatively scarce. However, variables such as length, similarity, initial strengths of relationships among stimuli, and rate of presentation are of demonstrated significance. As these data are discussed by other participants in this volume, they can be ignored here.

PAIRED ASSOCIATES AND CONNECTED DISCOURSE

The several continua along which connected discourse and lists can be considered extremes were identified previously as form, grammatical function, and patterning of orders by rules. Of concern here are transformations of paired-associates situations to connected-discourse situations, or the converse. General similarities in component stimulus-response relationships or structures of these situations that permit such transformation are examined in some detail. Paired-associates and, particularly, connected-discourse situations are then compared with respect to other classes of variables. Finally, paradigms for conceptualizing and for investigating transfer from one situation to the other are considered.

Similarities of Structure

Typically, paired-associates situations involve a list of an arbitrarily chosen number (k) of units exemplifying $1:1$, $n:1$, $1:n$, or $n:n$ patterns or pairings or, sometimes, combinations of these patterns of pairing. As a corollary of manipulative separability of functions as stimuli and as stimuli for responses, acquisition is specified in terms of the strengthening of the relationships between those stimuli assigned a stimulus function and the responses to those stimuli assigned a function as stimuli for responses. Moreover, the terminating responses must be of a specified form such as pronouncing or spelling an entire nonword or word correctly within a particular anticipation or recall interval. During the acquisition of paired associates many changes in both observed and inferred stimulus-response elements and relationships may also occur (Goss, 1963; Goss and Nodine, 1965, pp. 111–124). But until the specified changes in the relationships between the designated stimuli and terminating responses are obtained, acquisition of the list of one or more paired-associates units is incomplete.

With paired-associates situations thus conceived, the lists employed in most paired-associates experiments are simple in the extreme, since they generally consist of one or a few units of a particular pattern with stimulus and response members that are relatively simple in form. Each paired-associates unit can be elaborated to increasing resemblance to a list and to connected discourse. However, in contrast to acquisition of lists and connected discourse as conventionally executed, the stimuli of paired-associates units are divided into those with a stimulus function and those with a response function.

Instead of elaborating paired-associates units to resemble lists and connected discourse more closely, each list or unit of connected discourse, such as a sentence, could be converted into a $1:1$ paired-associates unit. Moreover, analytically the stimuli of lists and units of connected discourse can often be transformed into several $1:1$ units, one or more $n:1$ units, $1:n$ units, $n:n$ units, or combinations of these units. For example, a list whose stimuli were selected on the basis of membership in one to k taxonomic categories can be transformed into a paired-associates situation involving one to k $1:n$ or $n:1$ patterns. In each learning task unit the name of each taxonomic category is included explicitly either as the stimulus member with stimuli in that category as response members, or as the response members with stimuli in that category as the stimulus members.

In the same way, a sentence or set of sentences in which the "subject" of each sentence is the name of the taxonomic category, and the "predicate" is a list of names of instances, can be transformed into $1:n$ or $n:1$ paired-associates situations. Indeed, the transformation is easier because the name of the taxonomic category is explicit in the "subject" of the sentence. "Subject" and "predicate" could be reversed, in which case the corresponding transformation would be $n:1$ and $1:n$.

Elsewhere in this volume, Barbara S. Musgrave and Jean Carl Cohen explore in detail such transformations from paired-associates to connected-discourse situations, and the converse. They also show the manner of transformation for sentences whose stimuli are heterogeneous with respect to taxonomic category or denotative reference. Accordingly, such transformations need not be examined further here.

Comparison with Respect to Classes of Variables

Among the classes of variables common to paired-associates and to connected-discourse situations are (*a*) patterns of pairings of stimuli that are designated stimulus members and response members, (*b*) strengths and patterns of initial stimulus-response relationships, and (*c*) percentages and patterns of occurrence of stimuli. Also common to these situations are possible formats of presentation and various temporal parameters. The stimuli of these situations can vary with respect to meaningfulness and related attributes, similarity, familiarity, and number of and associations among elements. Many other classes of variables are also shared, including instructions to respond discriminatively to features of complex stimuli whether induced by the experimenter or by the subject.

Patterns of Pairing. As suggested above, the one or more sentences of connected discourse can be transformed into $n:1$ or $1:n$ paired-associates situations. Other sentences might be transformed into $1:1$ or $n:n$ paired-associates situations or into various derived patterns or pairings.

The trial-to-trial randomization of paired-associates units and of particular pairs within units characteristic of paired-associates learning could be realized in connected discourse. Thus, with a compound sentence exemplifying $1:1$ pairings such as "Long-horned grasshoppers are Tettigoniidae, short-horned grasshoppers are Acrididae, click beetles are Elateridae, blister beetles are Meloidae," the order of occurrence of each component simple sentence could be varied randomly from trial to trial. Alternatively, the order of occurrence of paired associates can be constant from trial to trial. Also, just as for paired-associates situations, the pairings of each common and scientific name could be unidirectional or bidirectional.

As a transition between paired associates and connected discourse, each component simple sentence could be presented with each common name and "are" as the stimulus member, with the scientific name being the response member. Or the common name might be the stimulus member with "are" plus the scientific name being the response member.

Strength and Pattern of Initial Stimulus-Response Relationships. As Rosenberg has shown for phrases or form class pairs (1965), the strength of relationships between stimuli of connected discourse situations can be varied, and does influence rate of acquisition. With respect to the illustrative sentence used above, the strength of the relationships of each common name to its paired and other scientific names might vary, as might the strength of the relationships among common and scientific names.[4]

Percentage and Pattern of Occurrence of Stimuli. Not all the stimuli of the sentence or sentences of connected discourse need appear on every trial. Thus, in each component simple sentence of the illustrative sentence used above, scientific or common names might be omitted in variations analogous to the manipulation of the percentage of occurrence of stimulus or response members in paired-associate experiments. Moreover, should both stimuli of particular pairs of scientific and common names be omitted in some trials, the arrangement could be regarded as a variation on the part-whole arrangement.

Format of Presentation. As noted above, sentences are typically acquired with trials involving study and test phases. However, as also noted, they could be and have been presented in a serial anticipation format. A closer approximation to the anticipation format would be to present the part of each clause or sentence designated as the stimulus with a requirement of anticipation of that part of each clause or sentence to be designated as the response. Complete sentences might be presented in the study phase with just those parts designated as the stimuli presented in the test phase. In the conceptual model Rothkopf (1965) proposed for learning from written sentences, he treats these and other aspects of format of presentation.

Temporal Variables. The duration of each stimulus of a sentence, the interval between each stimulus, and the interval between each sentence of a set and between repetitions of a set may be varied. Thus, for the illustrative sentence about insects used above presented under what is an approximation to an anticipation format of presentation, the durations of exposure for common names (with or without the common names) may be varied independently, as may be the interval between completion of this sequence for a particular simple sentence and the occurrence of the stimulus of the next.

The temporal variables of both anticipation and recall formats of presentation are described exhaustively by Nodine and Goss (1968, unpublished manuscript). Conceivably, as they suggest, these temporal variables can be reduced further to immediate contiguity and frequency of occurrence of stimuli and recognition responses to them both alone and in sequence. Similar, if not identical, parameters can be identified for connected discourse situations either when stimuli are presented successively or when they are presented simultaneously but with control of direction and duration of subjects' orientation toward parts of the sentences.

Meaningfulness and Related Attributes, Similarity, Familiarization, Number of and Association Among Elements. Each of these classes of variables is a property of stimuli or relationships of stimuli to recognition and to association responses. As shown in figures 2 and 3, relationships of stimuli to recognition and to association responses are among the observed and presumed stimulus-response relationships of the connected discourse situation and also of the list situation from the study phase of the initial trial to the test phase of the criterion trial.

The illustrative sentence on insects used above was selected because of relative simplicity of transformation to paired associates in a 1:1 pattern. Even for sentences that require more complex transformations, however, these several classes of variables are of demonstrated or potential significance for acquisition and other phenomena, just as they are of demonstrated or potential significance for acquisition as well as other phenomena of paired-associates situations.

Syntactic or grammatical structure of sentences is a class of variables that has been ignored here. One reason is the lack of data on acquisition and even more so on extinction, retention, and transfer as influenced by grammatical factors.[5] Another reason is the belief that differences in syntactic or grammatical structure are substantially or completely reducible to other classes of variables, such as strengths and patterns of initial relationships between and among the stimuli (strictly the stimuli, recognition, and association responses to the stimuli).

Strengths and patterns of initial relationships between and among stimuli (stimuli, recognition, and association response thereto) are, in turn, functions of variables from among the classes noted above, namely, percentages and patterns of occurrence of stimuli; format of presentation; temporal variables; meaningfulness and related attributes, similarity, familiarization-satiation, and number of and associations among elements of stimuli.

Reduction of syntactic or grammatical structure to these other classes of variables may, in some cases, fail to account for observed changes during acquisition and other phenomena with connected discourse. On these occasions two other classes of variables may prove pertinent. One class includes order and sequence of words, punctuation or intonation contours, definite and indefinite articles, and various prefixes and suffixes (bound morphemes), as well as auxiliaries. Another, related, class is basic sentence patterns consisting of extra-list associative responses that are names for grammatical categories or functions and particular orders of occurrence of these responses. This class reduces to patterns of relationships among these responses and of these responses to specific words that might enter into a sentence. In turn, both classes are conceived as reducible to percentages and patterns of occurrence of stimuli and other more basic classes of variables. Thus, no new concepts and principles are necessary (Goss, 1961c).

From the beginning of speech, the acquisition of names for

situations, objects, or classes of these stimuli, and of names for parts or properties of situations and objects makes a pervasive demand on humans. For particular situations or objects of several properties, the relationships of situations or objects to properties, and the converse, approximate $1:n$ and $n:1$ patterns of pairings, respectively. Because of contiguity, frequency, and perhaps other variables, the relationships for a situation or an object and its properties might be relatively stronger than relationships involving other situations or objects and their properties. Contingent on particular, later stimulus conditions, including instructions, responses of naming situations or objects and their properties should then occur together. The patterns of these occurrences would be or would approximate those described as noun phrases or as a noun phrase plus a verb phrase.

With elaboration to include similarity-dissimilarity based on form, position, and pattern, most, if not all, "phrases" of phrase-structure or constituent analyses (Johnson, 1965; Miller, 1962; Osgood, 1963) are conceived as derived from particular antecedent stimulus and stimulus-response conditions by means of general laws of learning such as contiguity, frequency, and similarity-dissimilarity. In such a general analysis of "how a sentence is actually manufactured or understood by users of the language" (Miller, 1962, p. 750), generative rules are viewed as empirical generalizations that are consequences of other conditions and laws. In apparent direct opposition is a conception of generative rules as innate with external data or appropriate stimulation serving to initiate-facilitate or to activate them (Chomsky, 1965).

Reasonably direct data on relationships between occurrences of words in particular order-sequences and antecedent-stimulus and stimulus-response conditions, particularly for young children, are scarce. However, there are no compelling data against an analysis of the genesis of syntactic structures in terms of particular antecedent-stimulus and stimulus-response conditions in conjunction with a few general laws of association. And there is ample precedent of the usefulness of extension of concepts and principles that have some basis in experimental findings with situations that are somewhat homologous to extra-laboratory situations.

Various arguments have been advanced against the preceding analysis of the genesis of syntactic structures. One of these arguments, perhaps the most frequently advanced in recent years, is Chomsky's (1957) criticism of a Markovian or finite-state theory of the generation of sentences on grounds of insufficient time for exposure to an "infinite" number of acceptable sentences and of inadequacy in dealing with embedding. Nothing in the analysis of classes of variables that determine acquisition and use of sentences outlined above entails the finite-state or Markovian theory criticized by Chomsky. For example, under appropriate conditions different constructions including self-embedding could be learned and then used to generate sentences. Osgood (1963, p. 742) takes exception to Chomsky's arguments on different grounds.

Another argument is in terms of a suggested reduction to concepts and principles of conditioning; it might be called guilt by conditioning. Thus, Miller (1962) describes an approach which he later summarizes as "by successive reduction of language to meaning to reference to conditioning." Prior to this summary he states: "I have no quarrel with that approach as long as we recognize that it treats only the simplest 1% of the psycholinguistic problem, and that our crucially important human skill in arranging symbols in novel and useful combinations is largely ignored" (p. 748).

An analysis in terms of antecendent-stimulus and stimulus-response conditions in conjunction with laws of association does allow for "arranging symbols in novel and useful combinations" and even permits specification of when such combinations might occur (e.g., Hull, 1930). It also allows for the occurrence of symbols in routine or conventional combinations or order-sequences. However, in applications of this or any other analysis, until criteria for novel-conventional and useful-useless dimensions are made more explicit, classification of particular combinations of symbols for particular subjects on particular occasions will remain difficult. When such classifications by these dimensions is possible, the percentage of combinations of symbols that are novel and useful can be estimated. Until then estimates of percentages of particular kinds of psycholinguistic problems will be fancies rather than facts.

Various advantages of tabular and other formats to textual exposition were mentioned earlier. These same advantages may often hold for acquisition with paired-associates situations as compared to acquisition with connected discourse situations. Thus, paired-associates situations do not involve transitional devices that distract and waste time and effort. Also, pairs of stimuli that are to be associated with each other are typically placed in close proximity in space and time and isolated from other pairs by randomization of orders of occurrence, instructions, the "mechanics" of presentation, and other factors.

In many sentences, words that are not part of the specified or more important relationships must be disregarded. Subjects often must search for and select the stimuli of the specified or important relationships so that the two or more stimuli of these relationships can be rehearsed in close temporal contiguity. Various devices can be and have been used to reduce these disadvantages of connected discourse. Stimuli that belong together can be placed together. The stimuli can be italicized or otherwise made more discriminable. Alternatively, paired associates can be made more difficult to learn by adding irrelevant elements to stimulus members, response members, or both. Theory and data concerning the conditions and consequences of selection of discriminable or critical parts among complex stimuli have been treated elsewhere (see, e.g., Goss, 1955, 1961b, 1961c, 1964a; Goss and Nodine, 1965, pp. 210–214; Rothkopf, 1965).

Transfer Between Situations

Both nonmediational and mediational analyses of transfer with paired-associates situations for two different lists each used once or one used twice have been schematized in detail (Goss, 1962, 1964c). Nonmediational analyses of transfer with list and connected-discourse situations have been schematized in these two sources as well. As mentioned earlier, except for lists presented by means of the serial anticipation arrangement, transfer from list or connected discourse situations to paired-associates situations, and the converse, has been of little concern either theoretically or empirically.[6] Once general similarities and differences between and among paired-associates, list, and connected-discourse situations have been identified, paradigms for transfer between and among these situations can be developed. In turn, these paradigms can guide both theory and experimentation.

The paradigms considered here are nonmediational. Moreover, they are limited to those particular lists and sentences that can be most easily transformed into paired-associates situations or that are transformations from paired associates that involve minimum embellishment in terms of transitional devices, redundancy, variations in sentence patterns to avoid monotony, and the like.

The paradigm of transfer considered first is that in which the stimulus and response members of the paired-associates situation are not changed when presented in lists or sentences. However, function words and other words would be added, and also punctuation and occurrence of some letters in upper case and others in lower case. Conversely, in changes from sentences to paired associates there are few differences between the stimuli of lists and sentences, except the elimination of most or all function words and any other words considered or known to be of little importance, as well as the elimination of punctuation and case. Paradigms of transfer in which some or all of the stimuli are changed are then considered.

Unchanged Stimuli. Although the stimulus and response members remain the same, the addition or elimination of function words, other unimportant words, punctuation, and case have been noted. Another dimension is changes in the order of occurrence of paired-associates units and of the corresponding subsets of stimuli of connected discourse. As suggested above, a variable order for paired-associates units and a fixed order for connected discourse is conventional, but not mandatory. Hence, variable-variable, fixed-variable, and fixed-fixed orders are also possible. Still another dimension of change involves combinations of unidirectional and bidirectional occurrence of stimuli as stimulus and response members.

In learning with paired-associates situations, duration of exposure of stimulus and response members, intervals between these exposures, and intervals between trials are controlled by the experimenter. In learning connected discourse with visual presentation, entire sentences or passages may be presented at one time or stimuli or subsets of stimuli may be presented sequentially. With auditory presentation, their occurrence is sequential. Whether presented all at once or sequentially, stimuli are grouped by punctuation or intonation. They may be grouped by other means such as spatial and temporal separation and coding by color, type case and face, or both.

Paired-associates situations are usually presented by devices and under instructions that minimize orientation toward and selection of the stimuli involved in the particular stimulus-response relationships to be strengthened. With connected discourse, such orientation and selection might also be minimized by the ways of grouping stimuli just noted, and by instructing or by training subjects in ways of grouping the stimuli when discriminable bases for grouping are present.

Almost certain to prove one of the most important dimensions of change is the extent to which stimuli that are paired or occur as pairs in paired-associates situations occur in the same spatial and, possibly, temporal relationships in connected discourse. Changes from such contiguity are essentially the same as the partial to complete reversal of pairings of the A–B_r change from one paired-associates list to another.

Stimuli that function as stimulus and response members in paired-associates situations might be paired in the opposite direction in connected discourse situations. The change is analogous to the A–B, B–A paradigm. An A–B, B_r–A paradigm can also be distinguished.

Determination of the relative significance of changes along the dimensions mentioned, and along others, will require extensive experimentation. But the general problems and methods of such experimentation are clearly continuous with available theory, methods, and findings.

With what might be designated the A–B, A–B paradigm, and possibly the A–B, B–A paradigm, findings for transfer from lists presented under the serial anticipation arrangement to paired associates in a 1:1 pattern, or the converse, can serve as some basis for predictions about direction and extent of transfer.[7] At present, contingent on conditions that are not yet easy to specify, transfer is likely to range from slightly or uncertainly negative to uncertainly and slightly positive (Jensen and Rohwer, 1965). At least as general differences between paired-associates and connected-discourse situations in conditions of presentation decrease, transfer should be increasingly positive. As is known both from observation of test performance and from data on retention tested by recognition, positive transfer does occur from connected discourse to those approximations of paired associates called fill-in or multiple-choice test items.

With approximations of the A–B, A–B_r and A–B, B_r–A paradigms, as reversal becomes more complete transfer should be increasingly negative. In general, transfer should be less negative with the A–B, B_r–A paradigm than with the A–B, A–B_r paradigm. Complicating predictions with all four paradigms are the allowances that must be made for effects of integration of recognition responses to stimuli and, perhaps, of greater response-mediated dissimilarity or similarity among stimuli (Goss, 1955, 1963).

The above paradigms can also be elaborated into those for retroaction and for proaction, respectively, by adding the A–B of the first list or by repeating the A–B, A–B_r, B–A, or B_r–A of the second list. Where positive transfer is expected from acquisition of the first list to acquisition of the second, retroactive and proactive facilitation should occur. Where negative transfer is expected, retroactive or proactive inhibition should occur.

Whether acquisition of the first and second list is for a certain number of trials or through achievement of a criterion of mastery, both lists are usually presented for several trials. A limiting case is alternation of lists from one trial to the next. With paired-associates and connected-discourse situations, alternation might be after phases of 1 to n trials. Conceivably, transfer would be influenced by the situation used first, and number of trials with one situation and then the other.

Changed Stimuli. Those stimuli that function either as stimulus or response members in paired-associates situations might be different in connected discourse situations, and both differences might obtain. Regardless of the magnitude of the difference, changed stimulus members are designated "D" and changed response members are designated "C." With the function or direction of the stimuli the same in paired-associates and connected-discourse situations, the resultant paradigms are analogous to the A–B, D–B; A–B, A–C; and A–B, D–C paradigms of transfer between paired-associates lists. When D and C are markedly different from A and B the condition serves as the control.

With the functions or direction of the stimuli reversed, three additional paradigms are generated: A–B, B_r–D; A–B, C_r–A; and A–B, C_r–D. The last of these paradigms holds only for differences between A and D and between D and C within the ranges of the generalization gradients. Beyond those ranges the A–B, D–C and A–B, C_r–D paradigms are identical.

When present, these differences in stimuli are over and above any of the differences in conditions of presentation noted above. Those conditions presumably hold across paradigms whether the stimuli are the same or different. For connected discourse presented all at once for subjects to read either at their own pace or within a certain amount of time, and for paired associates presented one at a time, the differences in conditions of presentation are such that, regardless of paradigm, little or no transfer might occur. As differences in conditions of presentation decrease, principles and resultant predictions regarding direction and extent of simple transfer, proaction, and retroaction for various of the paradigms for paired-associate situations should hold increasingly for simple transfer, proaction, and retroaction involving paired-associates and connected-discourse situations. For paired associates in a $1:1$ pattern, and possibly in a $n:1$ pattern, principles and predictions have been worked out in some detail, most recently by Dallett (1965) and Martin (1965).

Contingent on conditions of presentation, the mediational paradigms of table 3 (see p. 20), although developed for criterion or terminal paired-associates situations, may hold for connected discourse situations. Schematized elsewhere (Goss, 1962, 1964b) are some of the different combinations of prior experiences with paired-associates situations that are presumed to bring about the initial stimulus-response relationships of criterion or terminal paired-associates tasks shown in table 3. These paradigms of prior experiences might also be used to account for initial stimulus-response relationships of criterion or terminal connected discourse situations. And these paradigms can be extended to include prior experiences involving only connected discourse situations or both connected discourse and paired-associates situations. The resultant paradigms are too complex for presentation and explanation here.

APPLICATION TO PRODUCTION AND USE
OF INSTRUCTIONAL MATERIALS

Homologies between paired-associates situations and parts of tabular formats for the presentation of knowledge such as table 1 were described previously in considerable detail. Homologies between the structures of list and connected-discourse situations and those of both tabular and textual exposition formats were also described previously, but in less detail. Because of these homologies, and because of the many classes of variables common to laboratory situations and the formats for written instruction, principles of acquisition, possible extinction, retention, and transfer obtained in laboratory situations were presumed to be of pertinence in explaining those same phenomena with the written instructional formats. The greater the resemblance between the structure of a particular laboratory situation and a particular format, the more likely the significance of theory and data obtained with the laboratory situation for production and use of written instructional material in that format.

The transformations between paired-associates and connected-discourse situations considered in the previous section are essentially paralleled by the transformations from some kinds of textual exposition to tables, and the converse. Accordingly, on the basis of the homologies and commonality of classes of variables, principles of transfer involving paired-associates to connected-discourse situations might be expected to hold for transfer from the tabular format to textual exposition, and the converse.

Unfortunately, neither data nor detailed theory on transfer involving paired-associates and connected-discourse situations are now available. But the general nature of experimentation and theory was outlined in the previous section. Initially, theory and experimentation with the laboratory situations are likely to be developed for relatively simple paired-associates lists and sentences. Application of the resultant principles to simple transfer, proaction, and retroaction with formats of presentation of knowledge is likely to be confined to tables and textual exposition of limited amounts of knowledge. But there appears to be no principle that precludes successive elaboration of both laboratory situations and formats for presentation of knowledge.

Both as laboratory situations and as formats of presentation, diagrams, figures, and mathematical, logical expressions have not been treated in detail. For experiments on acquisition and other phenomena with diagrams like those shown in figure 1, however, the laboratory approach might be by selective successive presentation of each component relationship in the figure: all parts of a diagram might be masked except for the relationship of concern at a given point in acquisition; and subjects might be trained or instructed to orient toward, select, and rehearse each successive component relationship. Each component relationship might be presented in isolation from the entire figure as a paired associate or sentence. Following exposure of some or all of the simplest components in any one of these situations, they might be combined into progressively larger "parts" and then into the "whole." Or, they might be combined into the whole all at once. A similar approach might be employed for experiments concerned with acquisition and other phenomena with complex figures and mathematical, logical expressions.

GENERAL (S–R) CONCEPTS AND PRINCIPLES AND THE NATURE AND ORIGIN OF KNOWLEDGE

At the beginning the thesis was advanced that, directly or indirectly, many of the concepts and principles discovered and organized by near contemporary and contemporary S–R psychologists are pertinent to an understanding of the nature and origin of knowledge. Demonstrated in the preceding sections were continuity of approach, situations, and concepts, and principles from the simple situations of primary interest to most S–R psychologists through the relatively complex laboratory situations and formats for presentation of knowledge considered here.

The approach both here and in the theorizing and experimentation of S–R psychologists is the familiar one of simplification for more complete and more exact control, observation of changes in component stimulus-response relationships, and formulation of those changes, ultimately by mathematical representation. As more adequate explanatory concepts and principles for simple situations are developed, they are extended to more complex situations. Typically, complex situations are restructured into several component situations whose less complex stimulus-response elements and relationships or structures are homologous with the structures of the simple situations for which explanatory concepts and principles have been developed already. Often, concepts and principles for simple situations must be supplemented by composition rules or laws (Bergmann, 1953). Hull's (1952) use of the principles of conflict and chaining is illustrative of supplementation by composition rules. Continuity of situations is implicit in this approach. After the inevitable false extensions and overextensions, stimulus-response elements and relationships of simple situations will be manipulated more completely and more exactly. Homologous structures then will be discerned in more complex situations.

Continuity of concepts and principles is also implicit in this approach. Again after inevitable false extensions and over-extensions, concepts and principles will be evolved that will provide more complete and more exact explanations of change in the stimulus-response elements and relationships of simple laboratory situations. Supplemented by composition rules, these concepts and principles will be extended to provide more complete and more exact explanations of the more complex laboratory situations. Both the simple and more complex laboratory situations are homologous with many simple and complex extra-laboratory situations.

On the basis of homologous structures and commonality of classes of variables, supplemented on occasion by additional composition rules, concepts and principles discovered and organized in the laboratory are used to explain learning phenomena observed in extra-laboratory situations, including the various formats for presentation of knowledge. Such applications to learning phenomena in extra-laboratory situations should hardly be surprising; after all, many laboratory situations originated as simplified representations of extra-laboratory situations.

SUMMARY

The first of four objectives was specification of the general nature of scientific and other systematic knowledge with particular emphasis on conventional formats of presentation for written instruction and on common or possible laboratory situations. Relationships among formats were described and these formats, particularly tables and textual exposition, were compared with laboratory situations, particularly paired-associates, lists, and connected discourse. The stimulus-response elements and relationships or structures of the laboratory situations were described, and homologies between these structures and the structures of formats for presentation of knowledge were then outlined, as were classes of variables common to the laboratory situations and the formats.

The second objective was detailed consideration of similarities in structure between paired-associates and connected-discourse situations. The two classes of situations were then compared with respect to other classes of variables. Paradigms for conceptualizing and investigating transfer from one class of situations to the other were outlined.

The third objective was to expand the domain of immediate or potential application of concepts and principles discovered and organized by means of laboratory situations to development and use of written instructional materials. Of particular concern was the pertinence of theory and data on transfer from paired-associates to connected-discourse situations, and the converse.

The fourth objective was to demonstrate that, directly or indirectly, many of the concepts and principles discovered and organized by S–R psychologists are pertinent to an understanding of the nature and origin of knowledge. Continuities of approach, situations, concepts, and principles were noted.

NOTES

1. Some of the material in this paper emerged from a seminar on the learning of connected discourse at the University of Massachusetts during the spring of 1965. The other participants were Nancy J. Cobb, Jean Carl Cohen, Joseph Halpern, and Barbara S. Musgrave. Other material was developed as part of a research program on paired-associates learning under variations in occurrences of response members sponsored by the Training and Personnel Branch of the Office of Naval Research. Still other material was developed for a course, syllabus (Goss, 1964b), and mimeographed manuscript (Goss, 1962) on verbal behavior and learning. Finally, Louis E. Price made a number of useful suggestions, as did Helen L. Rowell.

2. Because paired-associates learning involves integrating and making available responses to response members, the list situation might be regarded as more "primitive" than the paired-associates situation. One reason for rejecting this view is that integration and availability of responses enter paired-associates learning as variables that range from complete integration-availability to essentially no integration-availability of the responses to be associated with the initiating stimuli. Quite conceivably, the starting point for discovery and

organization of principles of paired-associates learning should be lists in which integration-availability of both stimulus and response members is complete.

Another reason for rejecting this view are various differences between list and paired-associates situations. Thus, in the former situation, essentially all stimuli have the same dual function. But, as noted above, in the latter situation some stimuli are manipulatively separated as initiating stimuli while others are manipulatively separated as stimuli for responses. Still another reason for rejecting this view is the presupposition that acquisition of lists involves prior acquisition of recognition responses to the stimuli of lists. Such acquisition is more appropriately conceived in terms of the paired-associates situation, as are the presumed successive stages of integration of elements of response members necessary to make them available.

In addition, lists often consist of several subsets of stimuli with a presumed common implicit response for each subset (e.g., Bousfield and Cohen, 1956; Cohen, 1963). Such lists can be regarded as an implicit or incomplete paired-associates situation that involves several stimuli for each response. As noted below, this pattern of pairings is labeled $n:1$.

3. "Syntactical rules," as an example of conceptual schemes, have been treated elsewhere (Goss, 1961c). Such rules might influence acquisition and retention through one or more of the means mentioned there (p. 58). As suggested there, also, syntactical rules, as conceptual schemes, are probably of significance for behaviors that can be characterized as "composing" and "editing."

4. Individual differences are not included here as a separate category because such differences, when made more specific, often turn out to be already included in other classes of variables. Thus, individuals are likely to differ markedly with respect to strength and pattern of initial stimulus-response relationships. When these variables are specified for individuals or for homogeneous groups of individuals (Shapiro, 1965), they reflect individual differences. Individual differences with respect to meaningfulness and related attributes can also be determined and then allowed for or manipulated.

5. Some findings (e.g., Johnson, 1965; Marks and Miller, 1964; Martin and Jones, 1965; Martin, Davidson, and Williams, 1965) suggest that syntactical rules may influence acquisition of connected discourse. However, Martin and collaborators did not find this variable to be very potent; and their results may be restricted to noun-verb pairs that can be characterized as semantically fanciful. Unfortunately, Johnson's two- and three-phrase sentences apparently were not equated for attributes of the individual words other than Thorndike-Lorge counted frequency of occurrence.

Marks and Miller's sentences presumably represented the four combinations of syntactic and nonsyntactic, semantic and nonsemantic. The sentences representing these combinations were not equated for initial probabilities that the ith word of any one of the sentences evoked other words of that sentence, or of the other sentences. Thus, differences in rate of acquisition may reflect differences among combinations in such probabilities operating in unknown ways as sources of intra-sentence and inter-sentence interference.

At present, therefore, the importance of syntactic rules per se in learning phenomena with connected discourse cannot be regarded as established. In the particular example here, and for learning phenomena with connected discourse in the form of grammatically acceptable sentences, when other variables have been allowed for it seems doubtful that syntactic rules per se are of much importance. However, the matter is empirical.

6. That transfer from familiarization-satiation experiences to paired-associates learning constitutes another exception is a defensible position. Familiarization experiences, at least, have been conceived as a means to integration of recognition responses to stimuli and thereby to greater availability of those responses during subsequent acquisition of paired-associates lists in which those stimuli occur as stimulus members, response members, or both (Goss and Nodine, 1965, pp. 153–178; Underwood and Schulz, 1960).

7. For transfer from a paired-associates situation to the serial anticipation arrangement, k 1 : 1 paired-associates units might be transformed into a list of 2 k stimuli in which the stimuli of one paired-associates unit constitutes the first two stimuli, those of another unit the next two stimuli, and so on through the kth paired-associates unit. The general conditions of presentation typically differ so markedly that little transfer would be expected due to nonspecific factors. Prior acquisition with the stimuli of the list as paired associates might facilitate acquisition of anticipations of the second stimulus within successive pairs. But acquisition of anticipations of the first stimulus of the next pair as a response to the second stimulus of the prior pair might be retarded by interference from the R–S, or backward associations, between the second member of the prior pair and the first member of that pair.

For transfer from the serial anticipation arrangement to a paired-associates situation, a list of $2k$ stimuli might be transformed into k successive 1 : 1 paired-associates units. Again, the general conditions of presentation differ. Whereas the associations established previously between the first and second member of each unit might facilitate, the associations established between the second member of each pair and the first member of another pair might interfere. One basis for retardation would be interference with implicit rehearsal of members of pairs. Subjects might respond to the response member of a pair not with the stimulus member of that pair but with the stimulus member of another pair. In turn, this stimulus might elicit either the response member of the other pair or its own response member. Either would interfere.

Because of these and other considerations, transfer from paired-associates situations to the serial anticipation arrangement, or the converse, is not likely to be consistent in direction or marked in degree. As noted, available findings agree with this expectation. The same considerations hold for transfer from paired-associates situations to connected discourse, or the converse. Accordingly, similarity between general conditions of presentation is stressed here as a probable minimum condition for transfer between the two kinds of situations. Moreover, some provision must be made for similarity of the patterns and content of specific associations.

REFERENCES

Arnoult, M. D. Stimulus predifferentiation: Some generalizations and hypotheses. *Psychol. Bull.,* 1957, *54,* 339–350.

Battig, W. F., Allen, M., and Jensen, A. R. Priority of free recall of newly learned items. *J. verb. Learn. verb. Behav.,* 1965, *4,* 175–179.

Bergmann, G. Theoretical psychology. *Annu. Rev. Psychol.,* 1953, *4,* 435–458.

Bourne, L. E., Jr., Guy, D. E., Dodd, D. H., and Justesen, D. R. Concept identification: The effects of varying length and informational components of the intertrial interval. *J. exp. Psychol.,* 1965, *69,* 624–629.

Bousfield, W. A., and Cohen, B. H. Clustering in recall as a function of the number of word-categories in stimulus-word lists. *J. gen. Psychol.,* 1956, *54,* 95–106.

Bruner, J. S. The growth of mind. *Amer. Psychologist,* 1965, *20,* 1007–1017.

Calkins, M. W. Studies from the Harvard Psychological Laboratory (II.) D. Association (I.) *Psychol. Rev.,* 1894, *1,* 476–483.

———. Studies from the Harvard Psychological Laboratory (III.) B. Association (II.) *Psychol. Rev.,* 1896, *3,* 32–49.

Carroll, J. B. The critical need in the study of language. *College Composition & Communication,* 1962, *13,* 1–4.

Chomsky, N. *Syntactic structures.* The Hague: Mouton, 1957.

———. A review of B. F. Skinner's "Verbal Behavior." *Language,* 1959, *35,* 26–58.

———. *Aspects of the theory of syntax.* Cambridge: MIT Press, 1965.

Cobb, N. J., Farrick, N. C., Goss, A. E., and Gregory, B. N. Integration-availability of members of paired associates as functions of their meaningfulness and percentage of occurrence. Paper read at Eastern Psychological Association, Philadelphia, April, 1964.

Cofer, C. N. Further studies of clustering in the recall of nouns embedded during presentation in sentences. Department of Psychology, New York University, Tech. Rep. no. 2, Contract Nonr 285(47), 1961.

————. On some factors in the organizational characteristics of free recall. *Amer. Psychologist,* 1965, *20,* 261–272.

Cohen, B. H. Recall of categorized word lists. *J. exp. Psychol.,* 1963, *66,* 227–234.

Dallett, K. M. A transfer surface for paradigms in which second-list S–R pairings do not correspond to first-list pairings. *J. verb. Learn. verb. Behav.,* 1965, *4,* 528–537.

Dallett, K. M., and D'Andrea, L. Mediation instructions versus unlearning instructions in the A–B, A–C paradigm. *J. exp. Psychol.,* 1965, *69,* 460–466.

Deese, J. Influence of inter-item associative strength upon immediate free recall. *Psychol. Rep.,* 1959, *5,* 305–312.

Dewey, J. The reflex arc concept in psychology. *Psychol. Rev.,* 1896, *3,* 357–370.

Dollard, J., and Miller, N. E. *Personality and psychotherapy.* New York: McGraw-Hill, 1950.

Duncan, C. P. Mediation in verbal concept learning. *J. verb. Learn. verb. Behav.,* 1965, *4,* 1–6.

Earhard, B., and Mandler, G. Mediated associations: Paradigms, controls, and mechanisms. *Canad. J. Psychol.,* 1965, *19,* 346–378.

Ekstrand, B. R., and Underwood, B. J. Free learning and recall as a function of unit-sequence and letter-sequence interference. *J. verb. Learn. verb. Behav.,* 1965, *4,* 390–396.

Ellis, H. *The transfer of learning.* New York: Macmillan, 1965.

Frase, L. T. Validity judgments of syllogisms in relation to two sets of terms. *J. educ. Psychol.,* 1966, *57,* 239–245.

Gagné, R. M. The acquisition of knowledge. *Psychol. Rev.,* 1962, *69,* 355–365.

Gagné, R. M., Mayor, J. R., Garstens, H. L., and Paradise, N. E. Factors in acquiring knowledge of a mathematical task. *Psychol. Monogr.,* 1962, *76,* no. 7 (whole no. 526).

Garner, W. R., and Whitman, J. R. Form and amount of internal structure as factors in free-recall learning of nonsense words. *J. verb. Learn. verb. Behav.,* 1965, *4,* 257–266.

Gibson, E. J. A systematic application of the concepts of generalization and differentiation to verbal learning. *Psychol. Rev.,* 1940, *47,* 196–229.

Gomulicki, B. R. The development and present status of the trace theory of memory. *Brit. J. Psychol., Monogr. Suppl.,* 1953, no. 29.

Goss, A. E. A stimulus-response analysis of the interaction of cue-producing and instrumental responses. *Psychol. Rev.,* 1955, *62,* 20–31.

———. Early behaviorism and verbal mediating responses. *Amer. Psychologist,* 1961a, *16,* 285–298.

———. Verbal mediating responses and concept formation. *Psychol. Rev.,* 1961b, *68,* 248–274.

———. Acquisition and use of conceptual schemes. In C. N. Cofer (Ed.), *Verbal learning and verbal behavior.* New York: McGraw-Hill, 1961c.

———. Verbal behavior. Mimeographed manuscript, Univ. of Massachusetts, Amherst, Massachusetts, 1962.

———. Comments on Professor Noble's paper. In C. N. Cofer and B. S. Musgrave (Eds.), *Verbal behavior and learning: Problems and processes.* New York: McGraw-Hill, 1963.

———. Verbal mediation. *Psychol. Rec.,* 1964a, *14,* 363–382.

———. Verbal learning. Mimeographed syllabus, Univ. of Massachusetts, Amherst, Massachusetts, 1964b.

———. Response-mediated (mediate) association. Unpublished manuscript, 1964c.

———. Manifest strengthening of correct response of paired associates under postcriterion zero percent occurrence of response members. *J. gen. Psychol.,* 1965a, *72,* 135–144.

———. Paired associates and knowledge. Paper read at the American Psychological Association, Chicago, September, 1965b.

———. Paired-associates learning by young children as functions of initial associative strength and percentage of occurrence of response members. *J. exp. Child Psychol.,* 1966, *4,* 398–407.

Goss, A. E., and Cobb, N. J. Formation, maintenance, generalization, and retention of response hierarchies: The role of meaningfulness of response members. *J. exp. Psychol.,* 1967, *74,* 272–281.

Goss, A. E., and Greenfeld, N. Transfer to a motor task as influenced by conditions and degree of prior discrimination training. *J. exp. Psychol.,* 1958, *55,* 258–269.

Goss, A. E., and Nodine, C. F. *Paired-associates learning: The role of meaningfulness, similarity, and familiarization.* New York: Academic Press, 1965.

Goss, A. E., Nodine, C. F., Gregory, B. N., Taub, H. A., and Kennedy, K. E. Stimulus characteristics and percentage of occurrence of response members in paired-associates learning. *Psychol. Monogr.,* 1962, *76,* no. 12 (whole no. 531).

Goulet, L. R. Interlist response meaningfulness and transfer effects under the A–B, A–C paradigm. *J. exp. Psychol.,* 1965, *70,* 264–269.

Houston, J. P. Short-term retention of verbal units with equated degrees of learning. *J. exp. Psychol.,* 1965, *70,* 75–78.

Hull, C. L. Knowledge and purpose as habit mechanisms. *Psychol. Rev.,* 1930, *37,* 511–525.

———. *A behavior system.* New Haven: Yale Univ. Press, 1952.

Hunt, E. B. *Concept learning.* New York: Wiley, 1962.

Jahnke, J. C. Primacy and recency effects in serial-position curves of immediate recall. *J. exp. Psychol.,* 1965, *70,* 130–132.

James, C. T., and Hakes, D. T. Mediated transfer in a four-stage, stimulus-equivalence paradigm. *J. verb. Learn. verb. Behav.,* 1965, *4,* 89–93.

James, W. *The principles of psychology.* New York: Holt, 1890.

Jenkins, J. J. Mediated associations: Paradigms and situations. In C. N. Cofer and B. S. Musgrave (Eds.), *Verbal behavior and learning: Problems and processes.* New York: McGraw-Hill, 1963.

Jensen, A. R., and Rohwer, W. D., Jr. What is learned in serial learning? *J. verb. Learn. verb. Behav.,* 1965, *4,* 62–72.

Johnson, N. F. Linguistic models and functional units of language behavior. In S. Rosenberg (Ed.), *Directions in psycholinguistics.* New York: Macmillan, 1965.

King, D. J. Toward a theory of meaningful verbal learning. Albion Coll. Unpublished manuscript, 1966.

Koffka, K. *Principles of Gestalt psychology.* New York: Harcourt, Brace, 1935.

Köhler, W. *Gestalt psychology.* New York: Liveright, 1929.

Lacey, H. M. Mediating verbal responses and stimulus similarity as factors in conceptual naming by school age children. *J. exp. Psychol.,* 1961, *62,* 113–121.

Lewin, K. *Dynamic theory of personality.* New York: McGraw-Hill, 1935.

Marks, L. E., and Miller, G. A. The role of semantic and syntactic constraints in the memorization of English sentences. *J. verb. Learn. verb. Behav.,* 1964, *3,* 1–5.

Martin, E. Transfer of verbal paired associates. *Psychol. Rev.,* 1965, *72,* 327–343.

Martin, J. G., and Jones, R. L. Size and structure of grammatical units in paired-associate learning at two age levels. *J. exp. Psychol.*, 1965, *70*, 407–411.

Martin, J. G., Davidson, J. R., and Williams, M. L. Grammatical agreement and set in learning at two age levels. *J. exp. Psychol.*, 1965, *70*, 570–574.

McCullers, J. C. An analysis of some factors underlying intralist associative transfer in paired-associate learning. *J. exp. Psychol.*, 1963, *65*, 163–168.

———. Type of associative interference as a factor in verbal paired-associate learning. *J. verb. Learn. verb. Behav.*, 1965, *4*, 12–16.

McNeill, B. Developmental Psycholinguistics. In F. Smith and G. A. Miller (Eds.), *The genesis of language.* Cambridge: MIT Press, 1966.

Miller, G. A. Some psychological studies of grammar. *Amer. Psychologist*, 1962, *17*, 748–762.

———. Language and psychology. In E. H. Lenneberg (Ed.), *New directions in the study of language.* Cambridge: MIT Press, 1964.

———. Some preliminaries to psycholinguistics. *Amer. Psychologist*, 1965, *20*, 15–20.

Miller, G. A., and Selfridge, J. A. Verbal context and the recall of meaningful material. *Amer. J. Psychol.*, 1950, *63*, 176–185.

Miller, G. A., Galanter, E., and Pribram, K. H. *Plans and the structure of behavior.* New York: Holt, Rinehart & Winston, 1960.

Miller, N. E., and Dollard, J. *Social learning and imitation.* New Haven: Yale Univ. Press, 1941.

Musgrave, B. S. The effect of nonsense-syllable compound stimuli on latency in a verbal paired-associate task. *J. exp. Psychol.*, 1962, *63*, 499–504.

Musgrave, B. S., and Cohen, J. C. Abstraction in verbal paired-associate learning. *J. exp. Psychol.*, 1966, *71*, 1–8.

Nodine, C. F. Stimulus durations and total learning time in paired-associates learning. *J. exp. Psychol.*, 1965, *69*, 534–536.

Nodine, C. F., and Goss, A. E. Temporal parameters in paired-associates learning. Unpublished manuscript, 1968.

Osgood, C. E. *Method and theory in experimental psychology.* New York: Oxford Univ. Press, 1953.

———. On understanding and creating sentences. *Amer. Psychologist*, 1963, *18*, 735–751.

Peterson, L. R. Prediction of responses in verbal habit hierarchies. *J. exp. Psychol.*, 1956, *51*, 249–252.

Peterson, M. J. Verbal response strength as a function of cultural frequency, schedule of reinforcement, and number of trials. *J. exp. Psychol.*, 1956, *52*, 371–376.

Pikas, A. *Abstraction and concept formation.* Studia Scientiae Paedagogicae Upsaliensia VII, Institute of Education, Uppsala Univ., 1965.

Postman, L. The present status of interference theory. In C. N. Cofer (Ed.), *Verbal learning and verbal behavior.* New York: McGraw-Hill, 1961.

———. Unlearning under conditions of successive interpolation. *J. exp. Psychol.*, 1965, *70*, 237–245.

Reed, H. B. Factors influencing the learning and retention of concepts: I. The influence of set. *J. exp. Psychol.*, 1946, *36*, 71–87.

Richardson, J. The relationship of stimulus similarity and number of responses. *J. exp. Psychol.*, 1958, *56*, 478–484.

———. The learning of concept names mediated by concept examples. *J. verb. Learn. verb. Behav.*, 1963, *1*, 281–288.

Riley, D. A. Memory for form. In L. Postman (Ed.), *Psychology in the making.* New York: Knopf, 1961.

Rosenberg, S. The influence of grammatical and associative habits on verbal learning. In S. Rosenberg (Ed.), *Directions in psycholinguistics.* New York: Macmillan, 1965.

Rothkopf, E. Z. Some theoretical and experimental approaches to problems in written instruction. In J. D. Krumboltz (Ed.), *Learning and the educational process.* Chicago: Rand-McNally, 1965.

Saravo, A. C., and Price, L. E. Associative transfer in verbal paired-associates learning as a function of stimulus similarity. *Psychon. Sci.*, 1967, *8*, 315–316.

Schulz, R. W. Learning of paired associates as a function of pronunciability and percentage of occurrence of stimulus or response members. *J. verb. Learn. verb. Behav.*, 1965, *4*, 494–497.

Schulz, R. W., and Lovelace, E. A. Mediation in verbal paired-associates learning: The role of temporal factors. *Psychon. Sci.*, 1964, *1*, 95–96.

Sears, R. R. Functional abnormalities of memory with special reference to amnesia. *Psychol. Bull.*, 1936, *33*, 229–274.

Shapiro, S. S. Paired-associates learning in children. *J. verb. Learn. verb. Behav.*, 1965, *4*, 170–174.

Skinner, B. F. *Science and human behavior.* New York: Macmillan, 1953.

———. *Verbal behavior.* New York: Appleton-Century-Crofts, 1957.

———. *The technology of teaching.* New York: Appleton-Century-Crofts, 1968.

Slamecka, N. J. Retention of connected discourse as a function of duration of interpolated learning. *J. exp. Psychol.*, 1962, *63*, 480–486.

Spence, K. W. The nature of discrimination learning in animals. *Psychol. Rev.*, 1936, *43*, 427–449.

———. The differential response in animals to stimuli varying within a single dimension. *Psychol. Rev.*, 1937, *44*, 430–444.

———. Cognitive versus stimulus-response theories of learning. *Psychol. Rev.*, 1950, *57*, 159–172.

———. A theory of emotionally based drive (D) and its relation to performance in simple learning situations. *Amer. Psychologist*, 1958, *13*, 131–141.

Spiker, C. C. Experiments with children on the hypothesis of acquired distinctiveness and equivalance of cues. *Child Developm.*, 1956, *27*, 253–263.

Staats, A. W., and Staats, C. K. *Complex human behavior*. New York: Holt, Rinehart & Winston, 1963.

Tolman, E. C. *Purposive behavior in animals and men*. New York: Appleton-Century-Crofts, 1932.

Underwood, B. J. An evaluation of the Gibson theory of verbal learning. In C. N. Cofer (Ed.), *Verbal learning and verbal behavior*. New York: McGraw-Hill, 1961.

———. The language repertoire of some problems in verbal learning. In S. Rosenberg (Ed.), *Directions in psycholinguistics*. New York: Macmillan, 1965.

Underwood, B. J., and Schulz, R. W. *Meaningfulness and verbal learning*. Philadelphia: Lippincott, 1960.

Underwood, B. J., Ekstrand, B. R., and Keppel, G. An analysis of intralist similarity on verbal learning with experiments on conceptual similarity. *J. verb. Learn. verb. Behav.*, 1965, *4*, 447–462.

Voss, J. F., Thompson, C. P., and Keegan, J. H. Acquisition of probabilistic paired associates as a function of $S-R_1$, $S-R_2$ probability. *J. exp. Psychol.*, 1959, *58*, 390–399.

Wertheimer, M. Gestalt theory. In W. D. Ellis (Ed.), *A source book of Gestalt psychology*. New York: Humanities Press, 1950.

Wicklund, D. A., Palermo, D. S., and Jenkins, J. J. Associative clustering in the recall of children as a function of verbal association strength. *J. exp. Psychol.*, 1965, *2*, 58–66.

Wilmer, R. Osgood's transfer surface: Extension and test. *J. verb. Learn. verb. Behav.*, 1964, *3*, 274–279.

Wittlinger, R., and Voss, J. F. Acquisition of S_1-R, S_2-R paired associates as a function of S_1-R, S_2-R probability. *J. exp. Psychol.*, 1964, *68*, 407–412.

Discussion of
Professor Goss's Paper

MURRAY GLANZER

New York University

Professor Goss has done a very good, detailed, and thorough job on a complex topic. Since there is very little detail that can be added, I shall consider some general aspects of his paper that cover the fields of knowledge, connected discourse, instructional materials, and paired-associates learning. His paper sets forth a general approach in which all of these can be interrelated.

I will focus on one central aspect of the structure outlined, that is, the relation between paired-associates learning and connected discourse. A full analysis of this relation involves, either explicitly or implicitly, an analysis of the remaining relations. From one point of view, knowledge is incorporated into connected discourse or language, and instructional materials are a special case of language.

Paired-associates learning plays a very special role in the Goss paper. It is the embodiment of a particular point of view concerning language, an additive S–R view. By additive S–R view I mean a view of complex performance as generated by the addition, or concatenation of elemental S–R sequences. The paper is an attempt to apply an additive S–R approach—a very liberalized and complex S–R approach—to a variety of linguistic performances.

68

If I am permitted to oversimplify the paper in this way, then there are two points that have relevance to the Goss paper. One point is primarily based on logical or theoretical considerations. It comes from the linguist. The other point is primarily based on empirical findings. It comes from the verbal learning psychologist. These points are relevant not only to the Goss paper, but also to some of the other papers included in this volume. I shall, therefore, go over these two points in some detail.

THE LINGUISTIC POINT

The approach outlined by Professor Goss is relevant both to the understanding and the production of speech. Thus, in the analysis summarized in figure 2 (p. 35), a relation is specified between stimuli and stimuli produced by recognition responses to (extra-list) association responses, which are both other "ideas" and names for grammatical categories. There is another relation included in the figure that is labeled "Basic Sentence Pattern (Syntactical Rule)." I read these factors as carrying out in some way the analysis and organization of structured sentences. Is the approach outlined here adequate for language as described by linguists and logicians? The linguists, in particular Chomsky (1959, 1963), and logicians (e.g., Bar-Hillel, 1964) have considered an array of languages of different types. These range from the output of Turing machines, transformational grammars, and context-sensitive phrase structure grammars, to context-free phrase structure grammars and finite state grammars (or finite automata). The order of these different generating devices corresponds to increasing restriction in the grammar and increasing restriction in the output. The finite state grammar, which is the most limited of the devices listed above, is the only one that fits into a pairwise S–R approach. This statement holds even when both the S's and the R's are classes of events. (The use of mediators or any other mechanism to make stimulus or response classes does not change the basic characteristics of the approach.) Unfortunately, the finite stage grammar is not adequate for the job of generating anything like natural language. To generate that type of output requires a less restricted device.

There is a simple test to determine whether the model offered by Goss is sufficient to handle connected discourse. The test is to put the model into the form of a computer program and see whether it can generate connected discourse. On both logical and empirical grounds, there is reason to doubt that such a program can be devised.

I have claimed that, from the point of view of linguistic theory, language is too complex for the type of machinery being considered to handle it. However, I am not saying that nothing can be done about the various problems posed in the paper, nor that the data of concern are unclear. The classical psychological problems are there in clear form. The regularities that require study are readily available. People learn a variety of classifications and relations between stimuli and responses. They class together with a single implicit or explicit response a number of very different stimuli. For example, a child learns this type of classification when he responds to different plural sounds: /s/ as in cats; /z/ as in buds; /ɨz/ as in houses; /ɨn/ as in oxen; /−/ as in sheep. People give several different responses to a single stimulus, e.g., to the word "bear." They also give several different common responses to a set of several different stimuli. Thus the set /s/, /z/, /ɨz/ can also be responded to as indicating present tense with verbs, or the possessive with nouns. Possibly the clearest examples of acquired distinctiveness and acquired equivalence of cues also comes from speech−in the perception of phonemes. There are also very striking transfer effects. The frequently cited regularizing tendencies of children−"shooted" for "shot," "catched" for "caught"−are an example of this. It is clear that the regularities are there. It is also clear that these classifications, mediations, and generalizations are learned by very young children under the most haphazard and chaotic training conditions.

It is clear that these types of performance exist and that they can be learned by almost everyone. The question that remains concerns the adequacy of the additive S–R approach to the analysis of the process involved.

THE VERBAL LEARNING POINT

The linguistic point summarized above may sound arcane, or unrelated to practical events, or overly theoretical. It is, however, seconded or paralleled by another point that arises directly from empirical findings in the learning laboratory. This concerns the difficulty of demonstrating an underlying pair-wise organization in serial learning.

Instead of connected discourse (i.e., speech) let us consider serial lists in which the complications of "form, grammatical function, and patterning of orders by rules" are eliminated. A serial list of this sort should be a linear arrangement of S–R pairs. It follows, then, that there should be clear-cut positive transfer effects in going from serial list learning to paired-associates learning involving the same elements. Similarly, there should be clear-cut positive transfer effects in going from paired-associates learning to serial learning. There is little evidence of transfer in either direction, or positive effects found in studies involving transfer to derived serial lists.

It is not for lack of work that evidence of transfer effects is absent. Because of the popularity of the additive S–R view, such transfer effects have been assigned a major theoretical status and have been worked at extensively by Young (1962), Ebenholtz (1963), Jensen (1962), Jensen and Rohwer (1965), and others. The work is found under the label of the "specificity hypothesis" (Young), or the "sequential hypothesis" (Jensen and Rohwer).

I have raised these points because I think it is unstrategic at this point to limit approaches to practical problems on the basis of theoretical commitment. Theories have an important role in suggesting practical procedures when we are faced with practical problems. A number of these have been, of course, suggested in the Goss paper. I would like to leave the theoretical approaches flexible enough to suggest a variety of mechanisms for handling practical applications.

REFERENCES

Bar-Hillel, Y. *Language and information.* Reading, Mass.: Addison-Wesley, 1964.

Chomsky, N. On certain formal properties of grammars. *Information and control,* 1959, *2,* 137–167.

———. Formal properties of grammars. In Bush, Galanter, and Luce (Eds.), *Handbook of mathematical psychology,* vol. 2. New York: Wiley, 1963.

Ebenholtz, S. M. Serial learning: Position learning and sequential associations. *J. exp. Psychol.,* 1963, *66,* 353–362.

Jensen, A. R. Transfer between paired-associate and serial learning. *J. verb. Learn. verb. Behav.,* 1962, *1,* 269–280.

Jensen, A. R., and Rohwer, W. D., Jr. What is learned in serial learning? *J. verb. Learn. verb. Behav.,* 1965, *4,* 62–72.

Young, R. K. Tests of three hypotheses about the effective stimulus in serial learning. *J. exp. Psychol.,* 1962, *63,* 307–313.

Relationships Between Prose and List Learning[1]

BARBARA S. MUSGRAVE AND
JEAN CARL COHEN

Smith College

The aim of this paper is to analyze the task of learning the contents of a prose passage in experimental terms that have evolved in laboratory studies of verbal list learning. No experimental psychologist would deny that learning the contents of a prose passage is a task of great practical importance. School and college assignments, training programs of all kinds, governmental and business communications, and the products of mass communication media all attest to the omnipresence of learning from such materials. Yet there has been relatively little systematic, rigorously controlled, laboratory research on content learning from prose. A promising early attack on some of the methodological problems in the area then called "logical memory" or "memory for substance" (see Welborn and English, 1937, for a review of 83 studies) was virtually abandoned during the decades from 1935–1955, as efforts to establish a single, overarching Theory of Learning increasingly turned attention to "pure," "simple" test situations. Since the mid 1950s, content learning from prose has continued to seem to many behavioral scientists too complex and too global for profitable study. That is, the variables have been considered too numerous, too vaguely defined, too uncontrollable, and too apt to be interacting with each other in confounded fashion for research findings to hold much promise of yielding laws and principles of suitable generality.

But, today, in the second half of the 1960s, there are some new forces at work. For one thing, educational processes, human learning, and the study of natural language behaviors have all moved into top priority positions. Also, a great deal of information has accumulated in the intervening years about different kinds of simpler verbal phenomena that may be components of the learning that takes place with more complex materials — information, therefore, that may aid us in getting some sort of purchase on prose content learning. In addition, what is considered "suitable generality" has changed. Today, many psychologists are willing to explore behavior that occurs in relation to quite specific kinds of materials, or problems, or situations.

Therefore, perhaps it is time someone tried again, as did Welborn and English in 1937, to relate laboratory experiments on verbal learning to "substance learning" with prose materials. The present paper is such an attempt.

A review of more recent experiments using prose materials reveals various kinds of theoretical approaches and research directions, some more and some less closely related to the concerns of this paper. A number of studies have used verbatim memorization of passages as the learning task, and, inasmuch as the following discussion is not concerned with this task but with how the contents or substance of a passage might be mastered, these studies seem inapplicable except for two points of relevance. The first point is that some of these studies (e.g., Slamecka, 1960) have explicitly extended variables and tasks from list learning to successful predictions about prose learning. The second point is that some psychologists (e.g., Cofer, 1941; King, 1960), while primarily studying verbatim memorization, have explored ways to score the number of "ideas" successfully reproduced. Unfortunately, the "idea" has proved a slippery unit, not overly amenable to methodological elegance. A quite different research direction is found in efforts to calibrate prose difficulty by means of readability formulas, using such measures as number of syllables per word and number of words per sentence (Dale and Chall, 1948; Flesch, 1946), and such techniques as cloze procedure (Taylor, 1953). Analyses of prose from a different theoretical background have come from psychologists with linguistic interests who have used grammatical categories as units (e.g., Coleman and Blumenfeld, 1963; Johnson, 1965; Miller, 1962). Other psychologists have shown how isolated verbal units such as word associations are related to connected discourse (Deese, 1961; Rosenberg, 1966). Osgood (e.g., 1963) has perhaps done most to show that these several approaches and research directions are by no means mutually exclusive. He has utilized linguistic concepts as well as concepts from computer science, has investigated contextual effects with word-association techniques, and has provided a stimulus-response account of mediational processes in the understanding and creating of sentences.

The present paper is yet another effort, no more exclusive than the foregoing, to arrive at theoretically and methodologically valuable prose variables. As mentioned above, the approach to be taken is by way of variables and kinds of analyses developed from laboratory studies of verbal list learning. This is not to imply that the variables found to be effective in list learning are the only variables that influence prose learning. In fact, it may be that certain of the list-learning variables will prove to have only minor, if any, effects. Nevertheless, exploring possible relationships between list and prose learning may provide a way to avail ourselves of findings concerning variables that have in fact been shown to effect "simple" learning and that therefore should reasonably be considered in studies of prose learning. In addition, it must be admitted, we hope that this analytical attempt to relate list and prose learning will stimulate imagination in the study of written instructional materials.

Because a large number of extensions from paired-associate list-learning studies are included, the analytical units under discussion are frequently stimuli and responses. Others have approached prose using these units, and their work is perhaps most closely related to the discussion to follow. For example, Stolurow (1961) has incorporated a stimulus-response analysis into his discussion of programmed instruction. Rothkopf, too (e.g., 1962, 1963), has considered that the subject and predicate division of a simple, declarative sentence parallels the stimulus-response division. In addition, Newman and Saltz (1960) and Hall (1955) have applied list-learning principles to prose materials with stimulus-response test items.

Obviously, with exploration of relationships between list and prose learning the goal of this paper, its first purpose must be to provide a method of analyzing a prose passage into list-learning components. If this is accomplished successfully, the paper can then move on to its second purpose, which is to apply the concepts and principles of list learning to prose passages in some detail. A third purpose is to emphasize that analogies between list and prose learning are not sufficient, however persuasive; that, instead, relationships between these two types of materials should be submitted to empirical test. Hence, throughout the paper experiments using both prose and list materials within the same design will be suggested.

ANALYSIS OF RELATIONSHIPS AND INITIAL EXPERIMENTAL DESIGN

To best exhibit possible relationships between list learning and learning from prose passages, it seems wise to start with a passage and work backward from the many dimensions of prose to its simpler task components. The following example will serve to make the analysis of this section more concrete. Later, it will also be used to illustrate various methodological problems.

Sample Passage 1

Among the minerals found in Denton County is onlygon. It is typically found embedded in granite and is distinguishable by its powdery consistency. Onlygon is used primarily as an abrasive agent. The chief buyers of onlygon are construction companies.

Denton County also contains two other minerals, deleb and constro. Deleb is found in sand and constro in swampland. Each has a characteristic consistency: deleb is glutinous and constro grainy. Deleb is bought by electric companies for use as a solvent, whereas constro's chief outlet is to home owners as a heating element.

This passage was designed to make the easiest possible transition from lists to prose. Nevertheless, this simple passage is similar in structure to many passages in textbooks and elsewhere that describe and discriminate several items of the same class — for example, wild flowers, kings of England, stocks for public sale — on a set of descriptive dimensions. Analysis of more complex prose can wait until we see how we fare with simple prose.

Table 1

Contents of Passage 1

| | Items of Information | | | | | |
| | Shared Items | | Discriminating Items | | | |
Names	Identity	County	Location	Consistency	Buyer	Use
Onlygon	mineral	Denton	granite	powdery	construction companies	abrasive agent
Deleb	mineral	Denton	sand	glutinous	electric companies	solvent
Constro	mineral	Denton	swampland	grainy	home owners	heating element

The first step in analyzing such a passage as the one above is to convert it into a two-way table of information, such as is presented in table 1. With the passage in this tabular form, the underlying structure of the information contained in the passage may be perceived more easily and the relationships between its several parts can be considered one at a time. There are other ways that structure and relationships of parts might be represented abstractly. For example, an outline of the passage, a tree diagram, or a flow chart might be used. However, the matrix form given here reveals so many ways of applying the findings and principles of verbal list learning to prose, that we shall be content in this paper to explore this one rich haul exclusively.

One matter of supreme importance must be stressed here. To apply verbal learning concepts and principles successfully, it is critical to consider how the learning materials may interact with the task the learner is attempting to perform. In a laboratory or classroom, the experimenter or teacher selects the task and apprises the learner of this choice through the test that evaluates learning, and often, additionally, through instructions. For analytical purposes, then, the nature of the test is central to a description of the materials.

Verbal list-learning studies have used a variety of kinds of test — free recall, ordered recall, and paired-associate recall or recognition — for which the stimulus terms of the learning materials are provided on the test. Any of these kinds of test can be used to measure prose learning. For example, suppose that a student who has read sample passage 1 is asked, "What is onlygon's consistency?" This kind of test question is very like a paired-associate recall test, with the question serving as the stimulus and the answer associated in the prose as the correct response. With this similarity in mind, we can now attempt to apply what is known about paired-associate list learning to prose.

In this attempt, a second transformation of sample passage 1 may aid intuition. Earlier, the passage was transformed into a matrix. Suppose, now, the matrix is transformed into a paired-associate list with the marginals as compound stimulus terms and the cell entries as responses. Table 2 presents one such list for each of the three minerals.

Once the contents of the passage are presented thus in list form, many attributes of verbal material that have been explored, or are used as parameters, or are commonly controlled in list learning immediately come to mind as possible variables in prose learning. Length of list is such an attribute. So are the many dimensions of single verbal units such as meaningfulness, familiarity, frequency of occurrence, pronunciability, affect, and similarity both formal and semantic. Thus, conversion of passages into tables and tables into lists has demonstrable heuristic value, and the whole matter could be left at that. However, as mentioned above, one purpose of this paper is to urge that analogies drawn between list and prose learning be put to empirical test.

One reason for urging such tests is that if the predictions from list-learning studies concerning the influence of a particular

Table 2

Paired Associates from Table 1 with Marginals as Stimuli and Cell Entries as Responses

List No.	Stimulus	Response
	onlygon identity	mineral
	onlygon county	Denton
I	onlygon location	granite
	onlygon consistency	powdery
	onlygon buyer	construction companies
	onlygon use	abrasive agent
	deleb identity	mineral
	deleb county	Denton
II	deleb location	sand
	deleb consistency	glutinous
	deleb buyer	electric companies
	deleb use	solvent
	constro identity	mineral
	constro county	Denton
III	constro location	swampland
	constro consistency	grainy
	constro buyer	home owners
	constro use	heating element

variable were not confirmed, an experiment that used only prose passages would provide no way of deciding whether the analogy did not hold because of inherent differences between prose and lists, or whether the particular materials or testing procedures were for some reason not suitable for producing the expected effect in list learning either. A second reason is that the kinds of lists that can be derived from prose by way of tables are often, as will be seen later in this paper, rather complex affairs, on which little direct research has been done. In these instances, what needs testing is, first, whether predictions from simple list learning will hold for more complex lists, and then whether they will hold for prose passages. In many ways, it is an economy to make both extensions at once. It seems quite possible that our knowledge of list learning would gain as much as our knowledge of prose learning by examining the two in tandem.

To return to a simple illustrative problem and spell out how a list-learning variable might be applied to prose, comparison could be made between the learning of two lists differing along some particular verbal attribute, say, response meaningfulness, and two prose passages that differed similarly. The experimental design would then be a 2 x 2 arrangement, as shown in table 3.

Table 3

Design for Comparing List and Prose Learning

Kind of Task	Degree of Attribute	
	High Meaningfulness	Low Meaningfulness
List	Group I	Group III
Prose	Group II	Group IV

Such a design would require passages (and derived lists) differing in the meaningfulness of the response items to be learned. To exemplify this comparison, suppose the original passage were rewritten as follows:

Sample Passage 2

Among the navhobs found in Xoztyg County is onlygon. It is typically found embedded in engston, and is distinguishable by its quabrious consistency. Onlygon is used primarily as a monsodic agent. The chief buyers of onlygon are struation companies.

Xoztyg County also contains two other navhobs, deleb and constro. Deleb is found in nant and constro in winthland. Each has a characteristic consistency: deleb is plarious and constro pinty. Deleb is bought by sistic companies for use as a fitent, whereas constro's chief outlet is to hast owners as a larting element.

Obviously, this passage would reduce to a table identical to table 1 except that the cells would now contain very low meaningful entries. If the lists for the two list conditions were constructed as were those of table 2, with the marginals as compound stimuli and the cell entries as responses, the two lists would differ in response meaningfulness on test items constructed to parallel this stimulus-response division. Such lists would constitute only a minor extension of work on simple list learning — the extension from lists with single stimuli to those with compound stimuli. It seems eminently safe to predict that under the specified test condition the low-meaningful lists of group III would be more difficult than the high-meaningful lists of group I. (For the moment, the fact that variation in meaningfulness may be confounded with variation in associative strength among cell entries or between cell entries and marginals, is being disregarded.)

In addition to comparing the list conditions, however, we wish to compare list learning and prose learning. For this comparison, a common response measure is needed. Suppose that after equal numbers of exposures to passage or list, all four groups of subjects were given familiar types of test items, such as multiple-choice, matching, true-false, sentence completions, or fill-ins, with all test items maintaining the stimulus-response division of the lists — whichever one or combination of these were judged to be a fair test of learning from both kinds of training materials. If it is reasonable to predict that group I would score higher than group III on such a test, then, by analogy, we would predict that group II would score higher than group IV. If the prediction were confirmed, then the relevance of the two tasks would be supported. But would the differences be roughly equivalent? And how would group I compare with group II, or group III with group IV?

Suppose that prose groups II and IV together scored higher or lower than list groups I and III together. If such held true across a variety of passages and derived lists, then there must be factors at work in the prose that are not present in the lists or vice versa. However, it is important to remember that the prose is being compared with a specific kind of list. In the example above, the lists were constructed by using the marginals of table 1 as compound stimuli, and the cell entries as responses. This list would be an optimal one if the test asked such questions as "What is onlygon's consistency?" To whatever extent prose learners failed to perceive this kind of list in their study materials, they might be at a disadvantage on the test. Students, at least college-age students, may approach prose learning with note-taking habits, strongly entrenched by school learning, which set them to reduce prose to particular kinds of lists-for-memorizing. Such schoolwork habits may be an "individual differences variable" in the sense of remaining relatively constant across various sorts of learning situations for a particular student. On the other hand, perhaps the way students make "cram sheets" out of prose is governed importantly by particular properties of the prose. Such matters need empirical investigation.

DIFFERENT SORTS OF DERIVED LISTS

This section describes a number of different sorts of lists that in effect constitute alternate ways of representing the contents of a passage. These alternate lists suggest additional phenomena, concepts, and principles from the verbal-learning literature that can be applied to prose learning. As mentioned above, conceiving the prose in list form may provide more explicit ideas concerning what strategies a student might use in his approach to learning the substance of the passage, and also concerning the important interaction between study and test materials. Of course, these lists could also be used as the list materials in a comparison of prose and list learning. Consider the following variations:

1. *Placing the Column Headings as Part of the Responses Instead of the Stimuli.* Thus, ONLYGON LOCATION — GRANITE becomes ONLYGON — LOCATION GRANITE. When a verbal item moves from the stimulus side to the response side, experimentation suggests that the importance of particular attributes may be altered. For example, similarity is apparently of greater importance on the stimulus side, meaningfulness on the response side. In addition, if the column headings become responses, there are no longer eighteen stimuli with one response each, but three stimuli each with six different responses that form, in effect, a response hierarchy. Consequently, studies of verbal hierarchy-learning become relevant to this analysis.

2. *Placing the Row Headings as Part of the Responses Instead of the Stimuli.* Thus, ONLYGON LOCATION — GRANITE becomes LOCATION

— ONLYGON GRANITE, or perhaps LOCATION — GRANITE (ONLYGON), with ONLYGON placed inside parentheses to indicate how this term might be presented when the subject was told it need not be produced overtly. Shifting the row headings from the stimulus to the response side reduces the list from eighteen units to six and from simple PA-learning to hierarchy-learning. Comparing this version of the lists with the preceding one, it may be asked in some future experiment whether it is more efficient to learn the total contents of table 1 by learning three six-pair lists or six three-pair lists.

3. Placing the Row Headings or the Column Headings as Titles for Each List. Thus, ONLYGON LOCATION — GRANITE, ONLYGON CONSISTENCY — POWDERY, etc., becomes

ONLYGON
LOCATION — GRANITE
CONSISTENCY — POWDERY
etc.

In such an arrangement, each list is named by its own appropriate list-marker. Conceiving the lists as arranged in this fashion will be considered in more detail later under the topics of context and transfer.

4. Presenting the Row Headings and the Column Headings First as Lists Before Presenting the PA Units. Thus, the student would learn the three-item list ONLYGON, DELEB, and CONSTRO, and also the six-item list IDENTITY, COUNTY, LOCATION, CONSISTENCY, USE, and BUYER before learning the cell entries. Such presentation prior to PA-learning has not been explored explicitly, although it is close enough to familiarization techniques to make the findings from familiarization studies relevant.

5. Presenting a Single Stimulus Element as Stimulus for a List of Responses. In this arrangement each marginal would be a stimulus to be associated with its appropriate row or column entries conceived as a serially-learned list or integrated multi-unit response. Thus, instead of the pairs ONLYGON LOCATION — GRANITE, ONLYGON CONSISTENCY — POWDERY, etc., these would be collapsed into one pair consisting of a single term as stimulus and six terms as response: ONLYGON — MINERAL, DENTON, GRANITE, POWDERY,

ABRASIVE AGENT, CONSTRUCTION COMPANIES; and using a column heading as stimulus, and the list of items in the appropriate column of cell entries as responses: LOCATION — GRANITE, SAND, SWAMPLAND. Here, clearly, serial list learning and/or categorical clustering is involved and the relationship between what is called serial-learning and what is called response-integration or response-learning is exhibited. Doubtless learning such as that in section 4 above would also be required to completely master the contents of the passage or table.

6. *Placing the Column Headings and Cell Entries as Compound Stimuli with the Row Headings as Responses.* Thus, each set of six stimuli would have one response, as shown in table 4.

Table 4

Paired Associates with Column Headings and Cell Entries as Stimuli and Row Headings as Responses

List No.	Stimulus	Response
I	identity mineral	onlygon
	county Denton	onlygon
	location granite	onlygon
	consistency powdery	onlygon
	use abrasive agent	onlygon
	buyer construction companies	onlygon
II	identity mineral	deleb
	county Denton	deleb
	location sand	deleb
	consistency glutinous	deleb
	use solvent	deleb
	buyer electric companies	deleb
	etc.	

Such an N-to-1 pairing resembles the arrangements used in concept formation studies, and findings from these studies may be applicable. However, a more intricate analysis than will be made at this time is required to clarify the relationships between the two situations.

7. *Placing Row Headings and Cell Entries as Compound Stimuli with Column Headings as Responses.* This way of presenting the

material in table 1 is a variation of section 6 above, and also will be discussed later in the section on concept formation.

8. Combining the Lists for Each Mineral Into One Total List. Something of this sort was implied when the lists were reduced from eighteen units to three or to six. But such reduction involved a change from simple, discriminative PA-learning to hierarchy-learning in which, under the anticipation method, the learning of the group of appropriate responses for each stimulus does not necessarily result in subjects' anticipating the particular response that will follow each stimulus on every trial. Had the stimuli for list learning remained the eighteen stimuli for eighteen responses, however, there would still be choices as to whether the list should be separated into a series of learning tasks, with practice to criterion for each task, or combined into one. As given, the lists have a systematic grouping device—that is, in list I of table 2 the stimulus element ONLYGON is in first position in every stimulus compound; in list II, the stimulus element DELEB is in first position in every compound, and so on. But, suppose these lists were mixed together into one long, unsystematic list. Would it then make any difference if three mixed pieces of the list were learned, each to criterion, with the final trials given on the whole list; or if all training consisted of presentations of the whole mixed, ungrouped list? These cases clearly involve part-whole learning and make relevant the studies on this topic done with PA material.

KINDS OF PASSAGES AND DERIVED TABLES

When tables and lists are derived from passages, it becomes apparent instantly that various passages may reduce to tables of various sorts. Consider, for example, the following matters:

1. Orthogonality. Both passage 1 and its variant, passage 2, reduce to completely orthogonal tables. However, such did not necessarily have to be the case. For example, each mineral might have been distinguished by a set of separate items. Thus, the passage might have read as follows, retaining the same first paragraph as given in passage 1.

Sample Passage 3

Among the minerals found in Denton County is onlygon. It is typically found embedded in granite, and is distinguishable by its powdery consistency. Onlygon is used primarily as an abrasive agent. The chief buyers of onlygon are construction companies.

Denton County also contains two other minerals, deleb and constro. Each has a characteristic color: deleb is blue and constro orange. Deleb was named by John Adams. It is closely related to mercury. Constro sells for $9.80 a pound. Recently, *The New York Times* has commented on it. (See table 5)

Obviously, table 5 differs from table 1 in a variety of ways and, hence, the lists derived from the two tables would differ. Table 5 has only twelve different cell entries, whereas table 1 has fourteen; but table 1 has only six column headings, whereas table 5 has eleven. It is instructive to attempt to deduce, from findings concerning list learning, which table would be the easier to learn.

Some insights into the nature of this problem can be gained from multivariate information theory (Garner, 1962). The tabular representation of prose presented in this paper permits an easy transition into applying the concepts and mathematical manipulations of the theory. For example, Garner has explained that non-orthogonal arrays can differ not only in the amount but also in the form of the uncertainty.

2. *More Than One Entry per Cell: Multiple Responses, Definitions, and Examples.* Suppose passage 1 had said: "Onlygon is found embedded in granite and in marble." Such a change would produce two cell entries for onlygon in the column headed LOCATION. Or suppose the word "granite" had been followed by the defining phrase "i.e., any natural igneous rock formation of visibly crystalline texture." The definition serves as a restatement of the cell entry GRANITE and would constitute a second entry in the cell. The alternative phrase may make the information of the cell more or less memorable depending on subjects' prior knowledge, or on attributes of the phrase, such as meaningfulness. Or suppose the first paragraph of the passage had been extended by the sentence: "Onlygon has been found, for example, in granite deposits in both the north and the south part of Denton County." Obviously, changes of these sorts would require changes in the derived lists as well as the tables.

Table 5

A Non-Orthogonal Table

| | Items of Information | | | | | | | | | |
| | Shared Items | | Discriminating Items | | | | | | | |
Names	Identity	County	Loca-tion	Consist-ency	Buyer	Use	Color	Named by	Related to	Price	Comment
Onlygon	mineral	Denton	granite	powdery	construc-tion co.	abrasive agent					
Deleb	mineral	Denton					blue	John Adams	mercury		
Constro	mineral	Denton					orange			$9.80 per lb.	N.Y. Times

3. Number of Columns and Number of Rows. Three points are involved here. First, it is obvious that for an orthogonal table an increase in either the number of columns or the number of rows would increase the length of the passage and the number of items in the list. Second, perhaps it should be noticed that increasing the number of rows or columns is not the only way to lengthen the material to be learned because, as mentioned in the preceding section, this can be done by adding more items within cells.

Third, it may be that the ratio of number of columns to number of rows has a subtle influence on the ways subjects might organize their learning task. For example, it may be that at least English speakers think of the information contained in a passage as having an overall subject-predicate organization. Thus, they may approach a passage first asking what the passage is about (what its topic is), and then noting what the passage says on this topic. It seems reasonable to suppose that discrepancy between number of rows and number of columns is one of the cues used to decide what the topic of a passage is.

4. Number of Shared Items and Number of Discriminating Items. Shared items is another and perhaps in some cases decisive cue for deciding what the topic of the passage is. What use subjects can make of this cue presented in list rather than prose form remains to be seen.

The ratio of number of shared items and number of discriminating items is a dimension along which passages can vary from all shared items to all discriminating items, although these extremes are probably rare. A short passage with all shared items might read as follows:

Sample Passage 4
Among the minerals found in Denton County are onlygon, deleb, and constro. They are moderately priced and enjoy steady sales. All three require only surface-mining and may be moved by truck.

The resultant table 6 indicates that the content of this passage contains only six cell entries and, hence, only six responses, if, as in table 2, the marginals are used as compound stimuli and the cell entries as responses. Of course, the number of different

Table 6

A Table Composed Exclusively of Shared Items

	Items of Information					
Names	**Identity**	**County**	**Price**	**Sales**	**Type of Mining**	**Type of Moving**
Onlygon	mineral	Denton	moderate	steady	surface	truck
Deleb	mineral	Denton	moderate	steady	surface	truck
Constro	mineral	Denton	moderate	steady	surface	truck

responses in table 6 could be increased until it equaled the fourteen of table 1 by simply extending the number of column headings in table 6 to equal the number of cell entries in table 1. Whether such an extended table 6 would make a more difficult learning task, presented in either prose or list, than table 1, is an empirical question of considerable interest.

5. Partially Shared and Partially Discriminating Items. There are passages that reduce to a hybrid sort of table in which some of the cell entries are shared by two or more row headings but discriminate between these and one or more others, as shown in table 7. Such a table presents a picture of considerable confusion and accentuates the possibility that certain ways of constructing the lists may be far more effective than others. At the present writing, one can do no more than guess which kind of list would prove the best list-making strategy for this table. One guess proceeds with the following logic: the main hazards in table 7 are acquired-equivalence of row headings and related inter-row errors; therefore, all efforts should be made to integrate across rows, and the list described in section 5 under "Ways of Constructing Derived Lists," which suggests using the row headings as stimuli and a serial list of cell entries across rows as responses, would be the most effective.

The repetition of partially shared items in this table calls multivariate information theory to mind again. Notice that each of the last four columns contains only two responses. From column to column the pattern made by which rows contain the same response changes. Thus, for the column concerning loca-

Table 7

Partial Sharing of Items Between Rows

Names	Items of Information					
	Shared Items		Partially Shared and Partially Discriminating Items			
	Identity	County	Location	Consistency	Buyer	Use
Onlygon	mineral	Denton	granite	powdery	construction companies	abrasive agent
Deleb	mineral	Denton	sand	glutinous	construction companies	solvent
Constro	mineral	Denton	granite	glutinous	electric companies	solvent

tion, the two responses alternate. In the next column, repetition of response occurs in the last two rows; while in the third column, it occurs in the first two rows. Because there are only these three possible patterns of repetition, the fourth column must present a redundant pattern if only two responses are used. To this extent, then, the passage contains contingent uncertainty. This form of uncertainty could have been vastly augmented, of course, by having the same pattern of repetition in each of the four columns.

6. Discriminability Between Columns. In learning the information in table 1, it seems highly unlikely that subjects would make intercolumn errors. For example, if subjects were asked what consistency onlygon had, it is hard to believe that anyone would answer, "Construction companies." Doubtless, cell entries in this situation are discriminable by columns because there are associations among the cell entries of a given column, or between cell entries and their column heading, or because they do not exist across the entries of one column and the heading of another, or because of linguistic features that identify cell entries as appropriate parts of speech in regard to column headings, or because of diverse, complicated interactions of the foregoing factors.

Surely, the variant of table 1, which could be derived from passage 2 written with nonsense syllables, would run far more risk of intercolumn errors. The syllables, except for modest plausibility as certain parts of speech, and in this way having some association to certain words in the passage, have little association with each other in columnar groups.

In some instances, a suitable way to measure the degree of association between cell entries of a given column might be one of the word-association indices (Marshall and Cofer, 1963), and a suitable way to measure association between column headings and column cell entries might be by categorical norms (Cohen, Bousfield, and Whitmarsh, 1957). However, even if CONSISTENCY never elicited POWDERY, GLUTINOUS, or GRAINY, and these never elicited each other in word-association or categorical norms, it seems unlikely that ONLYGON CONSISTENCY would elicit ELECTRIC COMPANIES as a response. Doubtless, additional ways of measuring intra- and inter-columnar associations can be found.

7. *Discriminability Between Rows.* So strong are the "categorical imperatives" of the column headings in table 1 that it may be difficult to imagine a passage with associations within row cell entries strong enough to make inter-row errors unlikely. But consider a passage of the following kind:

Sample Passage 5

Among Mr. Jones's special friends in the apartment building is Jennifer. Jennifer is three years old. Her greatest interest is in playing house with her dollies. As a special treat for Mr. Jones, she occasionally presents him with a mudpie she has baked all herself.

The apartment house contains two other of Mr. Jones's special friends: Ruth and Katherine. Ruth is a young career girl and Katherine is a middle-aged housewife. Each has a consuming interest: Ruth's is her job as a portrait photographer, Katherine's is French cookery. Ruth occasionally gives Mr. Jones tickets to photography exhibits, whereas Katherine offers tempting pastries.

Clearly, although the general format of passage 5 is the same as that of passage 1, passage 5 would run less risk of inter-row error. If, in addition, the row cell entries were more strongly associated to the row headings, inter-row error might be further minimized. For example, suppose in passage 5 the child had been named Betsy, the career girl, Miss Dalshaw, and the French cook, Madame de Beauvelour. These three names are not only more discriminable than Jennifer, Ruth, and Katherine, but also more highly associated with at least some of the row cell entries.

8. A Fully Coded Matrix. It is possible to imagine a table in which all cell entries are related to the row and column headings in such a systematic way that if the row and column headings were learned and the systematic principle grasped, the cell entries would be duducible. Consider table 8. In table 8, the material to be learned reduces to a list of row headings, a list of column headings, and a principle for deriving cell entries. Materials of this sort are reminiscent of those used by Esper (1925). Would this coded table be easier to learn than table 6, which consists entirely of shared items?

9. Different Ways of Writing a Passage. There are many ways prose passages may differ and yet contain essentially the same items of information, i.e., reduce to the same table. It is quite possible that such variations in the writing influence learning. In addition, the way the passage is written might make a difference in the form of the lists used to compare list and prose learning.

To take a simple example, the information in table 1 could be presented in three paragraphs instead of the two used in passage 1, by writing separate paragraphs for DELEB and CONSTRO, instead of presenting information about these two minerals alternately within one paragraph. Such a difference in the form of the passage suggests a comparable difference in the form of derived lists. Although it has been convenient thus far in this discussion to represent passage 1 by three PA lists, one for each mineral separately, this was done only to make the simplest transition from table to list. Now, this matter needs to be examined more closely and qualified.

It seems reasonable to hold that lists I, II, and III as given in table 2 would be more faithful to a three-paragraph passage that took up each of the minerals in turn, than to passage 1. For passage 1, lists II and III should doubtless be mixed together with such pairs as DELEB LOCATION — SAND and CONSTRO LOCATION — SWAMPLAND following one another. This matter will be mentioned again in connection with transfer problems.

To take another simple example of how the organization of

Table 8

A Coded Matrix of Nonsense Syllables

Row Headings	Column Headings		
	MIZ	HEB	NAV
COS	CIZ	CEB	CAV
JEX	JIZ	JEB	JAV
SUL	SIZ	SEB	SAV

the passage might vary, the different kinds of items of information given in passage 1 about onlygon, deleb, and constro follow one another in approximately the same order. That is, for each of the three minerals the passage tells with one exception about identity, county, location, consistency, and so on, *in that order*. Of course, such regularity need not be so. Probably the passage is more readily mastered because of this regularity, but no studies have yet yielded data on this point.

There are many other properties of a group of prose passages, each of which would reduce to the same table, that might influence content learning, or "reading comprehension." Syntax is a powerful variable. Perhaps the way a passage is written — in such simple, analyzable ways as which items are used as subjects and which as predicates of sentences — is influential. Also, such differences would probably interact with the way the test items following learning were constructed (Rothkopf, 1963).

10. Other Kinds of Passages. The sample passages presented above share the quality of being simple, descriptive passages, written in a style designed to convey straightforward information of an unembroidered sort. There are, of course, many other sorts of prose, such as narrative, logical, or imaginative. Preliminary consideration of such sorts of passages indicates that they, too, have much in common with ordinary list learning, but detailed consideration of such kinds of passages is outside the scope of this paper.

ADDITIONAL LEARNING PHENOMENA AND SITUATIONS

Intrapassage Facilitation or Interference

Representing the contents of a prose passage as a table, and then considering the kinds of lists that can be derived from the table, reveals kinds of intrapassage transfer problems that may be involved in learning from prose. In general, transfer has been conceived as the effect of one task on another. However, if a single task is of sufficient length and complexity — as, for example, the learning of an entire prose passage — one may wish to examine the possible effects of one part of the task on another part. In analyzing prose learning, one may wonder how learning the information contained in one paragraph or section will influence learning that of a second paragraph or section. If there is successive intrapassage facilitation between paragraphs, the task of mastering the contents of the whole passage should be significantly easier than if there is successive intrapassage interference. Extensive exploration of interlist transfer problems has provided a number of principles that can be applied to prose learning once passages are translated into paired-associate lists. To consider the relationships involved, it may be helpful to translate passage 1 more abstractly than was done in tables 1 and 2. This more abstract translation can be seen in table 9.

Table 9

Paired-Associate Lists for Sample Passage 1 in S–R and Transfer Theory Notation

	Lists		
Kind of Item	I. AB–C / AF–G	II. DB–C / DF–H	III. EB–C / EF–I
Shared	$S_1S_2-R_1$	$S_8S_2-R_1$	$S_9S_2-R_1$
	$S_1S_3-R_2$	$S_8S_3-R_2$	$S_9S_3-R_2$
Discriminating	$S_1S_4-R_3$	$S_8S_4-R_7$	$S_9S_4-R_{11}$
	$S_1S_5-R_4$	$S_8S_5-R_8$	$S_9S_5-R_{12}$
	$S_1S_6-R_5$	$S_8S_6-R_9$	$S_9S_6-R_{13}$
	$S_1S_7-R_6$	$S_8S_7-R_{10}$	$S_9S_7-R_{14}$

The structure of table 9 is, of course, the same as that of tables 1 and 2 because all three tables represent passage 1. In table 9, list I represents the information to be learned about onlygon, list II that about deleb, and list III about constro. The shared items have the same responses across lists, R_1 and R_2, which represent the cell entries mineral and Denton of table 1. In addition, the stimuli for the first two pairs have common elements across lists, S_2 and S_3, which represent the column headings IDENTITY and COUNTY of table 1. But the compound stimuli of these two first pairs also each contain one element that differs across lists while repeating in the two pairs. These elements are S_1, S_8, and S_9, which represent the row headings ONLYGON, DELEB, and CONSTRO of table 1. Thus, the shared items that compose the first two pairs would be, in transfer terms, across lists I, II, and III, simply continued practice on a two-pair list of S_2-R_1, S_3-R_2 were it not for the distinguishing stimulus elements S_1, S_8, and S_9. In the usual transfer notation, modified for compound stimuli, the first two pairs across the three lists might be written AB–C, DB–C, EB–C, with A, D, and E referring to the row headings of table 1, B to the column headings, and C to the cell entries. This notation does not do justice to the complexity of these pairs, because it does not indicate that the A, D, and E items remain constant within lists. Nevertheless, use of this notation may aid in relating list and prose learning.

The last four pairs in each list represent the discriminating items of table 1. Again, stimulus elements S_1, S_8, and S_9 remain constant across pairs within lists but differ across lists, whereas elements S_4, S_5, S_6, and S_7 differ within lists but are constant across lists. For these four pairs, the responses also differ across lists. This situation can be written AF–G, DF–H, and EF–I, which again does not adequately reveal that the A, D, and E terms remain the same across pairs within lists, but it does have the virtue of showing something of the structure of the passage in traditional transfer terms. If the A, D, and E items are disregarded for the moment, the shared and discriminating items of information in passage 1 are seen as two different transfer situations: the shared items as continued practice B–C, B–C, B–C, from which positive transfer would be predicted; and the discriminating items as the learning of three successive sets of new responses to the same stimuli, F–G, F–H, F–I, from which negative transfer would be predicted. The effects of the A, D, and E stimulus elements are unpredictable, as no transfer experiments have been done using compound stimuli of this sort.

The continued-practice transfer paradigm, B–C, B–C, B–C, and the paradigm for new responses to the same stimuli, F–G, F–H, F–I, are, of course, only two of the transfer situations that have been explored in the learning of lists. If list and prose learning are thought of as related, it becomes of interest to wonder what sorts of passages and table might result from other sorts of transfer list situations. All the kinds of transfer could, of course, be presented systematically. However, for brevity's sake, only one additional situation will be considered: the re-pairing paradigm in which stimuli and responses of the first list are reshuffled for the second list and reshuffled again for any subsequent lists, the so-called A–B, A–B$_r$ paradigm. Consider table 10, in which all the responses reappear as cell entries across rows and columns. It seems reasonable to expect that such a table would be vastly more difficult to learn than any of the tables presented previously. Notice that numbers were used as cell entries in this illustration. Numbers serve the purpose here precisely because they are equally suitable as responses for all column headings. Certain words, but not all, share this property.

Table 10
AB–C, DB–C$_r$ Transfer Situation

	Items of Information					
				Re-Paired Items		
	Shared Items		Dollars per ton of ore	Tons per box car	Import duty per 1,000 tons of ore	Dollars per ton refined
Names	Identity	County				
Onlygon	mineral	Denton	10	12	14	12
Deleb	mineral	Denton	12	14	10	10
Constro	mineral	Denton	14	10	12	14

For example, if the row headings were campus organizations, such as the Debate Club, the Mathematics Club, and the Senior Class; and the column headings were President, Vice-President, and Secretary-Treasurer, conceivably (although just barely) the same three boys — Jim, Bob, and Dick — would occupy the positions interchangeably. Or the cell entries might all be words that reflect a range of values, but the cutting points are less precise than numbers (hence, more qualitative than quantitative), such as high, medium, low; or acute, moderate, imperceptible. These word scales could be extended to as many terms as human subjects could be shown to discriminate. Another way to arrange acceptable duplication of cell entries across columns is by careful selection of column headings. To sum up, applications of the A–B, A–B$_r$ transfer paradigm to prose materials is especially relevant to, but limited by, those situations in which cell entries are equally acceptable across columns.

Another problem concerns the type of list that would parallel a particular passage. In section 8 above concerning different ways of constructing derived lists, and in section 9 above concerning different ways a passage might be written, mention was made of the possible intermingling of the lists in table 2. Inter-pair transfer might well be quite different for an intermingled list I–II–III or an intermingled list II–III than for separate lists. One reason for this is that lists having compound stimuli or compound responses can incorporate some, at least, of the strong organizational features usually associated only with prose, and these may powerfully affect inter-pair transfer. What is meant here by "organizational feature" as applied to lists has been exhibited perhaps most clearly in table 9, where certain stimulus elements remain the same across pairs within a list but appear in only one list, while others occur uniquely within lists but reappear across lists. Thus, the subject is provided cues for grouping or otherwise arranging or organizing the material to be learned. It seems reasonable to suppose that such cues might be more or less salient, depending on whether the subject can survey the total task or is presented with successive segments of it. A major facet of subjects' behavior when confronted with a task possessing such organizational cues is selective attention.

Cue Selection

That subjects do not necessarily use as functional stimuli all components of nominal, experimenter-presented stimulus compounds is now well documented (Cohen and Musgrave, 1964; Cohen and Musgrave, 1966; Musgrave and Cohen, 1966; Underwood, Ham, and Ekstrand, 1962). This phenomenon may markedly affect the comparability of transfer effects in list and prose learning depending on the way the lists are presented. For example, if the three lists of table 2 are presented for mastery one at a time, it would seem reasonable that when subjects are presented list I they would quickly recognize that the first stimulus element (ONLYGON or, more abstractly, S_1) does not aid with the discrimination of particular pairs. In fact, this element increases stimulus similarity. Consequently, the efficient strategy in such a list would be to disregard this element, S_1, because it would engender intra-list negative transfer. But, when the next task, list II alone or lists II and III intermingled, is presented, disregard for the first stimulus element in each compound would have differing effects on the shared and discriminating items. The shared items would become more alike if the S_1, S_8, and S_9 items were disregarded, and, hence, there should be more positive transfer of a B–C, B–C, B–C kind. But, by the same token, the discriminating items would become more alike, and, hence, there should be more negative transfer of an F–G, F–H, F–I kind. Thus, for the task of learning all the contents of the table, either as lists or prose, cue selection after the first list or first paragraph, might well be governed by the ratio of shared to discriminating items.

Context

Much has been made recently (e.g., Postman, 1962) of the possibility that subjects who have learned several lists of paired associates successively and are then asked to perform again on the first list, are aided in doing so by having associated the whole first list, as a particular list, with stimuli of a contextual rather than a task sort. Thus, a subject might remember the first list specifically as the one learned on Monday, when it was cloudy, and he had just come from a history examination.

If context cues can thus operate to reduce inter-list interference, then perhaps the stimulus elements in first position in the stimulus compounds of tables 2 and 9 (ONLYGON, DELEB, and CONSTRO, or S_1, S_8, and S_9) may similarly serve as list-markers to distinguish lists and thus mitigate transfer effects. Perhaps the best list arrangement for this mitigation is the one discussed in section 3 of the part of this paper labeled "Ways of Constructing Derived Lists"—i.e., by presenting the row headings of table 1 separately from the list of shared and of discriminating items. Thus, in the window of a memory drum, the term ONLYGON might appear prior to presentation of list I, DELEB prior to list II, and CONSTRO prior to list III. Whether such "context" items would serve to differentiate lists and thus alter transfer effects remains to be explored empirically.

Mediation

Presumably, mediation effects occur when some part of a stimulating situation or task overtly or covertly activates a particular response, or responses, thus producing stimuli which then influence the subject's final behavior in the situation. Such effects can be subsumed under the topic of transfer, and are surely related to cue selection, context, and concept formation. They are discussed separately here in order to make several points that seem particularly appropriate to this heading.

Perhaps of especial interest in relating simpler verbal situations to prose is the phenomenon called "mediated priming" (Amster, 1964; Cramer, 1964; Musgrave, Cohen, and Robbins, 1967) in which several words, each associated with a given response, are presented as compound stimuli in a word-association task. The result in some cases has been to elicit the desired response more frequently under this condition than when only a single word is presented alone as stimulus. It is possible that in a prose passage some such priming takes place, with the consequence that, as the passage proceeds, the subject is increasingly set to find paired stimuli and responses appropriate to each other, and, hence, more readily learned.

On the other hand, primed interference may take place. For example, consider the following simple descriptive passage:

"The dog ran down the trail, stopped, and listened. The bark of the pine trees was wet with rain and the wind howled in the branches." Presumably, associations to "dog" and "listened" cause the reader to first misinterpret the word "bark." Whether the misinterpretation, even if it constituted interference in the first reading, would detract from or enhance acquisition or delayed recall is not known.

Concept Formation

Concept formation and concept identification have been discriminated roughly in terms of the amount of totally new information a subject must acquire in the two processes. Thus, the formation of concepts involving experience with totally new defining attributes seems a more primitive and more difficult job than simply learning to identify which combination of already familiar attributes results in correct labeling of concept exemplars. Prose is, of course, ideally suited for communicating the kind of information used in concept identification. That is, the subject can simply be told the correct combination of attributes instead of being given a series of experiences from which to make his own deductions.

As to concept formation as such, it is doubtless unlikely that verbal statements can substitute effectively for sensory experience. But, suppose sensory experience is not directly involved. Surely prose, particularly if it is extended to include mathematical statements, can communicate raw or primitive information about the nature of attributes entirely new to the reader, which are so abstract as to be perhaps best set forth in verbal statements, as witness texts in such areas as introductory physics. In addition, prose is well-suited to telling the learner the identity of newly presented concept-exemplars. Thus, in passage 1, the subject is told that onlygon, deleb, and constro, which are no more than nonsense words to begin with, are the names of minerals. With this identification, the subject can bring to bear whatever information he has about the concept "mineral." For example, he may know at once that the three names label inorganic substances. Should this or should this not be included in the derived table under the SHARED ITEM column heading? It should not, because the passage does not include an explanatory phrase such as "Among the minerals, and thus inorganic substances, found in Denton County . . ." Of course, list learners should be left as uninformed as prose learners as to the implications of the label "mineral."

As for contributions toward an understanding of concept formation or identification that can be drawn from studies of list learning, the most compelling idea has been that these processes are analogued by PA lists in which more than one stimulus is associated with the same response, so-called $n:1$ pairings (Goss, 1961). At several points in the preceding sections, tabular analysis has been made of passages that could then be transformed into lists containing $n:1$ pairings. These different tables and different lists present rather different problems, which need to be considered individually.

For example, all shared items are $n:1$ pairings, if it is assumed that (as in tables 1 and 2) ONLYGON IDENTITY and DELEB IDENTITY are indeed different stimuli despite their common second element, for in each case the response is MINERAL. Such an effect is even more pronounced, of course, for an all-shared-item passage such as passage 4, represented in table 6.

Table 4, which presents paired associates with column headings and cell entries as stimuli and row headings as responses, contains $n:1$ pairings in that for each set of informational items there is the name of one of the minerals as response. It is important to notice that the stimuli of each set or list are not instances of the concept class to which the concept label refers. Instead, they are discrete items of information concerning that class. These items of information are not restricted to defining attributes. Nor are they restricted to those matters that can serve to discriminate onlygon, deleb, and constro from each other. To the extent that this situation is not like the usual concept formation situation, consideration of the $n:1$ pairings that can be derived from a prose passage may prove quite valuable by forcing a reassessment of our usual notions of concept formation. To indicate something of the complexity involved, a few detailed comments will be included in this account, which perforce must be too brief to analyze the problem adequately.

In the usual concept formation task, each of the stimuli typically contains relevant and irrelevant attributes. The subject's task is first to discriminate between these two kinds of aspects. He discovers that the irrelevant aspects are paired with more than one response and hence cannot be used to identify the situations in which a particular response is correct. In table 4, the stimulus IDENTITY MINERAL is irrelevant in this way; that is, it is irrelevant to the learner's choosing between the responses ONLYGON, DELEB, or CONSTRO. But, it is not irrelevant to an attempt to define one of these terms. Thus, if one wished to test whether a subject had learned the concept for which one of these responses was the label, and, therefore, asked the subject to try to formulate the concept, he might quite properly begin his formulation in the time-honored way by saying, "Onlygon is a mineral that . . . "

The stimulus COUNTY DENTON, however, is quite a different matter. This stimulus is irrelevant to the choice between the three responses, and, in addition, may be irrelevant to the definition of any of these terms. Neither the passage nor the derived lists tells us whether Denton County contains other minerals than these three. Nor are we told whether these three occur outside this county.

In considering the discriminating items of table 4, and how they might relate to the $n : 1$ concept formation situation, we may find it helpful to consider also table 5 (the non-orthogonal table in which, in the main, different items of information are given for each mineral) and table 7 (the table of partially shared and partially discriminating items, which exhibits confusing patterns of overlap between cell entries). In table 5, none of the items of information could be discarded as irrelevant aspects on the grounds that they were paired with more than one of the mineral names since none of them is doubly paired. In table 7, none can be discarded as irrelevant despite double pairings. Instead, in table 7, the duplication forces integration across rows. It is hoped that these brief comments will stimulate efforts to relate laboratory studies of concept learning to learning with prose materials.

EXPERIMENTAL PROBLEMS

Throughout the foregoing discussion, there have been comments to indicate how an experimental attack on prose learning might be mounted through what is already known about list learning. The purpose of the present section is briefly to draw these comments together and to consider more sharply some of the specific, methodological problems involved.

Kinds of Materials

Earlier sections of this paper have enumerated kinds of lists and kinds of passages. Obviously, the number of 2 x 2 combinations of kind-of-list x kind-of-passage that await exploration with the basic design suggested in table 3 is extensive. Hopefully, it will become even more extensive as experimentation yields additional, perhaps quite new, insight into both prose and list learning by virtue of bringing the two together in one design. Fortunately, not all the variations of list and passage need be manipulated simultaneously.

Concerning the kinds of lists which might be constructed, three points are pertinent. First, some lists may be more appropriate than others in terms of faithful representation of particular passages. For example, a list based on passage 1 that presented the items of information in exactly the order in which they occur in the prose would be preferable to a list which, say, presented all the informational items pertaining to onlygon first, then all items relating to deleb, and then all items for constro. Similarly, where a label (e.g., "constro" or "location") appeared as the subject of a sentence in the prose passage, it would be preferable to use the same label as the stimulus term in the comparable list item.

Second, the selection of some lists rather than others may be based on hypotheses concerning the most effective way to learn the material. For example, in section 5 above it was suggested that possibly the contents of table 7 would be learned most effectively by learning responses serially across rows. A prose passage of this table, however, might not be organized in this fashion. A list that is ordered in exactly the way that the items in the prose passage are ordered, though, might not be learned as quickly as a list which changed the order of items.

Third, it is possible that valuable information can be gained, at least of a preliminary sort, by having subjects themselves produce materials. That is, subjects could be asked to write passages from lists, or lists from passages, or both from tables. This exercise might reveal guidelines as to which passage-list combinations are most analogous to common study practices.

Thus far, a comparison of prose learning and list learning has been considered. It is possible that table learning might also prove fruitful. Thus, were the same information to be presented in prose, in a table, and in a list, there might result revealing differences in learning efficiency. Few studies have been made of learning from tables. One such study, by Anderson and Ross (1955), shows that the learning of a given cell entry will depend, in part, on its position in a row and column. Discovery of other factors that are important in learning from a table may throw light on learning of the prose from which the table is derived.

Certain other problems regarding materials also must be considered. For example, among the flaws in passage 1, mentioned earlier, is the number of words in comparable items of information: onlygon is used as an *abrasive agent*, and deleb is used as a *solvent*. Little is known of the learning of compound responses, although it is probable that both response differentiation and response integration would be relevant concepts. Either compound responses or mixed single and compound responses can be considered as problems to be investigated in and of themselves. Until these studies are conducted, however, it would seem wiser to include only one-word responses.

Another problem mentioned previously, exemplified in passages 1 and 2, is the amount of association between cell entry and column heading, or among the cell entries. As these passages now read, there are stronger associative links in the high-meaningful passage 1 than in the low-meaningful passage 2. If effects of meaningfulness are to be investigated, these differential associative links must be controlled. This particular kind of difficulty is illustrative of the sorts of methodological problems that may arise because of the highly interwoven relationships present in prose.

Kinds of Procedures

Experimental work comparing list and prose learning would require practical decisions concerning such procedural matters as method of presentation and type of response measure. Adaptation of present procedures used to study list learning may yield fresh insight into that process.

The first problem is to equate practice across passages and lists. In the past, lists typically have been presented piecemeal by presenting one item or pair at a time. The usual reading of prose provides far more opportunity to glance ahead or back, and thus, perhaps, to have a better overall view of the learning task, which in turn might well activate more appropriate organizing strategies for mastering the information presented.

Equating can go either way: (1) lists can be presented whole, written on a single sheet of paper for easy, overall perusal; or (2) prose can be presented piecemeal by either successive cards, memory drum, slide, or movie projector. Piecemeal presentation of prose brings up the problem of what, precisely, the pieces should be. Might words be presented, one at a time, after the fashion of a serial list? Or phrases? Or clauses? Or sentences? Of course, a single word is not the equivalent of a paired-associate pair, and a single phrase or clause or sentence may contain several such pairs. Different methods of presentation of passages and lists might produce different effects even with one combination of kind-of-passage and kind-of-list, but only research can tell.

To return to one presentational possibility mentioned above, that of exposing the words of a passage one at a time, it is extremely important to remember that the general purpose of this program is not to compare PA and serial anticipation learning. In other words, neither list nor passage learning is intended to be rote in the sense of verbatim learning. Instead, the effort is to explore a task much more similar to modern school-assigned tasks than is verbatim learning, which, until as recently as fifty years ago, occupied a great deal of school time in class recitation of Latin declensions, multiplication tables, memorization of poetry, Bible passages, Shakespearean soliloquies, orations, declamations, and so on.

Today, great stress is laid instead on a process called "comprehension," or "understanding," and this is tested by some such method as multiple-choice, fill-in, matching, or essay questions. Thus, the student is expected to learn the informational contents of the material and to be prepared to demonstrate this learning under a number of conditions, including generating his own prose sentences and paragraphs to embody it.

Laboratory use of types of tests typical of school situations has several things to recommend it. Experimental findings may thus be more directly applicable, and school habits, which might transfer into the laboratory as a learning set that governs how the learner conceives what he is supposed to be doing, would not suffer disruption.

However, one needs to be alert to methodological problems involved in choice of test items and testing procedures. Certain types of tests are more like prose than like lists (essay questions, sentence fill-ins), whereas others are more like lists than prose (matching). Similarities between practice and test conditions may favor one kind of material over the other and thus create an artificial difference. One solution is to make use of several different kinds of items with each subject.

When and how frequently the tests are given are procedural variables that may interact with type of test and deserve very careful attention. Tests could be given following every learning trial or could occur after specified numbers of trials. If the former procedure is adopted, there is the possibility that the subject's way of processing the material will be markedly affected. For example, prose learners might stop reading the prose and simply scan it for answers to specific questions. Meanwhile, list learners might cast their lists into more proselike form during learning trials. Thus, list and prose learning might be made more alike depending on the nature of the items and the time of testing.

Clearly, the experiments suggested in the foregoing discussion are attempts to construct transition experiments, to use Underwood's phrase (1964), in so far as they are designed to explore prose learning through what is known about list learning. But, in addition, as the previous discussion has mentioned, list learning cuts across many other so-called areas, such as transfer, concept formation, context, and mediation. Consequently, explorations of prose and complex-list learning are directed toward greater unification of these areas as well.

NOTES

1. Appreciation is expressed to the U.S. Public Health Service for their support of the writers' research efforts in verbal learning with compound stimuli (MH-08156). The writers also thank A. E. Goss for his helpful comments.

REFERENCES

Amster, H. Prediction of convergent associations from the frequency of responses to single words. Paper read at Psychonomic Society, Niagara Falls, October, 1964.

Anderson, S. B., and Ross, S. Memory for items in a matrix. *Amer. J. Psychol.*, 1955, *68*, 595–604.

Cofer, C. N. A comparison of logical and verbatim learning of prose passages of different lengths. *Amer. J. Psychol.*, 1941, *54*, 1–20.

Cohen, B. H., Bousfield, W. A., and Whitmarsh, G. A. Cultural norms for verbal items in 43 categories. Under Contract Nonr-631(00), between the Office of Naval Research and the Univ. of Connecticut, 1957. (Tech. Rep. no. 22).

Cohen, J. C., and Musgrave, B. S. Effect of meaningfulness on cue selection in verbal paired-associate learning. *J. exp. Psychol.*, 1964, *68*, 284–291.

———. Effects of formal similarity on cue selection in verbal paired-associate learning. *J. exp. Psychol.*, 1966, *71*, 829–838.

Coleman, E. B., and Blumenfeld, J. P. Cloze scores of nominalizations and their grammatical transformations using active verbs. *Psychol. Rep.*, 1963, *13*, 651–654.

Cramer, P. Successful mediated priming via associative bonds. *Psychol. Rep.*, 1964, *15*, 235–238.

Dale, E., and Chall, J. A formula for predicting readability. *Educ. Res. Bull.*, 1948, *27*, 11–20.

Deese, J. From the isolated verbal unit to connected discourse. In C. N. Cofer (Ed.), *Verbal learning and verbal behavior.* New York: McGraw-Hill, 1961.

Esper, E. A. A technique for the experimental investigation of associative interference in artificial linguistic material. *Language Monogr.*, 1925, no. 1.

Flesch, R. *How to test readability.* New York: Harper & Bros., 1951.

Garner, W. R. *Uncertainty and structure as psychological constructs.* New York: Wiley, 1962.

Goss, A. E. Verbal mediating responses and concept formation. *Psychol. Rev.*, 1961, *68*, 248–274.

Hall, J. F. Retroactive inhibition in meaningful material. *J. Educ. Res.*, 1955, *46*, 47–52.

Johnson, N. F. The psychological reality of phrase-structure rules. *J. verb. Learn. verb. Behav.*, 1965, *4*, 469–475.

King, D. J. On the accuracy of written recall: A scaling and factor analytic study. *Psychol. Rec.*, 1960, *10*, 113–122.

Marshall, G. R., and Cofer, C. N. Associative indices as measures of word relatedness: A summary and comparison of ten methods. *J. verb. Learn. verb. Behav.*, 1963, *1*, 408–421.

Miller, G. A. Some psychological studies of grammar. *Amer. Psychologist*, 1962, *17*, 748–762.

Musgrave, B. S., and Cohen, J. C. Abstraction in verbal paired-associate learning. *J. exp. Psychol.*, 1966, *71*, 1–8.

Musgrave, B. S., Cohen, J. C., and Robbins, D. M. G. Convergent popular associations in a word-association task. *J. verb. Learn. verb. Behav.*, 1967, *6*, 840–843.

Newman, S. E., and Saltz, E. Effects of contextual cues on learning from connected discourse. *Amer. J. Psychol.*, 1960, *73*, 587–592.

Osgood, C. E. On understanding and creating sentences. *Amer. Psychologist*, 1963, *18*, 735–751.

Postman, L. Transfer of training as a function of experimental paradigm and degree of first-list learning. *J. verb. Learn. verb. Behav.*, 1962, *1*, 109–118.

Rosenberg, S. Associative factors in the recall of connected discourse. *Psychon. Sci.*, 1966, *4*, 53–54.

Rothkopf, E. Z. Learning from written sentences: Effects of order of presentation on retention. *Psychol. Rep.*, 1962, *10*, 667–674.

———. Learning from written sentences: Within-sentence order in the acquisition of name-clause equivalences. *J. verb. Learn. verb. Behav.*, 1963, *2*, 470–475.

Slamecka, N. J. Retroactive inhibition of connected discourse as a function of similarity of topic. *J. exp. Psychol.*, 1960, *60*, 245–250.

Stolurow, L. M. *Teaching by machine*. U.S. Dept. Health, Education, and Welfare. Washington, D.C.: U.S. Government Printing Office, 1961. OE-34010 Cooperative Research Monogr. no. 6.

Taylor, W. L. "Cloze Procedure": A new tool for measuring readability. *Journ. quart.*, 1953, *31*, 415–433.

Underwood, B. J. The representativeness of rote verbal learning. In A. W. Melton (Ed.), *Categories of human learning*. New York: Academic Press, 1964, pp. 47–78.

Underwood, B. J., Ham, M., and Ekstrand, B. Cue selection in paired-associate learning. *J. exp. Psychol.*, 1962, *64*, 405–409.

Welborn, E. L., and English, H. Logical learning and retention: A general review of experiments with meaningful verbal materials. *Psychol. Bull.*, 1937, *34*, 1–20.

Discussion of
Professors Musgrave's and Cohen's
Paper[1]

SLATER E. NEWMAN
North Carolina State University

Barbara Musgrave and Jean Cohen have proposed a study of the relationship between prose and list learning. Initially they plan to deal with descriptive, information-bearing passages, passages that are definitional in character and in which there appears to be an equivalence between the stimulus term (i.e., the subject of a declarative sentence) and its response term (i.e., the predicate). They have proposed that the prose passage be translated into a table, and the table into a list. A series of 2 x 2 experiments would be done in which one manipulation would always be List x Prose. Some variable, whose effects on simple list learning are already known, would also be manipulated. By this they hope to determine whether predictions from simple list learning will hold for more complex lists, and then in addition whether they will hold for prose passages.

Since Musgrave and Cohen plan to determine the extent to which predictions from simple list learning hold for learning from complex lists and from prose passages, it is useful to examine the conditions under which paired-associate learning is *ordinarily* studied in the laboratory.[2] Here are some of the characteristics of the laboratory situation:

110

1. The materials
   a. All stimulus terms are from the same class of items, as are all response terms.
   b. Each stimulus term appears with only one response term, and each response term with only one stimulus term.
   c. Each stimulus term is a single item (e.g., trigram or word), as is each response term.
   d. Each pair is unrelated to any of the other pairs in the list.
   e. Each stimulus term appears on the left side of the list and each response term on the right.
2. The pairing trials
   a. Every pair in the list is exposed for the same period of time on a particular trial.
   b. Exposure time is the same for each pair from trial to trial.
   c. Each pair appears only once on a trial.
   d. The order of the pairs varies from trial to trial.
3. The test trials
   a. A test follows each pairing trial.
   b. Each item is tested on each test.
   c. Only one test item is presented at a time.
   d. On the test the stimulus term is presented and recall of its response term is required.
   e. The stimulus term appears in the same form on the test as it did on the pairing trial.
   f. The test interval for each item is the same within a test trial.
   g. The test interval for each item is the same from trial to trial.
   h. The order of the items on the test differs from test to test and from the orders used on the pairing trials.

It is evident that laboratory study of paired-associate learning is characterized by several factors. The first is stringent experimenter control of the order of and the amount of time available for training events and test events. The second is S's knowledge, usually at the beginning of training (but after he has heard the instructions) and almost certainly after the first test, of how he will be tested: e.g., what the specific test items are, the length of time he has to respond, and whether the test order is the same as the pairing order. Since the rate at which S learns from a list or from a prose passage is probably strongly affected by the degree to which he has control over his own training (cf. Newman, 1957) and by what he knows of the conditions of the test (cf. Postman and Jenkins, 1948; Underwood, 1963), I would propose that very early in their research program, Musgrave and Cohen run several List vs. Prose experiments: (1) under both experimenter-controlled and subject-controlled training and test conditions, and (2) where the degree to which S is informed about the conditions of the test is varied.

Where S is given control over his own training or testing (e.g., he is limited only in the amount of time he has to study the items or to perform on the test), information should probably be obtained also about the way he trained or tested himself (e.g., the order in which he studied the pairs, or in which he presented the items to himself on the test). Such information can in turn be related to characteristics of the pairs, as well as to S's performance on particular items on each test.

Musgrave and Cohen have chosen to deal with rather complex tasks, those more usually dealt with in paragraphs than in lists. Theirs is a bolder beginning than I would make. I would choose, first, to compare simple list learning with simple prose learning. Initially, I would try to determine the effects of variables that appear to distinguish simple lists from simple prose, perhaps variables even as seemingly minor as (1) the format in which the items are presented (i.e., list vs. paragraph) and (2) the addition of one word (e.g., "is") or one of a class of words (e.g., verbs) between each stimulus term and its response term (cf. Glanzer, 1962; Rohwer, 1966). I would retain the 2 x 2 design and would, as mentioned above, study the effects of variables such as (1) and (2) above under both experimenter- and subject-controlled study and test conditions, and where information to S about the conditions of the test had been manipulated. Thus, sometimes the design would become 2 x 2 x 2 or 2 x 2 x 2 x 2.

The major contribution of the Musgrave-Cohen paper appears to me to be their suggestion that the sentences in descriptive, prose passages be analyzed into stimulus and response terms, and that these then be entered into a table in which the interrelationships between such terms would be likely to become evident. Use of this procedure can be expected to lead to the identification of a number of learning tasks that are quite common outside, though perhaps not inside, the learning laboratory. (Several such tasks have been presented by Musgrave and Cohen.) A comprehensive taxonomy of learning will have to deal with tasks such as these. A comprehensive technology of training will have to include recommendations for training on such tasks.

Finally, I would like to comment on the use of results from "learning research," whether we study list learning or prose learning in or out of the laboratory. It seems reasonable to me to assume that eventually our findings will be made use of, not only by other researchers and by those who theorize about learning, but also by those who prepare instructional materials (the book publishers, the makers of instructional films, slides, recordings, television programs, and "programmed" materials) and by teachers, who sometimes have the task of preparing instructional materials for use with their classes, and who also have to decide on the sequence in which a set of varied materials is to be presented.

There is another use of our research findings, one which may be even more important than any of those which I have yet mentioned: that is in training students to train themselves. We may look forward to the time when, as soon as the child starts his formal training (perhaps even before, if we can make the appropriate information available to parents and get them to serve as teachers) he will begin to learn how to taxonomize the various learning tasks with which he is confronted (perhaps making tables will play a role here). He will learn a set of procedures to be used with each learning task, and he will learn how the self-training procedures must be changed, as a function of certain characteristics of a task. (It will, of course, be necessary to determine first the age at which children are able to learn such skills.)

Let us suppose, for example, that the student has to learn the capitals of each of the New England states. He will, in his "learning-to-train" training, have learned:

1. To classify this as a particular kind of task (i.e., a paired-associate task).

2. That ordinarily with paired-associate tasks (a) response-learning should be done first, stimulus-term discrimination should be done next, and finally associative-learning should be done in which each response term is associated with its stimulus term; (b) during response-term learning, the response terms should always be studied in the same order; (c) initially the pairs should be studied in the same order and S should test himself in that order; later S should test himself using several different random orders.

3. Under certain circumstances other procedures should be used with paired-associate tasks (e.g., if the stimulus terms are very similar to one another, stimulus-term discrimination training should precede response-term learning).

If research findings are to be used to foster skill in self-training, there are several implications:

1. A substantial effort will be necessary for: (a) developing a taxonomy of learning tasks (cf. Melton, 1964), (b) identifying procedures to be used with particular tasks, and (c) identifying the characteristics of each kind of task that make necessary a change in procedure, or in sequence of procedures.

2. A program will have to be developed for training students to train themselves (i.e., to accomplish tasks 1a, 1b, and 1c above). Training would probably be begun as soon as S entered school (perhaps before, if parents were trained to instruct their children and were willing to do so) and would be continued throughout public school. The time of introduction would be determined by the age at which the child was capable of learning such skills.

3. A method will have to be devised for identifying the research-based information that should be fed into the training

program (i.e., as new information became available from research, the program would have to be revised) and for making this information available (a) to those charged with the responsibility for training others to train themselves, and (b) to those who had already learned how to train themselves.

It is apparent that there is much to be done. The approach proposed by Musgrave and Cohen, particularly as it relates to the development of a taxonomy, should prove useful in integrating into educational practice the results from both laboratory and nonlaboratory research.

NOTES

1. This paper was prepared during the author's tenure of a United States Public Health Service Special Research Fellowship (1-F3-MH-30, 116-01) at the Institute of Human Learning, University of California, Berkeley. The Institute of Human Learning is supported by grants from the National Science Foundation and National Institutes of Health.

2. It is assumed here that the items are presented visually (though most of the conditions would be the same were some other mode of presentation used) and that a pairing-test procedure (also called the "study-test" or "recall" procedure) rather than the anticipation procedure is employed. The pairing-test procedure probably resembles more closely than does the anticipation procedure the conditions under which a prose passage is ordinarily read (i.e., S ordinarily reads the entire passage before he is tested on its contents). See Cofer (1941) and Newman and Saltz (1960) for examples of experiments in which pairing-test procedures have been used to study learning from prose materials.

REFERENCES

Cofer, C. N. A comparison of logical and verbatim learning of prose passages of different lengths. *Amer. J. Psychol.*, 1941, *54*, 1–20.

Glanzer, M. Grammatical category: Rote learning and word association analysis. *J. verb. Learn. verb. Behav.*, 1962, *1*, 31–41.

Melton, A. W. The taxonomy of human learning: Overview. In A. W. Melton (Ed.), *Categories of human learning*. New York: Academic Press, 1964.

Newman, S. E. Student vs. instructor design of study method. *J. educ. Psychol.*, 1957, *48*, 328–333.

Newman, S. E., and Saltz, E. Effects of contextual cues on learning from connected discourse. *Amer. J. Psychol.*, 1960, *73*, 587–592.

Postman, L., and Jenkins, W. O. An experimental analysis of set in rote learning: The interaction of learning instruction and retention performance. *J. exp. Psychol.*, 1948, *38*, 683–689.

Rohwer, W. D., Jr. Constraint, syntax, and meaning in paired-associate learning. *J. verb. Learn. verb. Behav.*, 1966, *5*, 541–547.

Underwood, B. J. Stimulus selection and verbal learning. In C. N. Cofer and B. S. Musgrave (Eds.), *Verbal behavior and learning: Problems and processes.* New York: McGraw-Hill, 1963.

Verbal Units in the
Learning of Connected Discourse

NEAL F. JOHNSON

Ohio State University

During the past decade, the interest in the learning and utilization of complex behavior has increased manyfold. That statement is nowhere more true than in the area of verbal behavior. If one were to plot the yearly percentage of reported studies in the area of verbal learning and verbal behavior that use, in some way, connected discourse as either stimulus or response materials, I am certain it would show a marked positive acceleration. That situation has come about mainly because of an increasing awareness of the inadequacy of some of our earlier and more simple conceptions of the learning process. It is interesting to note, however, that what changes have occurred have not involved our conception of the basic building block of learning (i.e., association). Rather, these changes have involved some modification of our conception of what is a stimulus and what is a response, and a recognition that learning is not quite as mechanical as initially assumed (e.g., see Hull, 1930, for a description of the somewhat more mechanistic view).

These considerations become particularly important if one is to evolve some conception of the process of learning from written instruction, because it is abundantly clear that there is no easy separation between stimulus and response terms. The prob-

117

lem is further complicated by the fact that even if we could divide a communication into stimuli and responses, each of the stimuli and responses would consist of many elements or words, and we would still be left in the position of trying to describe the associative interrelations between: (1) members of the stimuli, (2) members of the responses, and (3) the members of each stimulus and each of the members of its associated response.

As a first step in formulating a means for disentangling the problem, it may be worthwhile to examine the process of communication as discussed by Mowrer (1954). Basically, his argument is that a sentence is a conditioning device whereby the meaning associated with a predicate is conditioned to the subject of a sentence. He assumed that after hearing a sentence, part of the mediating response hierarchy originally aroused by the predicate would then be elicited by the stimulus as well. In addition, he suggested that such sign-sign learning involved the transferring of hierarchies rather than new learning.

Mowrer pointed out that if sentences do fulfill the above function, then communication can be viewed as the transfer of meanings from sign to sign and from person to person. While he suggested that the former kind of transfer is the most important, as far as understanding the basic psychological processes underlying language is concerned, it should also be noted that communication does not occur unless such sign-to-sign transfer occurs from person to person. In fact, the Skinnerian (1957) conception uses the outcome of such person-to-person transfer as the basic condition for language acquisition.

The appropriateness of such a model of the communication process seems clear from the examples used by Mowrer. For example, in a sentence like *Tom is a thief*, the idea that both *Tom* and *thief* have meanings that may be characterized as a hierarchy of mediating responses is very easy for most of us to understand, and there is an increasing volume of empirical support for such a supposition. Furthermore, we have a fairly sound understanding of the process whereby part of the hierarchy originally elicited by *thief* would, after the learner heard the sentence, be elicited by *Tom*. The simplicity of the situation suddenly deteriorates, however, when we are faced with trying to account for

Tom is not a thief in the same terms. Does introducing the operator *not* make hearing the sentence an extinction trial? The situation becomes even more difficult when considering the kind of
sentence we customarily encounter in everyday discourse. For
example, *That rather small boy who ran away lives in a rather shabby
house near the railroad tracks that I dislike seeing* would be extremely
difficult to explain.

THE UNIT PROBLEM

As these considerations would suggest, the problem encountered when trying to understand the process of learning through
oral or written communication is not so much that of explicating
the concept of an association or defining the conditions under
which it is established as it is that of trying to define the nature
of the stimuli and responses that become associated. Therefore,
what appears to be lacking is a conceptual system to explain what
becomes associated with what. Stated in more general terms, we
might ask whether it is possible to characterize complex stimuli
and responses as single entities or units.

The Stimulus Side

UNSTRUCTURED STIMULI. The importance of supposing some
kind of unitization process on the stimulus side has recently been
demonstrated in the work on stimulus selection. The basic effect
is that when a complex stimulus appears in a paired-associate
(PA) task, the subjects are more able to give the correct response,
after learning, to some of the components of the complex stimulus than to others. Those data suggest that early in learning subjects fractionate a stimulus into its components and then select a
single component as the effective stimulus. As a result of that
effect, Underwood (1963) has stressed the importance of dif-
ferentiating the nominal (experimenter defined) from the functional (subject defined) stimulus.

One of the first studies demonstrating the selection effect was
that by Weiss and Margolius (1954). They used a PA task in
which each of the stimuli consisted of a color patch and a pair of
nonsense syllables (80 percent association value), with the re-

sponses being common words. The learning continued to a criterion of one perfect trial, and twenty-four hours later they were tested for their retention of the list. On the retention test the subjects were divided into three groups: one group received the entire original stimulus, another only the colors, and the last only the nonsense syllables. The results indicate that the group that saw the entire compound on the test trial did rather well, but the groups that saw only one of the components on the test trial were significantly poorer in their performance. The interesting result, however, was the fact that the performance of the group presented with the colors was significantly better than the performance of the group seeing only nonsense syllables. Therefore, these two classes of cues were not equally effective in eliciting the response.

There are several interpretations of these data (Underwood, 1963), but, broadly speaking, they can be sorted into two categories: those which suppose that subjects learn the responses to individual components of the stimulus, and those which suppose that subjects integrate the stimulus into some kind of configuration that represents the functional stimulus that elicits the response.

Underwood, Ham, and Ekstrand (1962) examined the issue by using a method similar to that used by Weiss and Margolius. Color patches were used as one component of the stimuli; the other was a trigram. For some subjects the trigram was an English word, and for others it was a low association value nonsense syllable. The subjects learned the task to a criterion of one perfect trial, and forty-five seconds later continued the learning trials with either the original stimulus or one of the two components. For the group that had the low association value trigrams paired with colors during original learning (OL), the performance with the colors alone was as good as when both the color and the trigram were presented. There was also significant transfer to the trigrams. Underwood (1963) suggested that this result rules out the configuration hypothesis, for certainly if that were true it would be difficult to explain the 100 percent transfer to the colors.

In order to eliminate the possibility that the subjects in the

Underwood, Ham, and Ekstrand (1962) experiment simply paid no attention to the low association value trigrams, Jenkins and Bailey (1964) had the subjects spell the trigrams before giving the response during original learning. Their data indicate that the spelling had no effect on the results.

There is also evidence that subjects may select letters as the functional stimulus when the stimuli are single trigrams. Yum (1930), in a study of generalization, found that if after learning the letters in a nonsense syllable stimulus were changed, there was more disruption (or less generalization) when the initial letter was changed than when other letters were changed. Underwood (1963) reported a study by Mattocks in which subjects learned responses to low association value trigrams. After learning, the subjects were questioned regarding how they had learned the list. The results indicated a marked tendency for the subjects to use only the first letter of the stimulus.

Similarly, Jenkins (1963) had subjects learn numbers as responses to low association value CCCs. During learning, they were required to spell the trigram before responding. Learning continued to a criterion of two perfect trials, after which the individual letters from the trigrams were presented and the subjects asked to give the appropriate number response. His results indicate that even with the rather high degree of original learning and the forced attention to all the letters, there was a marked selection effect, with the initial letter eliciting almost twice as many correct responses as the medial letter and the final letter falling about halfway between the other two.

There have also been several studies that used somewhat more complex verbal forms as the stimulus components. In the study mentioned above by Underwood, Ham, and Ekstrand, while all the subjects had a color patch as one of the stimulus components, part of them had low association value trigrams as the other component, while others had three-letter English words. Both groups showed a marked preference for the color patch as the functional stimulus, but it also was clear that the English words were more effective than the nonsense forms. An incidental finding related to that effect is the Jenkins and Bailey (1964) demonstration that in the Underwood, Ham, and Ekstrand situation, if the subjects were tested by presenting just the color names, they would do about as well as when the color patch is presented.

Jean Cohen and Barbara Musgrave (1964) had subjects learn letters as responses to stimulus compounds that consisted of two trigrams. The trigrams were either 100 percent association value English words (H-trigrams) or 10 percent association value nonsense syllables (L-trigrams). Four groups of subjects learned the lists, which differed in the nature of their stimulus compounds (i.e., HH, HL, LH, and LL). Learning continued to a criterion of two consecutive perfect trials. On the test stage the subjects were presented with either the compound used during original learning, or one of the two components. The only difference between the components for the HH group and the LL group was the position of the trigram in the stimulus complex (i.e., first or second). The combined results of the LH and HL groups allow for assessing the effect of meaningfulness on selection. The results indicate that while stimulus meaningfulness had an appreciable effect on selection—regardless of the position of the most meaningful item—there was a position effect only for the LL group, with the item in the first position eliciting more correct responses on the test stage.

In a similar study, Ken Jacobus (1965) had subjects learn digits to stimulus compounds consisting of three trigrams that varied in pronounceability, i.e., high (H), medium (M), and low (L). There were six possible orders in which the three trigrams could appear (HML, LMH, MLH, etc.). On each randomization of the list, one of the six stimuli appeared in each of the six possible orders, and each stimulus appeared in each of the six possible orders in one of the six randomizations of the list. In addition, one-sixth of the subjects had each of the randomizations as his first trial. Therefore, for each subject, position of the trigrams was completely counterbalanced across randomizations. For individual items, position on the first trial was counterbalanced across subjects. After original learning, the eighteen trigrams were presented individually for two unreinforced trials, and the subjects were asked to give the digit with which it was associated during original learning. The highly pronounceable trigrams elicited the most correct responses, the medium pronounceable the next most, and the low pronounceable trigrams the fewest correct responses. The function was almost perfectly linear. It is interesting to note that the results reported by Underwood (1964) and Cohen and Musgrave would suggest that these differences between the trigrams cannot be attributed to differential ease of using the trigrams as stimuli, because when they are used individually as single stimuli in separate lists, the learning rates for the lists were not that different, and the test-stage performance was highly similar.

In an extention of these results, Jacobus was concerned about the effect of varying the presentation rate and degree of learning on the differential use of the components. The task he used was exactly the same as in the previous study, except the presentation rate was either 1 sec.: 1 sec., 2 sec.: 2 sec., or 4 sec.: 4 sec. In addition, the total presentation time for each item was either 48 sec., 96 sec., or 144 sec. As in the previous study, each subject was scored for the number of correct responses to high, medium, and low trigrams on the test stage.

The results indicate that the variation in the presentation rate had no effect on the tendency to use the stimulus components differentially. However, as degree of learning increased, there was an increase in the tendency for the highly pronounceable trigrams to elicit more correct responses than the mediums, which, in turn, elicited more than the lows. It appeared from the results that the subjects maintained the same selection strategy throughout learning. Furthermore, when Jacobus compared a group of subjects that had just reached a criterion of one perfect trial with a group that had between fifteen and twenty over-learning trials, he found the latter group to show a significantly greater discrepancy in their performance to the three kinds of trigram than the group that had just reached criterion. That result would suggest that subjects do not attempt to pick up the unused components as learning progresses.

Recently, evidence has been reported that questions the Jacobus conclusion regarding selection during overlearning. In their study, James and Greeno (1967) used CVC English words and nonsense syllables as the stimulus compounds, and varied the extent to which the subjects had mastered the list before they were tested for stimulus selection. One group of subjects was stopped in their learning of the list when they reached a criterion of one-half of the items correct. Another group was allowed to continue until they had reached a learning criterion of one perfect recall. The third group learned to one perfect recall and then was given ten overlearning trials. On the test stage, the subjects were presented with the individual stimulus components and asked for recall of the responses.

The results indicate that as degree of learning increased, there was an increase in the subjects' ability to give the correct response to the most preferred stimulus component (i.e., the words). For the nonsense syllables, however, the subjects had a very low probability of recall and the group that learned their list to 50 percent and the group that learned it to 100 percent were approximately equal. The group that had ten overlearning trials showed a marked increase in their ability to recall the response when the nonsense syllables were presented. James and Greeno interpreted their data as indicating that subjects use a strong selection strategy during the course of acquiring the material, but once they had learned the list they attended to other stimulus components.

One way of reconciling these data with those of Jacobus is to suggest that the James and Greeno conclusion is correct, and that the Jacobus data indicate that fast learners select more than slow learners. All of the subjects in the Jacobus study had the same amount of study time, and the subjects in his overlearning group were those individuals who had learned the list most rapidly. The subjects who had just reached a criterion of one perfect in that period of time were also those subjects who had learned the list most slowly. Therefore, considering the James and Greeno data, it might be most reasonable to suppose that the Jacobus data indicate that fast learners select more than slow learners.

An overview of these studies, which have used unstructured materials, indicates quite clearly that one cannot suppose that a learner will utilize all parts of a stimulus complex that has been presented to him. It appears as if subjects adopt a strategy of least effort, and identify that component of the stimulus complex which is both unique with respect to the other stimuli and involves the least amount of learning on his part.

It is likely that during the early stages of learning, a learner searches among the components of complex stimuli to find those which will be most effective. That search process is supported, in part, by both the Jacobus and the James and Greeno studies. During the early phase of learning in both these studies, there was an increase in the tendency for all stimulus components to elicit the correct response. However, after the first few trials, there was no more gain in the tendency for the least preferred components to elicit the response, while the most preferred components increased rapidly. If, during the early phase of learning, subjects do search around for a convenient component, it would be expected that all components would gain some tendency to elicit the response. Once a single component has been identified, however, only that component should show an increase in the tendency to elicit the response.

The overlearning data of James and Greeno are of some interest in that they indicate that subjects do tend to pick up other components after their performance has become perfect. It should be pointed out, however, that the increase in effectiveness of the least preferred components was not very great, even during overlearning. Therefore, even overlearning will not insure complete stimulus utilization.

The Jacobus data would indicate that the above problems are more critical for fast learners than for slow learners. It could be that one of the factors that retards learning for a slow learner is the fact that he attempts not only to learn the response and the stimulus-response association, but also to integrate the stimulus. If that is the case, then the term "slow learner" may not be an appropriate label for these subjects, because their retarded performance could be attributable to the fact that they attempt to learn more than "fast learners."

One final point regarding these studies is that the preferred components tend to be the most codable components. In the Underwood, Ham, and Ekstrand study, the selection of the verbal item was enhanced by increasing its meaningfulness. In the Cohen and Musgrave study, as well as the James and Greeno, the most meaningful CVC was selected. In the Jacobus study, the subjects tended to select on the basis of pronounceability. These data might suggest that subjects prefer components that can be most conveniently handled as a single stimulus unit (i.e., highly codable). Furthermore, it is important to note that the Jenkins study indicates that subjects will not use all of the components of a stimulus that is difficult to code, even when they are forced to react to all of the components during learning (e.g., saying all of the letters).

If subjects select the most codable items, there is a possibility that these items are not further fractionated. That is, one of the properties of a codable element may be that it is not readily fractionated, and that the subjects can treat it as a single unit. For example, if a stimulus complex consisted of a highly pronounceable item and one that is not very easily pronounced, it may be that the disregarded component is the one that would have to be further fractionated into components (e.g., individual letters) before it could be used efficiently. The Jenkins experiment indicated that if a poorly coded trigram is presented to the subject, the subject will fractionate it into individual letter components, and use one of them as the functional stimulus. On the other hand, it may be that if Jenkins had used highly pronounceable CVC combinations (e.g., POG), the subjects may have treated the trigram as a single unit and made no attempt to fractionate it into individual letters.

That idea was examined in a study by Postman and Greenbloom (1967). They pointed out that the subjects may use an entire trigram as a stimulus, and on the test stage they use the given letter as a stimulus for recalling the other letters in the trigram. Under that interpretation, the previous results would be taken as representing the differential ability of the subjects to use the individual letters for recalling the other letters in the trigram, which, in turn, elicited the response. In their experiment they collected data on the ability of subjects to give the correct response to individual letters, as well as examining the extent to which subjects could recall other letters in the trigrams. During original learning, half the subjects had easy-to-pronounce trigrams as stimuli, and the other half had hard-to-pronounce trigrams. They report that there did appear to be some selection of the initial letters of the hard-to-pronounce trigrams (in accord with the data of Jenkins), but for the rest of the letters in those trigrams, and all the letters in the easy-to-pronounce trigrams, the ability to give the response to the letter was highly correlated with the subjects' ability to recall other letters. The data appear to suggest that, at least for easy-to-pronounce trigrams, the subjects treated them as stimulus units and that the individual letters varied in their effectiveness as cues for reinstating the stimulus unit.

These data would indicate that stimulus fractionation and selection does not invariably occur when a complex stimulus is presented. If subjects can be provided with some device that allows them to code the stimulus into a single entity (e.g., pronunciation), then fractionation will not occur. In part, the concept of codability can be defined in terms of a tendency for subjects to respond differentially to the components. The Postman and Greenbloom data indicate clearly that such differential responding was considerably greater for CCCs than for CVCs.

STRUCTURED STIMULI. The above considerations would suggest that if subjects are presented with structured materials, the structure might provide a coding device such that the subjects will treat the materials as a single unit rather than as a set of components. The problem is to evolve some conception of the way in which the sequence might become integrated in such a way that it can be represented with a single mediating response or code. An illustration of the direction such a conception might take is the work reported by Cliff (1959) on the way adverbs and verbs combine. In addition, recent developments in semantic theory (Katz and Fodor, 1963) have been specifically concerned with this issue, and Osgood (1963), capitalizing on these models, has offered a general schema with which the psychologist might work.

One of the psychological implications of grammar is that it might define both perceptual units and response units. There is a great deal of work on the effect of structure on response integration (see the following section), but there has been much less work on its effect on perceptual units. One of the clearest cases is a study by Fodor and Bever (1965). Subjects were presented with a sentence in one ear, and in the other ear they heard a click that occurred somewhere within the sentence. Immediately after hearing the sentence, the subjects were instructed to write out the sentence and indicate exactly where the click occurred.

The results indicated that the accuracy of locating the click was considerably greater if it occurred in the boundary between two surface-structure constituents than if it occurred somewhere within a constituent. They also demonstrated that the effect was not dependent upon pauses occurring at constituent boundaries, because the effect occurred when there was no pause between constituents. Furthermore, their results indicate that when subjects make errors in locating clicks that occurred with a constituent, there is a tendency for these errors to be in the direction of the nearest constituent boundary. These data suggest that the subjects perceived the sentences in terms of units that conformed to the grammatical structure of the sentence.

The mere fact that subjects use grammatical structure to define perceptual units does not guarantee that these units are so codable that the subjects will not fractionate them into components. In particular, the ease with which subjects can learn numbers of various parts of speech seems to vary as a function of the part of speech. For example, Glanzer (1962) has demonstrated that, depending upon the nature of the context, function words and content words are learned at different rates. In addition, Mandler and Mandler (1964) have demonstrated that within sentence contexts, various parts of speech are differentially easy to acquire. Among content words, there is some evidence (Johnson, 1965, 1969) to indicate that adjectives and adverbs are learned somewhat more slowly than are other parts of speech.

It is interesting to note that the items which are most difficult to learn (i.e., modifiers) are those items which can be dropped from a language sequence without violating the grammatical rules that define the units. If subjects differentially respond to the components of linguistic units (i.e., stimulus select), the disregarded components should be those which can be dropped without violating the structural integrity of the sequence. Underwood (1963) suggested that one way to avoid such single component selection might be to have all of the components for any stimulus appear in several of the stimuli. In that case, any one stimulus would be composed of a unique *combination* of the components. The subjects would not be able to master the task unless they attended to all components and learned their relations.

One final question regarding coding of linguistic stimuli concerns the way the stimuli are integrated. The Postman and Greenbloom study indicated that even with codable stimuli there are differences among the components in their effectiveness as a cue for eliciting the rest of the stimulus components. That is, even in cases where the subject has not fractionated the stimulus and selected a component, there are still wide differences among the components in the probability that they will elicit the response in the absence of other components.

A similar phenomenon has been demonstrated with language materials (Blumenthal, 1967; Blumenthal and Boakes, 1967). In these experiments, subjects learned sentences in a free-recall task. At the time of the test, they were prompted with various words from the sentences. The results indicate that even for well-integrated sentences, there was variation in the effectiveness of the various words in the sentences as prompts, with the subject of the sentence being the most effective prompt. Therefore, even if subjects do not fractionate a stimulus unit during learning, it cannot be supposed that all of the elements within the unit are equally effective in eliciting the response.

The Response Side

As in the case of the stimulus, there is a question as to the extent to which the response, or predicate, side of a sentence can be conceptualized as a unit that, as a single entity, can be conditioned to the stimulus. The fact that response selection can occur, and that it is a function of variables similar to those affecting stimulus selection, has recently been demonstrated by Postman (personal communication). He used a paired-associate task, but two responses were paired with each stimulus and the subjects told that either one of the responses would be considered correct. Learning was continued until the subjects gave a correct response to all the stimuli on two trials, although it was unnecessary to give the same correct response on both trials to any one stimulus. The most surprising result was that the subjects settled on one response to each stimulus very early in learning. Postman examined the responses that were given on the earlier trials to determine how much response switching had occurred. He found that the responses given on the last trial accounted for 98 percent of all the responses!

Generally, the problem of response selection is not important in communication, because if alternatives are acceptable it may make little difference which is acquired (e.g., paraphrasing). However, in those instances where there are alternatives and it is necessary for the subjects to learn the entire set as responses to the stimulus, it is important to recognize that selection can occur and it is an extremely strong effect.

Regarding the problem of response unitization, a recent study (Johnson, 1965) illustrated one approach to the issue. It was assumed that what subjects treat as a response unit would be apparent in their behavior to the extent that those response elements that come from the same unit should be highly dependent response events. For example, during the learning of response sequences, the subjects should tend to recall the elements from the same unit in an all-or-none manner. A paired-associate task was used in which sentences were learned as responses to digits. The learning followed the standard anticipation procedure, and they learned eight digit-sentence pairs. It was assumed that the subjects would treat the phrases as units and, therefore, words from the same phrase would be more dependent as recall events than words from different phrases. The dependency was measured by computing the conditional probability that each word in the sentence would be wrong, given the preceding word was right. It was expected that these transitional error probabilities would show spikes on the transitions between phrases. The results showed that such spikes did occur and, furthermore, the pattern of transitional-error probabilities (TEPs) reflected the entire phrase structure of the sentences.

These results were taken as support for the supposition that subjects tend to use grammar to break a sentence into functional sub-units. In an effort to determine the effect of such sub-units on learning, another study (Johnson, 1968) was conducted in which subjects learned sentence segments as responses in a paired-associate task. It seems reasonable to assume that sentences like *The friend of my father gave us a ride* and *The father of my friend gave us a ride* would be equally probable in the language. Therefore, *father of my* and *of my father* should be equally probable as segments. However, the latter is a unit and the former is not. To determine the effect of the unit on learning, one group of subjects learned sequences like *of my father,* another learned *father of my,* and a third learned scrambled sequences like *my of father.* In addition, three more groups learned sequences produced in the same manner, but based on simple four-word predicates (e.g., *hit the small ball*). As expected, for both major groups, the phrases were learned more rapidly than the equally acceptable, but nonphrase sequences. The latter sequences, however, were learned more rapidly than the scrambled sequences. In addition, for both groups, the nonphrases fell about 65 percent of the way between the phrases and the scrambled sequences. These data were taken as further support for the hypothesis that subjects unitize grammatical response sequences.

Recently, some studies on hesitation phenomenon in learning have offered further support for the hypothesis that subjects produce responses in terms of functional units. Martin (1967) has presented data which indicate that during learning subjects tend to hesitate at the boundaries of major constituents in sentences, and he suggested that these hesitations reflect unit decisions on the part of the subjects. In another study, Suci (1964) identified the location of pauses in subjects' spontaneous speech. He then constructed a list of learning materials for each subject. In one case, this consisted of the spans of words that occurred between pauses (i.e., units). In another case, an equal number of words occurred in each response segment, but the sequences did not begin and end at points where the subject had hesitated (i.e., partial units). His results indicate that the units were learned significantly more rapidly than were the partial units.

These considerations would suggest that if subjects do use

grammar to define functional response units, the relevant units for conditioning are these larger segments rather than individual words. In addition, the phrase-learning experiment indicated that learning is facilitated when the responses conform to these units, even when the control group learns equally probable and acceptable sequences.

Stimulus-Response Learning

The data available on the integration of sentence parts is rather limited, but that which has been collected suggests that the process is not very simple and we must use caution in generalizing from data gathered using unstructured material. While these considerations have been reviewed elsewhere (Johnson, 1968), it may be worthwhile pointing out some of the more critical issues.

In an experiment by Tulving and Patkau (1962), an attempt was made to examine the way subjects use sequential constraints when recalling response sequences. They used several approximations to English, and controlled for both word frequency and nonsequential associations. When doing this, they found that there was little change in the subjects' ability to recall sequences from a first- to a fifth-order approximation, but there was a sharp increase in performance from the fifth order to text material. Janine Frankart (1964) found, paradoxically, that when she gave subjects specific word-to-word associations prior to learning sequences representing various orders of approximation, the facilitating effect occurred only for very low orders of approximation. For the English-like material, there was no facilitating effect whatsoever. In conjunction, the two studies would suggest that the kind of sequential constraints that are encountered in connected language material may not be characterizable in terms of word-to-word associations, and the strategy subjects use for learning structured material may not be the same as they use for unstructured material.

That conclusion received added support in another experiment (Johnson, 1966) in which subjects were given specific word-to-word associations between words within sentences, which they later learned. It was hypothesized that subjects might use something like a word-to-word association when trying to integrate an adjective-noun (A–N) transition within a sentence, but they might not use such an association when integrating a noun-verb (N–V) pair that represented the subject-predicate transition. Therefore, it was predicted that the prior association should facilitate the integration of the A–N transition, but not the N–V transition. That result was obtained. In addition, the pre-experimental strength of the A–N pair was greater than the N–V pairs. Therefore, if these word pairs are put into random strings, the A–N transition should be learned more rapidly than the N–V transition, according to the Frankart data. In addition, if subjects do use word-to-word associations when learning random sequences, as the data suggest, then the absolute amount of change as a result of building in a prior habit should be greater for the N–V transition than for the A–N transition because the pre-experimental strength of the N–V transition is less (i.e., the increment added to habit strength as a result of a learning experience decreases as prior strength increases). Therefore, given the same relative difficulty of learning the A–N and N–V transitions in sentences and random strings, the effect of a prior learning experience should facilitate the A–N transition more than the N–V transition in sentences, but the reverse effect should occur in random strings.

It appears, then, that the nature of the associative system that subjects use in language may not be the same as for unstructured sequences. Unfortunately, the available data does not give a very clear understanding of the system, but it does suggest that subjects associate large response units rather than individual words.

One way to conceptualize these response units is to assume that they are stored in memory in terms of a single unitary code. In fact, it might be most meaningful to view a response unit as any behavioral sequence which is stored in the same code. If that were the case, then it would not be meaningful to talk about associations between individual response items, but rather the nature of the associative system that relates one code to another code. That is, subjects may not form interresponse associations, but rather establish associations between the codes that integrate these responses into units.

The concept of coding can be illustrated by a recent unpublished experiment. Subjects learned letter sequences as responses to digit stimuli. The sequences were structured by introducing blank spaces between certain of the letters. For example, the subjects learned sequences consisting of nine letters that appeared on the study trials as three groups of three letters each (e.g., 1–SBJ FQL ZNG). Prior data had indicated that subjects use the blank spaces to define behavioral units.

After the subjects had learned the first two pairs to a criterion of approximately 80 to 90 percent correct, they were asked to learn a second set of two pairs structured in the same manner. On the second list, the letters were the same as those used in the first list except for one letter in each of two chunks. For example, if a first list response was SBJ FQL ZNG, then the second list response might be SXJ FQT ZNG. If subjects store the members of a unit in terms of a single memory code, then changing one letter will change the entire code. Therefore, if one letter is changed on the second list, there should be a tendency for the code representing that unit in the first list to be forgotten. On the other hand, the one unit that had no change should have the same code on both the first and second list and, therefore, it should not be forgotten, Therefore, letters that were common to both first and second list, and that appeared in units that had no change (e.g., ZNG), should be retained very well, whereas letters that were common to the two lists, but appeared in a unit that had a change (e.g., S, J, F, and Q), should show considerable forgetting. Finally, the specific changed letters (B and L) should also show forgetting.

The control group learned the first list and then worked on a puzzle during the time the experimental groups were learning their second list. In comparison to the control group's performance, recall by the experimental groups of the unchanged units gave no evidence for forgetting. The unchanged items that appeared within a unit that had a change (i.e., a changed code) showed a 50 percent loss with respect to the control group, while there was a 60 percent loss for those specific items that were changed. This difference in the recall of the two types of un-changed letter was interpreted as indicating a loss of the code for the unit that had a change. The fact that changing one mem-ber of a unit has a relatively uniform effect on all of the other members, offers support for the idea that the members of a unit share a common storage in memory.

An effect similar to the above has been demonstrated with sentence materials, as well. In a recent study (Johnson, 1969), subjects learned sentences like *The tall boy saved the dying woman.* For half the subjects, the terminal words (i.e., the objects) were scrambled among the sentences so that the sentences were mean-ingless. If subjects use the constituent structure of the sentences to define units, and these are stored in memory using a single code, then any unit that contains the difficult item should be difficult to learn, but those units that do not contain that item should be somewhat easier. The results indicate that scrambling the objects made learning the entire predicate rather difficult, but had little or no effect on the subject of the sentences.

CONCLUSIONS

In both written and oral communication, the informing ma-terial that is presented to a subject is usually quite complex. While it is clear that increasing complexity has an effect on learn-ing rate, the above considerations would suggest that it may also have an effect on what is learned. That is, it is becoming increas-ingly clear that learners adopt a principle of least effort in a learning situation, and attend only to those aspects of the task which are needed to attain a high level of performance. Those components of the task which the teacher considers important, but which the learners need not use, will tend to be disregarded. Furthermore, the effect seems to occur regardless of whether the materials are viewed as a stimulus or whether they are viewed as a response. Consequently, it seems necessary to introduce into any learning situation devices that force the learner to attend to all of the components of the learning materials.

From a theoretical point of view, it seems meaningful to view the learning of structured materials as the learning of the relationships among codes that represent large response segments, rather than the learning of relationships among individual response items. That point of view would suggest that when preparing learning materials, it is important to keep in mind the kind of behavioral unit that is most convenient for the learner to use during learning.

For example, suppose a sentence fill-in format were to be used in a programmed instruction situation. The complete sentence might be, *The brown car is near our house.* If the subject of the sentence was the stem (*The brown car ___ _____ ____ _____*), with the predicate (*is near our house*) as the response, the task would require the learner to use convenient response units. On the other hand, if the stem consisted of *The brown ____ __ _____ ____ house,* and the response was *car is near our,* neither the stem nor the response would conform to convenient units. Consequently, one would expect both stimulus selection (Postman and Greenbloom, 1967) and a retarded rate of response learning (Johnson, 1968; Suci, 1964).

The results of two studies (Glanzer, 1962; Johnson, 1961) offer rather specific support for that expectation, In the Johnson study, the stimuli were sentence frames that consisted of an article, adjective, noun, and verb, in that order. For half the subjects, the stimuli consisted of a sentence with a blank in the adjective position, and for the other half the blank appeared in the noun position. In both cases, the subjects were required to learn a nonsense word as a response, and were instructed to respond by saying the sentence with the nonsense word in the correct position. For both groups, the response consisted of a convenient unit, regardless of whether one considers the response the specific word or the sentence. However, the groups did differ in that the subjects with the noun missing in the stem did not have a complete unit as a stimulus. These subjects learned the lists significantly more slowly than the groups for whom only the adjective was missing. Therefore, both to improve learning rate and avoid item selection, it is important that both the stimulus and the response conform to convenient units for the learner.

REFERENCES

Blumenthal, A. L. Prompted recall of sentences. *J. verb. Learn. verb. Behav.*, 1967, *6*, 203–206.

Blumenthal, A. L., and Boakes, R. Prompted recall of sentences. *J. verb. Learn. verb. Behav.*, 1967, *6*, 674–676.

Cliff, N. Adverbs as multipliers. *Psychol. Rev.*, 1959, *66*, 27–44.

Cohen, J. C., and Musgrave, B. S. Effect of meaningfulness on cue selection in verbal paired-associate learning. *J. exp. Psychol.*, 1964, *68*, 284–291.

Fodor, J. A., and Bever, T. G. The psychological reality of linguistic segments. *J. verb. Learn. verb. Behav.*, 1965, *4*, 414–420.

Frankart, J. On the relationship between grammaticalness and the utilization of short-range associations. Unpublished doctoral dissertation, Ohio State Univ., 1964.

Glanzer, M. Grammatical category: A rote learning and word association analysis. *J. verb. Learn. verb. Behav.*, 1962, *1*, 31–41.

Hull, C. Knowledge and purpose as habit mechanisms. *Psychol. Rev.*, 1930, *37*, 511–525.

James, C. T., and Greeno, J. G. Stimulus selection at different stages of paired-associate learning. *J. exp. Psychol.*, 1967, *74*, 75–83.

Jacobus, K. The effects of total exposure time, pronounceability, and presentation rate on stimulus selection. Ohio State Univ., 1965.

Jenkins, J. Stimulus "fractionation" in paired-associate learning. *Psychol. Rep.*, 1963, *13*, 409–410.

Jenkins, J., and Bailey, V. Cue selection and mediated transfer in paired-associate learning. *J. exp. Psychol.*, 1964, *67*, 101–102.

Johnson, N. F. The cue value of sentence frames for the acquisition of speech categories. Unpublished doctoral dissertation, Univ. of Minnesota, 1961.

———. The psychological reality of phrase-structure rules. *J. verb. Learn. verb. Behav.*, 1965, *4*, 469–475.

———. The influence of associations between elements of structured verbal responses. *J. verb. Learn. verb. Behav.*, 1966, *5*, 369–374.

———. The influence of grammatical units on learning. *J. verb. Learn. verb. Behav.*, 1968a, *7*, 236–240.

———. Sequential verbal behavior. In T. Dixon and D. Horton (Eds.), *Verbal behavior and general behavior theory.* Englewood Cliffs, N.J.: Prentice-Hall, 1968b.

———. The effect of a difficult word on the transitional-error probabilities (TEPs) within a sentence. *J. verb. Learn. verb. Behav.*, 1969, *8*, 518–523.

Katz, J., and Fodor, J. The structure of a semantic theory. *Language,* 1963, *39*, 170–210.

Mandler, G., and Mandler, J. M. Serial position effects in sentences. *J. verb. Learn. verb. Behav.,* 1964, *3*, 195–202.

Martin, J. G. Hesitations in the speaker's production and listener's reproduction of utterances. *J. verb. Learn. verb. Behav.,* 1967, *6*, 903–909.

Mowrer, O. The psychologist looks at language. *Amer. Psychol.,* 1954, *9*, 660–694.

Osgood, C. On understanding and creating sentences. *Amer. Psychol.,* 1963, *18*, 735–751.

Postman, L., and Greenbloom, R. Conditions of cue selection in the acquisition of paired-associate lists. *J. exp. Psychol.,* 1967, *73*, 91–100.

Skinner, B. *Verbal behavior.* New York: Appleton-Century-Crofts, 1957.

Suci, G. The validity of pause as an index of units in language. In H. Levin (Ed.), *Project literacy reports no. 2.* New York: Cornell, 1964, pp. 50–57.

Tulving, E., and Patkau, J. Concurrent effects of contextual constraint and word frequency on immediate recall and learning of verbal material. *Canad. J. Psychol.,* 1962, *16*, 83–95.

Underwood, B. Stimulus selection in verbal learning. In C. Cofer and B. S. Musgrave (Eds.), *Verbal behavior and learning.* New York: McGraw-Hill, 1963.

———. The representativeness of rote verbal learning. In A. Melton (Ed.), *Categories of verbal learning.* New York: Academic Press, 1964.

Underwood, B., Ham, M., and Ekstrand, B. Cue selection in paired-associate learning. *J. exp. Psychol.,* 1962, *64*, 405–409.

Weiss, W., and Margolius, G. The effect of context stimuli on learning and retention. *J. exp. Psychol.,* 1954, *48*, 318–322.

Yum, K. An experimental test of the law of assimilation. *J. exp. Psychol.,* 1931, *14*, 68–82.

Discussion of
Professor Neal F. Johnson's Paper

WENDELL W. WEAVER

University of Georgia

In his paper, Johnson proposes the thesis that early concepts in language study are inadequate because of the distorted conception of "what is a stimulus and what is a response." He finds the central problem of language to be that of "trying to define the nature of the stimulus and response that became associated."

A large part of the paper is devoted to an investigation of the literature and attempts to find evidence of a unitization on both the stimulus and response sides. From this review of the literature, the conclusion is drawn that evidence in the papers reviewed supports "some kind of unitization process on the stimulus side," while the unitization hypothesis on the response sides is given many qualifications.

At times, in his paper, Johnson seems to be using "stimuli" and "responses" as units involved in some measurement, that is, stimuli being anything presented to the subject in terms of a nonsense syllable unit or a word unit, and responses being reports that have been elicited by the experimenter's directions to the subject. This attitude is not maintained, however, and in many cases "stimulus" and "response" are used in positions that imply that there is some identifiable distinction in connected discourse between "stimulus" and "response." For example,

139

there is the statement, "There is no easy separation between 'stimulus' and 'response' terms." Actually, there is an easy measurement separation; one simply chooses what he would have as a stimulus and applies it. The demonstration that there is a difference "in reality" may be impossible.

It is indicative of the shifting of the problem from a measurement situation to a question of some "absolute unitization" that an appeal is made to a language model — Mowrer's. The process involved now is not simply "stimulus-response," but a "mediating response hierarchy" elicited by the stimulus and a "transferring of hierarchy." The "stimulus-response" relationships are no longer input-output relationships of measurement, but rather are now part of an explanatory mediated-conditioning language model. Several times in the paper there is a shift from the measurement use of the terminology to an explanation of what is going on when the language is underway, without clear guides to the changing scene.

The most interesting part of the paper is a report of one of Johnson's research studies, which attempts to demonstrate a particular unit of language, or, more precisely, to indicate that language units are multiple when considered in terms of words, rather than single word-by-word units. The method used is a so-called "paired-associates learning situation" in which a number is presented as a stimulus and a normal English sentence is the response member of the pair. The task of the subject is the rote recall of the sentence on presentation of the number. The dependent variable is the transitional error probability, which is computed from the number of improper elements, or improper sequences, at each particular word in the sentence. The results are that transitional error probabilities tend to be high at boundaries defined by phrase-structure rules, and tend to be low within these boundaries.

Here one should note carefully the nature of the learning task. Learning is that of a particular sample from a well-known set of orders of English sentences, and a particular sample of a well-known set of English words. The subject is given the tape recorder-like task of repeating back by rote the material the experimenter has presented. This is an atypical human learning situation. The individual is rarely required to reproduce, verbatim, material that is extended beyond the range of immediate memory, material that he already knows well as far as its semantic and structural characteristics are concerned. On the other hand, there is no doubt that this particular task did produce results that fitted (statistically) hypothesized events. In the subjects involved in this particular situation, certain language elements are perceived together with a higher degree of probability than are other language units. Nevertheless, the method excludes the powerful factors, in fact the crucial factors, for the learning of continuous prose, of semantic variability and structural complexity.

The problem of the manner in which the sentence is decoded is approached by Johnson (1964) with the supposition that immediate constituents might have "psychological reality": that is, the subject may "deal with structured language material as a hierarchy of response units of increasing inclusiveness." Johnson's idea of the way decoding operates is that "word function" is decoded rather than "meaning." The subject decodes the subject and predicate, and the predicate is stored in short-term memory; whereas the subject of the sentence is decoded as "article" and "modifying noun." "Modifying nouns" are stored in short-term memory, whereas "article" is decoded into the unit word "the."

The overwhelming impression of these descriptions (not only in Johnson's paper, but in the descriptions of other linguists) is that structure is the vehicle controlling word choice, rather than assigning control of word to the "message." This position would be more tenable if the sentence, in isolation, could be demonstrated to be "the unit" of language. If one considers an individual listening to even so short a passage as one hundred and fifty words comprising ten or eleven sentences, the informational load becomes staggering. Furthermore, the processing task does not end here. In an informal, natural language situation, the passage is extremely unlikely to be entirely in subject-predicate form. The speaker assumes situation commonality, and the listener must include in his decoding factors other than the auditory language sequence. These intrusions are an integral part of the decoding, yet the situation does not seem to have a formal, sequential, interpretive function such as that proposed here for the sentence.

Even more telling against Johnson's construction is the information load his model places on short-term memory. Short-term memory just does not seem to be this good. Generally, it proves to be the bottleneck in the channel of communications. It stretches credence to assign short-term memory the function of handling high-speed interchanges, meanwhile holding large and small constituents in abeyance. For example, when the predicate and the "modified noun" are in short-term memory together, the predicate is stored first, but the "modified noun" must come out first in the decoding, a type of reversal the human nervous system always has had difficulty handling.

The question of the descriptive veracity of the model is secondary to its predictive qualities. What does the model predict? Chiefly, that in rote memorization immediate constituents isolated by phrase-structure rules tend to have low "transitional error probabilities" within the phrase-structure, and higher "transitional error probabilities" between phrase units in the structure. The same effect may be predicted by other hypotheses, for example, the pattern of distributional constraint operating on various word units differentially. However, the variations in structure per se, when separated from the effects of a selection of particular content words, have not been shown to have an effect on the learning of the substantive content of the message.

Developmentally, knowledge of structure seems to occur early in the history of the normal human being. At about one and a half years of age, he is producing grammatical "two-word" utterances—grammatical here meaning that words are produced in their proper sequence. At five years of age, typically, without "formal" instruction the child is using correctly the major structural forms of the language (see McCarthy, 1954). By about ten years of age, the material to which the child is being exposed by his instructors has similar sequential constraint to that of "average adult prose" (Carterette and Jones, 1963). For the human, the structure of the language seems an easily acquired, necessary but not sufficient skill for communicating. Perhaps this is why it is so difficult to find important learning variables connected with the structure of the language.

In his paper, Johnson demonstrates a kind of learning, but it is not the type of learning one is ordinarily concerned with in written instruction. Further, it is difficult to find anywhere in psycholinguistic research satisfactory demonstrations of specific effects of language structure on learning, if one exempts from consideration studies dealing with the number and type of "content" words and the length of clauses or sentences.

Constraint increases at function words, as shown by the small number of words subjects can produce in a particular time period, for example, five minutes, with such word deletions. One might assume that language decoding requires a search pattern, which consumes time according to the size of the distribution that must be searched, or that some matching situation goes on, with greater latency according to the length of the unit to be matched. Under either of these conditions an immediate constituent will emerge as an artifact of the constraining situation based on the word unit alone. Even when the immediate constituent consists of two or more lexical items (for example, "red car"), linguistic logic is confounded with sequential constraint, because the sequence "car red" is not as common in English; that is, statistical frequencies for the sequence "red car" would be higher than frequencies for "car red."

Johnson mentions mediating responses several times in his paper. There are important considerations with regard to units of language, but we are only able to consider them through our measurements. Learning is always an interaction between what is happening now and what has gone on before, and what has gone on before is "inside" the organism. Stimulus-response psychology (with behaviorism the general psychological philosophy) in its beginnings attempted to ignore the "inside" of the organism. As behavioral researchers attempted to study more and more complex phenomena, a measurement problem arose. In many, and the most interesting, cases the stimulus could not be identified directly with the response. One solution to the problem was to ignore potential stimuli and concentrate on analyzing responses. The other major tack was to posit some internal operation providing a logical explanation for the dissociation of stimulus and response.

These speculations did not come about because psychologists were particularly interested in these internal operations, but because what needed to be explained required particular kinds of transformations that could only be occurring internally. The idea of mediation as an explanatory construct came into psychology as a response to these difficulties. Mediation acts like a buffer system, or an "internal stimulus-response," triggered by the outside stimulus. For stimulus-response psychology, its most powerful quality was the bridging of delay; thus, temporal noncontinuity could theoretically be tolerated between stimulus and response.

In verbal behavior, it is particularly important to have a mechanism that can explain delay. It is easily observed that a verbal stimulus may trigger verbal behavior out of all proportion to the verbalizing itself; an extremely small stimulus may elicit an extremely large response, as when a man says to his wife, "Shut up!" It is not very difficult, perhaps, to explain these kinds of responses in the light of a conditioning history, but it is much more difficult to explain how the history came to be preserved in the central nervous system, or somewhere in the organism, or somewhere in the world, in a physical form that will allow its reconstruction and reactivation by another stimulus at a later time.

Association cannot be understood without an "inside" of some sort. It implies at least two entities that come together. Generally, one is given perceptually (the stimulus), while the other must be somewhere physically extended in order to associate. It is difficult to imagine where the locus of this association might be, unless it is "inside." Our use of input-output relationships should include attempts to study this dimension—what the "inside" looks like—by inferring from the only information we have the responses of the organism under various stimulations.

It is especially difficult to explain associations of the nature of those which Johnson considers in his discussion of Mowrer's assumption that, in a sentence such as "Tom is a thief," a hierarchy of meanings attached to the word "thief" are ultimately connected to the designation "Tom." In this case it is obvious that Tom is a substantive, that is, he is perceptually designatable. He has a physical reality. On the other hand, "thief" does not designate such an entity. The label "thief" designates a set of relationships, or a group of attributes, that are applied to a particular complex of behaviors. There are relationships between physical entities involved, but there is no one physical entity that can be pointed to and designated "thief." "Thief" implies a sequence of behavior in relation to particular physical objects in the environment, and in relationships between sets of relationships, such as the attributes of property, personal ownership, social morality, character, etc.

What is the "hierarchy of meanings" to which the term "Tom" is applied? There are certainly no sets of representations of external reality in the sense of substantiality. The sole reality is a set of learned attributes of a particular kind of behavior. If the association of "Tom" to "thief" is made, then the substantiality "Tom" is associated with the set of attributes that only have a unitary existence within the nervous system of an individual. Certain attributes are correlated "inside" the individual, and it is this correlation that makes the term "thief" an entity. However, it is difficult to show that the word itself has a unitary basis, which consistently arouses the *same* set of attributes, let alone to consider that all of these attributes are conditioned as a package to an entirely separate referent. The logic of a deterministic science needs to account in some fashion for such terms as "thief," as well as for even more abstract terms — those that have even less contact with substantiality. At this point it is important again to have a clearer view of the "inside" of the organism.

The major difficulty in looking for units of language is that language behavior is based on a long history of organismic action and reaction. When one presents a stimulus to a human organism, he is presenting an input to a highly organized and constantly reorganizing collection of neurophysiological relationships. However timid one is about inferring what goes on internally in the organism, there are few nowadays who would be so bold as to affirm that nothing goes on within the organism.

If one is dealing with written instruction and he shows an individual (an early adolescent, let us say) this passage from Hamlet: "What is a man, if his chief good and market of his time, be but to sleep and feed? A beast. No more," one may expect a response and get none, or one not connected with the stimulus at all. There is nothing in the lexical content of the passage that should pose difficulty. The words are all common: man, good, market, time, sleep, feed, beast. These separate lexical elements of the passage are relative to the experience of the early adolescent, and on a vocabulary test the great majority of early adolescents would have little difficulty dealing with the words in this passage. On the other hand, much more is implied by this passage than meets the eye in the lexical content.

In the first place, this is a question that answers itself, a literary device that requires added learning beyond the actual content of the passage. The quotation may also be read as a philosophical question, in which case a whole set of relationships, a whole set of experiences, a whole set of learning is implied. It is easy to assign this interpretive reading to an existence in some mythical never-never land, but the scientific psychologist must logically assume that, in some fashion, there are elements, attributes, signs, symbols laid down somewhere within the organism as a result of the contact of this individual with his culture, and the internalization of the attributes of his culture.

Typically, the early adolescent has not had this kind of contact and has not internalized these kinds of experiences; there is nothing "inside" to allow the interpretation of the "What is a man?" type. I tried out this passage on a group of early adolescents that tend to congregate around my house. The vocal responses to my stimulus was indicative of the internal state of the early adolescent in regard to this kind of task. They ranged from a high of "Oh, it sounds like Shakespeare," to a low of "Are you nuts!"

If one attempted to develop a knowledge of these types of relationships in early adolescents through written instruction, he would not have the simple task of defining terms, although some special exercise on the analogous use of "market" might add a little to the interpretation. The task would center on having the individual read other verbal material relating the kinds of structures implied by such questions as "What is a man?" Orientations would have to be developed that would lead the individual to search for answers to generalized questions. The learner would have to recognize that he needs to go beyond the use of the word "man" to designate a male human. In some way, through his learning, there would have to develop an internal set of constraints that would isolate "man" as a generic term, standing for the entire species. A set of information would need to be developed on considerations of the large question of "humanness." A great part of this verbal behavior might be built on contrasts between man and the rest of the animal world. Part of this contrast would be understanding laid down in the organism of the ubiquitous, biological, survival orientation of the lower animals, against the symbolizing, abstracting, "not living by bread alone" propensities of the human being.

Even with such an apparently simple stimulus as "What is a man?" one certainly would not expect from his newly educated organism a unitary response. Rather, expectations would be of a whole array of verbal behavior triggered by the stimulus, but nevertheless internally distributed and organized and available as an output carrying beyond the output of any individual's previous output, if the subject becomes creative.

What is the unit of language in this case? Whatever it is, it can only be categorized arbitrarily as stimulus-response in a traditional sense because the ostensible stimulus, "What do we mean by 'what is a man'?" does not stimulate many individuals at all. Rothkopf's "mathemagenic behaviors" (Rothkopf, 1965) and the term "inside" in this paper are large constructs that do not exist in any discernible, physiological unit. Scientific logic leads one to assume that there are physiological units involved; that is, actual physical entities ordered in time or space that represent all of the elements and relationships of behavior. But when the investigator comes into contact with the language, the unit has long since been amalgamated into the on-going continuity of the verbal behavior. It is relatively useless to speculate about the nature of the "inside," except at those points where a particular theoretical point of view can be shown to order data parsimoniously, and, further, requires an assumption of an "inside" as part of its parsimony.

When one talks about the "inside" of the organism it is strictly a rhetorical device, for the organism cannot be partitioned, in reality, into such categories. There is always a relationship between what is "inside" and what is "outside." The problem of the relationship of the language "inside" to the physical reality "outside" is a problem of semanticity. The linguist C. A. Hockett makes this comment on semanticity, "Linguistic signals function in coordinating and organizing the life of a community, because there are associative ties between signal elements and features in the world . . ." (1963, p. 8). A central consideration of any practical use of laboratory results, or of theoretical models, of linguists or of psychologists, is that the experiment or the theory must make some semantic sense. The very power and force of language, the reason for its use in society, is the ability it gives the organism to represent what is happening on the outside of the organism. Hockett sums up his view on semanticity by saying, ". . . in short, some linguistic forms have denotations" (ibid.).

As noted above in the discussion of "Tom is a thief," denotations are of at least two types. In one case denotation is a direct perception of a physical entity; in another case it is the inferences from a set of perceptual attributes that a set of relationships characterizable internally as an entity exists. This view seems to modify, somewhat, Hockett's conception of association as the relation of "single elements" to "features in the world." Hockett's analysis needs modifying because "features in the world" do not come into the nervous system as "features in the world." These "features in the world" must themselves be given some sort of transduced representation; that is, they must be encoded into the neurophysiological code of the nervous system. Actually, then, only certain coded correlates of "features in the world" are present in the nervous system. Therefore, the association is between the signaled attributes of "features in the world" and signal elements that involve the internal language of the organism.

Further complicating the analysis of associations is that for some associations the individual produces words in common with other individuals. For other associations, the individual will produce associates unique to himself. This kind of data seems often to approach the dichotomy of language made by Saussure (1959) in which he designates language potentially communicable from one individual to another as "la langue," and language which an individual uses himself in a specific individual manner as "la parole." There is a good bit of data on the associational nature of "la langue," but little data that examines "la parole." Gathering this data would involve noting the associational patterns of particular individuals and analyzing the ways in which language organization differs within the same individual. In fact, there are few analyses of the consistency of language production of individuals. Weaver and Bickley (1967a, 1967b) have used a cloze situation to relate the predictability of language productions of individuals, predicting their own production to the same individual's ability to predict the language production of others. Using this sort of measurement, differences can be demonstrated between the internal language of the individual and the language as the individual communicates.

This brings one no closer, however, to defining a unit of language. In relation to Johnson's paper, the point here is that associations are also measurement constructs, and the sequential grammatical associates are interwoven with paradigmatic lexical associates so that constituents of phrase size are confounded with constituents of word size (and, of course, of constituents of syllable size or of phoneme size if these prove relevant).

Underlying Johnson's analysis of the decoding of the sentence, indeed, underlying all transformational analyses of language, is the idea of a hierarchy. This has been a very convenient term with which to express inferred relationships that seem to come from data selected from the language behavior of individuals (especially when this data is averaged across individuals). Psychologists, keeping up with the times, have also adopted this construct as explanatory of the way the language is organized "inside" the individual. Again, the concept has potential for misleading when one divorces it from its measurement context.

In Johnson's study, the largest category of the hierarchy is the "sentence." A part of this category is the subordinate constituent "noun phrase," and a part of this category is the even more subordinate constituent "article." Eventually, the final constituent is reached—the word "the." The decoding proceeds within the sentence, and there is no apparent reason for extra-sentence effects to affect the coding. On the other hand, Shepard (1963) has demonstrated that with randomly selected natural language passages the effect of context increases monotonically with the size of context on both sides of a target word. There is little effect after forty words of context (on both sides) are added, but this is still beyond the limits of the typical sentence. Weaver and Bickley (1966) have shown that the effect of context outside the sentence on words within the sentence does not have the monotonic effect Shepard demonstrates with his random passages. The effect on different words in the sentence is from no effect at all to very pronounced effects. Nevertheless, the conclusion from the findings is that there are extra-sentence constraints on certain lexical items and on certain words that change the *structure* of the sentence (i.e., under some conditions subjects switch grammatical categories).

Johnson seems to take the word "unitizing" literally, and he is looking for a combination of particular components of a complex stimulus within the organism, which collapses on itself in such a way as to trigger a specific unitary response. There is also the idea that the unity, visualized as ultimately collapsing to give the unitary stimulus, is the immediate constituent of a grammatical analysis of the sentence. Since this is a conditioning model, the important question is, "How did these phrases become conditioned originally?" It would seem that if one is to use specific stimuli under such a conditioning model there would need to be specific reinforcement of each stimulus unit; otherwise, how would the unit become differentiated at all?

It is difficult to conceive how this reinforcement could come about. Other models of the development of language in the child, such as that of Brown (1965), picture language development with the child presenting segmented language models— primarily of the content words of the language—and receiving from the caretaker, usually the mother, standard expansions of these smaller models. Whether these conditions obtain or not, they certainly provide us with observational units by which we can attack the problem of learning in the child. So far, neither immediate constituent analysis nor recorded conditioning histories have provided such convincing developmental demonstrations. One would expect, for example, that the child, rather than selectively emitting content words in the language, would instead emit phrases modeled on the immediate constituents of the sentence. Why this does not occur needs explanation.

A number of contemporary investigators (Chomsky, 1966; Hockett, 1963; Fries, 1952; Katz, 1966) strongly hold to the position that there are two, or more, major subsystems in language. Nevertheless, the force of the semantic element in language—the desire to use the language to mean something—is such an overriding consideration in analyzing the language, that it is dubious whether studies that do not include considerations of semanticity can help us much in analyzing the naturally produced language. It is difficult to see how phrase-structure grammars, any more than traditional grammar, can provide principles for a technology of written instruction.

REFERENCES

Brown, R. *Social psychology.* New York: Free Press, 1965.

Carterette, E. C., and Jones, M. H. Redundancy in children's texts. *Science,* 1963, *140,* 1309–1311.

Chomsky, N. *Cartesian linguistics.* New York: Harper & Row, 1966.

Fries, C. C. *The structure of English.* New York: Harcourt, Brace, 1952.

Hockett, C. F. The problem of universals in language. In J. H. Greenberg (Ed.), *Universals of language.* Cambridge: MIT Press, 1963.

Johnson, N. F. A model of sentence generation. Paper read at American Psychological Association, Los Angeles, September, 1964.

Katz, J. J. *The philosophy of language.* New York: Harper & Row, 1966.

McCarthy, D. Language Development in Children. In L. Carmichael (Ed.), *Manual of child psychology.* New York: Wiley, 1954.

Rothkopf, E. Z. Some theoretical and experimental approaches to problems in written instruction. In J. D. Krumboltz (Ed.), *Learning and the educational process.* Chicago: Rand-McNally, 1965.

Saussure, F. de. *Course in general linguistics.* Trans. by C. Bally and A. Schehaye. New York: Philosophical Library, 1959.

Shepard, R. N. Production of constrained associates and the informational uncertainty of the constraint. *Amer. J. Psychol.,* 1963, *76,* 218–228.

Weaver, W. W., and Bickley, A. C. Constraint on sentence elements of context external to the sentence. Paper read at the Southeastern Psychological Association, New Orleans, April, 1966.

———. Some differences in encoding and decoding messages. *J. of the Reading Specialist,* 1967a, 7, 18–25.

———. Structural-lexical predictability of materials which predictor has previously produced or read. *Proceedings, 75th Annual Convention, APA,* 1967b, pp. 289–290.

PART II

STIMULUS MEASURES AND CHARACTERIZATIONS OF PERFORMANCE

Developing a Technology of Written Instruction: Some Determiners of the Complexity of Prose[1]

EDMUND B. COLEMAN

University of Texas, El Paso

The major purpose of this paper is to initiate a systematic study of the stimulus dimensions that affect the learning of prose. A tidy portion of education can be defined as the learning of prose. To develop a technology for this portion of education — to develop a technology of written instruction — psychology must provide a systematic array of S–R functions that relates the stimulus dimensions of prose to measures of learning and understanding.

The literature of education abounds in experiments having conflicting results. This is largely due to the fact that investigators have only the crudest of scales for calibrating their stimulus materials, which fact in turn is due to the scarcity of controlled experiments in which the subject (S) learned sentences or higher levels of prose. Psychology boasts a profuse literature describing experiments in which S memorized lists of unconnected words or nonsense syllables, but it is not impossible that complex verbal learning is so complicated by interaction effects that such studies will provide only a trifling percentage of the S–R functions needed to predict the sort of verbal learning that we are really interested in: education, training, and the learning of language skills such as talking, understanding, reading, and writing.

155

As one example, studies of step size within the literature of programmed instruction include conflicting results that can be attributed to the fact that investigators have no precise way to quantify step size. Using a linguistic unit such as number of words and weighting this for complexity would seem a reasonable method, but there is no adequate weighting scheme. Response-calibrated weighting schemes such as cloze scores will be useful for some purposes, but the only stimulus-calibrated schemes are crude readability formulas.

Most of the stimulus dimensions (S-dimensions) that govern the complexity of prose are still waiting to be related to response measures (R-measures). One systematic way to taxonomize the S-dimensions would be according to the complexity of the R-measures they affect, perhaps beginning with dimensions that affect perceptual responses (legibility), moving on to those that affect word-for-word memorization (m, pronounceability), and finally coming to those that affect comprehension (content-word ratio, kernel-sentence ratio, syntactic structure).

Thus taxonomized, the S-dimensions would be arranged in a cone-shaped grid with those affecting perceptual responses located in the apex. (A relatively small number of S-dimensions affect perceptual responses, somewhat more affect word-for-word memorization, and a nearly infinite number affect comprehension.) There is a high negative correlation between the number of S-dimensions at a part of the cone and the number that have already been related to R-measures. A respectable percentage of those at the apex have already been related to measures of behavior, but almost none of those at the base have been. Obviously, a science must focus its resources at levels simple enough to reward abstract study. But since the base of this cone-shaped grid contains the sort of verbal behavior everyone else is interested in, it would seem the task of psychology to aid their speculative extrapolation by dotting this base with an array of systematically distributed S–R relations. The first step in the task is to develop a set of R-measures, especially measures of the higher cognitive processes such as understanding.

Many of the S-dimensions most likely to predict complex verbal behavior have already been taxonomized by linguists. It seems irresponsible not to relate their S-dimensions to an equally systematic array of R-measures. Traditionally, the dimensions have been investigated by two general methods, which can be called correlational and experimental. The first section of the present work presents a correlational study, the second presents a sample of controlled experiments.

THE CORRELATION STUDY

Studies of readability certainly investigate the S-dimensions of prose, and these studies have traditionally used the correlational method. Perhaps the correlational method is best illustrated by Gray and Leary's classic *What Makes a Book Readable?* (1935). The present section can be considered an extension of Gray and Leary that uses more reliable R-measures and additional S-dimensions suggested by recent advances in linguistics.

In the correlational method, the investigator constructs a scale of readability, or comprehensibility, or complexity, or the like. He selects a range of passages and scores each passage according to some R-measure, usually by having Ss read the passage and then counting the number of questions they can answer about it. Then the R-measures are correlated with various S-dimensions of the passages—mean length of sentences, mean number of prepositions, kernel/clause ratio, and the like.

The general weakness of such a correlational method is that the S-dimensions are correlated with one another and it is difficult to assign either individual effects or interaction effects. In addition to this general weakness, in the previous correlational studies the investigators were using a rather unreliable R-measure: the number of questions S could answer about the passage. An investigator can ask easy questions about difficult passages and vice versa. The questions one investigator would ask about the passage might bear little resemblance to those asked by another investigator. It would seem that cloze scores (Taylor, 1957) provide a more reliable measure of comprehensibility than number of questions answered.

Miller and Coleman (1967) have provided a scale of comprehensibility as measured by cloze scores. Their scale consists of thirty-six 150-word passages ranging from first-grade material to the most difficult technical prose. The comprehensibility of the thirty-six passages was measured by three variations of cloze tests.

One was the traditional cloze test with 20 percent of the words deleted. The second cloze test deleted only a single word in each passage and thus enabled Ss to use all the sequential constraint in the passage. The third required Ss to successively guess all 150 words, and he was given the correct word as he proceeded through the passage. Thus, he saw only the words preceding the one he was trying to guess and not those following it; he could use unilateral constraint only.

The summed scores for the three variations gives a measure based upon 2,400 responses per passage. This measure reflects the uncertainty of every word in the passage — guesses by sixteen Ss for each of the 150 words. This summed cloze score should be a highly reliable criterion of comprehensibility. Values for thirty-two S-dimensions were determined for each passage, and these dimensions were correlated with the summed cloze score. They were also correlated with each of Miller and Coleman's three variations of the cloze score.

RESULTS. The first four columns in table 1 give the rs of the thirty-two S-dimensions with the four cloze scores — the three variations and their sum. Note that these rs are surprisingly high, considerably higher than those reported in previous correlational studies of readability. Cloze scores are apparently a more reliable measure of a passage's comprehensibility than such measures as ratings or number of questions answered by readers.

Word Classes

It has been suggested that the proportion of certain word classes affects the comprehensibility of a passage. For instance, King and Cofer (1960) have investigated the adjective-verb quotient. Gray and Leary (1935) considered proportion of prepositions and certain classes of conjunctions. But before considering such proportions, it will be useful to study word classes in a more general fashion.

Table 1

Correlations for Four R-Measures and 32 S-Dimensions

	Sum	Clo	Cl_2	Cl_3	1 CW	2 CW_2	3 AN	4 CN	5 CN_2	6 V_c	7 V	8 V_n	9 Adj	10 A_2A_3	11 Adv_{man}	12 $Adv_{t\text{-}1}$	13 Adv	14 Pro	15 Pre	16 Let	17 Sy	18 1-S	19 Mor	20 Mi	21 Sen	22 Cl	23 Ker	24 Dif	25 Df_2	26 Rep	27 A^2_n	28 Ger	29 Inf	30 Par	31 SC	32 CC
Summed Cloze		97	96	96																																
20% Cloze			95	87																																
1-word Cloze				87																																
Every-word Cloze																																				
1 Content Word	39	38	37	37																																
2 $CW-V_cA_3$ CIRSU	-36	-41	-38	-29	10																															
3 Abstract Noun	-78	-78	-78	-70	44	-33																														
4 Concrete Noun	67	64	66	64	37	-08	-76																													
5 Con. N + $N_g N_f$	70	66	68	68	34	-05	-76	97																												
6 Verb copula	03	04	-03	13	13	-18	12	-04	-09																											
7 Verb-full	66	72	66	55	39	-34	-65	53	49	-16																										
8 Verb$_{nom}$	-76	-75	-72	-72	-22	38	81	-67	-71	09	-60																									
9 Adjective	-56	-54	-55	-53	-20	59	49	-52	-45	-23	-48	-60																								
10 Adject - A_2A_3	-51	-52	-49	-46	-18	66	43	-46	-38	-14	-58	-58	33																							
11 Adverb$_{man}$	-34	-33	-29	-33	28	25	34	-29	-35	-12	-07	48	-06	08																						
12 Adverb$_{t\text{-}1}$	25	25	21	25	27	-18	-35	23	23	-03	33	-32	-22	08	-00																					
13 Adverb	11	14	10	09	34	-04	-46	07	03	-08	28	-06	-22	29	88	27																				
14 Pronoun	58	60	62	48	57	-63	-62	38	35	01	56	-53	-52	37	-07	25	37																			
15 Preposition	-62	-65	-60	-57	-52	40	74	-47	-45	03	-71	55	41	40	15	-54	37	-69																		
16 Letter	-90	-87	-87	-85	48	45	83	-59	-64	08	-09	82	55	44	-07	34	-06	-57	58																	
17 Syllables	-90	-89	-88	-84	47	39	47	-59	-73	14	49	39	62	42	34	-18	37	-30	14	58																
18 1-Syl. Word	88	86	86	82	-43	60	38	47	-48	-06	-52	-42	-52	-30	-52	15	-26	-09	-10	-59	-89															
19 Morpheme	-88	-86	-86	-83	09	48	83	-59	-71	02	-57	86	89	53	43	34	-10	46	43	67	-58	-94														
20 Morph-inflect	-88	-87	-85	-82	-23	48	83	-68	-75	10	-65	89	89	46	47	-30	-15	-59	95	96	95	-89	97													
21 Sentence	57	52	51	60	-30	43	87	-73	-75	10	-65	89	89	50	48	38	38	43	43	65	96	95	-89	-43												
22 Clause	66	68	65	60	52	-52	-56	47	42	-04	34	39	-31	-33	-11	34	29	67	-60	-32	-45	-61	52	-59	67											
23 Kernel	-77	-77	-75	-70	-06	68	67	-59	-59	-06	-06	82	62	62	45	29	11	-57	74	74	74	-75	74	72	-32	-65										
24 Dif CW (TTR)	-64	-59	-53	-68	-27	48	35	-25	-22	-44	-52	30	30	62	17	41	-14	-39	41	48	52	-45	54	50	-58	-75	60									
25 Dif CW-syn	-56	-51	-43	-61	-25	47	30	-17	-14	-44	-49	30	29	61	13	-20	-16	-35	48	48	43	-36	43	40	-57	-72	57	60								
26 Repetition	49	38	34	60	50	00	-14	24	24	54	31	-35	29	-33	-09	15	10	26	-32	-28	-30	22	-28	-28	71	56	-29	57	-74							
27 Adject$_{nom}$	-57	-55	-59	-53	-07	11	45	-47	-47	24	-36	48	30	48	08	09	07	-24	27	51	49	-56	51	50	-25	-24	51	26	20	-14						
28 Gerund	-30	-28	-39	-26	14	26	17	-20	-22	-23	-15	29	18	26	20	17	31	-13	27	01	27	31	-37	51	23	-20	-28	01	10	04	21					
29 Infinitive	04	01	-04	10	18	-08	13	-02	-05	35	-22	18	19	17	-19	25	05	08	13	-13	05	01	24	24	01	-28	24	29	07	-05	-14	16				
30 Participle	-33	-31	-28	-33	-17	47	34	-20	-31	-19	18	23	60	-00	17	-19	25	-23	-29	24	26	-29	37	37	-25	40	42	43	39	-17	20	07	-56			
31 Sub. Conj.	-11	-07	-05	-15	-33	-31	02	-26	-15	11	14	06	-01	-22	-30	-36	-37	11	12	-03	01	02	06	-48	17	-22	-09	-15	-01	14	-13	22	-33	-07		
32 Coord Conj.	-10	-04	-04	-16	02	-03	-08	06	03	-41	-02	-08	-13	06	-14	-07	-08	13	-16	-03	-08	08	-04	-03	-33	-17	04	25	28	-24	05	14	-22	08	-06	

The cloze technique and the large sample of words in the present study permit a more detailed study of word classes than is currently available. We have a cloze score for each of the 5,400 words, and this sample of words is large enough to permit a fairly detailed analysis. The words were analyzed into forty-four word classes. In this analysis, only the traditional cloze scores were used; i.e., these are results from cloze tests that deleted 20 percent of the words in the passage.

CLASSIFICATION. The classification of the present paper is based on that of Fries (1952) because his volume is readily available and familiar to many psychologists. The conventional names of the word classes will be used, however, rather than those of Fries. The classification is given with examples of each word class in table 2. For some word classes, more detailed distinctions than those of Fries were made, and they are described in detail when these classes are discussed. The principal extensions were:

Nouns were analyzed into twelve subclasses, including six classes of abstract nouns that are listed with examples in table 2.

Nouns include Verb-er (agentives such as *farmer, driver*), V (verb)$_{nominal}$ (*knowledge, explanation*), and Aj (adjective)$_{nominal}$ (*beauty, cuteness*).

Verbs were analyzed into five classes, not counting Verb-er and V$_{nominal}$, all of which are adequately defined in most English grammars.

Fries' determiners (his class A) were analyzed into four subclasses:

A1 = articles such as *the, a, an, this, these, those, that.*

A2 = pre-determiners such as *each, any, more, some, all, most, few, both, half.* These are determiners (with the exception of numbers) that can fill the slot in _____ *of the fine old stone houses.*

A3 = possessive pronouns such as *your, their, his, my,* etc.

A4 = numbers such as *one, two,* etc.

The function words from B to O are as defined by Fries (Chapter 6). Their conventional names are given with examples in table 2. The classes from P to W are as follows:

P = verb particles such as go *out,* come *in,* get *up.*

Q = pro-verbs (Harris, 1957, p. 305).

Table 2

Cloze Scores of Word Classes

Content Words				Function Words			
Word Class	Example	No. of Words	Cloze	Word Class	Example	No. of Words	Cloze
Noun	atom	566	49%	A1 (article)	these	568	74%
Proper N	Venus	108	42%	A2 (predeterm.)	much	115	48%
$N_{fraction}$	side	33	43%	A3 (poss. pro.)	his	112	58%
N_{group}	covey	40	47%	A4 (number)	four	91	40%
N_{behave}	image	9	55%	B (modal auxil.)	could	206	75%
N_{unit}	mile	97	66%	C (not)	not	31	76%
$N_{process}$	chore	62	32%	D (adv. degree)	very	91	49%
$N_{language}$	space	128	27%	E (coord. conj.)	and	214	65%
$N_{adjunct}$	brick	28	38%	F (preposition)	from	595	67%
$N_{possessive}$	Joe's	5	45%	G (do)	do	10	85%
Verb-er	joker	16	45%	H (there)	there	4	75%
V_{copula}	is	117	76%	I (wh-words)	where	9	86%
V_{full}	hit	539	44%	J (subor. conj.)	since	175	55%
$V_{infinitive}$	to go	92	49%	K, L, M, N, O	oh	8	58%
V_{gerund}	going	35	19%	P (particle)	go *in*	35	61%
$V_{nominal}$	gift	125	21%	Q (pro-verb)	can +	19	48%
$V_{participle}$	going	67	22%	R (time, locate)	now	111	46%
Adjective	red	361	26%	S (address)	Mrs.	13	79%
$Aj_{nominal}$	depth	65	28%	T (to)	*to* go	101	90%
$Ad(verb)_{man}$	sadly	68	28%	U (pronoun)	you	326	72%
				W (sounds)	bam	5	95%

R = adverbs of location and time such as *here, there, away, now, then, again, soon, often, sometimes, once, before, always, too, also, on, home, upstairs.*

S = address such as *Mr., Mrs.,* etc.

T = *to* in infinitives.

U = pronouns (except A3, possessive pronouns).

W = sounds, as *bam* in *It went bam!*

RESULTS. In table 2, cloze scores are given for each of the word classes. The cloze scores are slightly higher than those previously reported (e.g., Fillenbaum, Jones, and Rappaport, 1963), probably because many of the passages were very simple, grammar-school prose.

DISCUSSION. The discussion should begin by explaining why I complicated Fries' classification by further analysis. The reason is that Fries' 1952 classification groups together a number of word classes that have opposite effects upon comprehensibility. Under his class 1 (nouns), for instance, Fries grouped together pronouns that have high cloze scores (U = 72 percent) and nominalizations that have low scores ($V_{nominal}$ = 22 percent). Similarly, adverbs of manner have low scores (Ad_{man} = 28 percent), while adverbs of time and location have high scores (R = 46 percent); V_{copula} has high scores (77 percent), while V_{full} (44 percent) has much lower scores.

In addition, the linguists who are developing generative grammars have found it necessary to analyze words into far more classes than was thought necessary by traditional grammarians. For instance, Lees' grammar (1960) listed forty-seven word classes. An extension of this grammar, which he distributed in mimeographed form in March, 1961, contained sixty-eight word classes. Some of these distinctions may be related to comprehensibility.

Some word classes are related to comprehensibility because their members are common familiar words; others are related to comprehensibility because they occur in syntactic constructions that are easy to comprehend.

From table 2, we can derive counts that will predict comprehensibility as measured by cloze scores; a passage is easy to comprehend if certain word classes predominate over others. For instance, a passage is easy to comprehend if function words (classes A through W) predominate over content words (noun, verb, adjective, adverb). It is easy to comprehend if concrete nouns (Proper N, Noun, Verb-er) predominate over abstract nouns ($N_{language}$, N_{behave}, $N_{process}$, $V_{nominal}$, $Aj_{nominal}$), if active verbs predominate over nominalized verbs, and so on. An investigator interested in readability can derive an astronomical number of suggestive proportions from table 2 — so many, in fact, that any of them must be regarded as an hypothesis for investigation rather than as a conclusion.

Content Word Ratio

Gray and Leary found an r of .26 between percentage of content words and comprehensibility. Since that time, Fries has presented a very full discussion of content words and function words. As a rough approximation function words can be considered to be the words that are not capitalized in titles, i.e., words such as articles, prepositions, conjunctions, and the like. Fries and Hockett (1958, Chapter 31) should be consulted for a fuller discussion. Perhaps the reader will appreciate the relation of comprehensibility to proportion of content words if he will compare a sentence with a high proportion of content words (*multiply all positive odd numbers in the even rows by the third even positive score*) to one with a low proportion (*multiply the first of the scores in that column by the second of the means*).

METHOD. The number of content words was counted in each of the thirty-six passages, and since all passages contained 150 words, this was equivalent to determining the content word ratio. Two definitions of content words were used, and the functions relating cloze scores to content word ratios were plotted for each. For the first definition, content words were defined as nouns, verbs, adjectives, adverbs, A4 (numbers), V_{copula}, R (adverbs of time and location), C (*not*), U (pronouns), L (*yes, no*), S (address), and A3 (possessive pronouns). For the second definition U, L, S, A3, V_{copula}, R, and C were not counted as content words.

RESULTS. By the second definition, the number of content words per 150-word passage ranged from 55 to 84. In figure 1, mean summed cloze score per passage is plotted as functions of the two content word ratios. The maximum summed cloze score for a passage would be 2,400: correct guesses by sixteen different *S*s for each of its 150 words. To facilitate comparison between S-dimensions, this figure and many that follow are labeled in z-scores. (Perhaps it is worth mentioning that labeling the S-dimensions in z-scores rather than raw scores has no effect whatever upon the shape of the function and the positions of the points). In this figure and many that follow, each point represents the mean of four passages. To facilitate direct comparison, the same four passages are averaged for corresponding points on every curve. In order to average the same four, it was necessary to average according to the dependent variable rather than according to the independent variable. In figure 1, and in most that follow, *r* is given for each function.

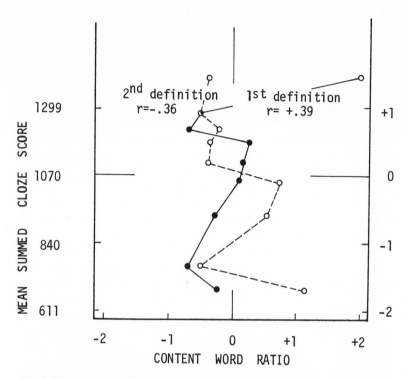

Fig. 1. Mean summed cloze score before reading plotted as a function of two different content word ratios (in z-scores). Each point represents four passages.

DISCUSSION. There is a moderately high relation between content word ratio and comprehensibility; however, the important point is not the absolute magnitude of the correlation, but the fact that it can be changed from positive to negative by changing the definition of "content word." Some justification for each of these definitions – or for a number of intermediate definitions – could be found in the literature. For instance, the first definition gives a positive correlation because it includes pronouns, and no less an authority than Fries defines a pronoun as a content word. The most satisfactory definition is probably the one represented by the dotted curve in figure 1, the one representing the second definition above. It has a negative correlation with the weighted cloze score ($r = -.36$). Passages containing many content words are relatively hard to understand. Actually, this stimulus dimension can be better studied using the controls of the experimental technique. Such a study is provided later in the experimental section of this paper.

Proportions of Concrete Nouns and Abstract Nouns

Although Gray and Leary mentioned the effect of abstract words on comprehensibility, they did not try to measure the proportion of abstract words. They argued that "in repeating several trial counts of abstract words in a selection, we noted frequent inaccuracies, probably for the reason that as a person becomes familiar with the many connotations of an abstract word the quality of abstractness is gradually lost."

It seems possible to define abstract nouns. Gorman (1961) describes a reliable method for classifying nouns as abstract and concrete. It is true that there are a few nouns that seem to be on the ill-defined border between abstractness and concreteness, but actually the majority of abstract nouns belong to classes that can be defined quite reliably. The effect of abstract nouns is great enough to overcome unreliability due to definition problems.

METHOD. In the present paper, two counts of concrete nouns were determined for each of the thirty-six passages. The first definition of concrete nouns does not include $N_{fraction}$ and N_{group}; the second definition does. Both counts of concrete nouns included agentives (*farmer*, *driver*) and proper nouns as concrete nouns.

Abstract nouns were defined as nouns belonging to the following classes of table 2: N_{behave}, N_{unit}, $N_{process}$, $N_{language}$, $V_{nominal}$, and $Aj_{nominal}$. In brief, they were nouns that did not describe objects that could be perceived by the senses.

RESULTS. The number of concrete nouns per passage ranged from 1 to 35. Table 1 gives the rs for the two concrete noun ratios: $r = .67$ for the count that did not define $N_{fraction}$ and N_{group} as concrete nouns, and $r = .70$ for the count that did. In figure 2, mean summed cloze scores are plotted as a function of the number of concrete nouns and the number of abstract nouns in

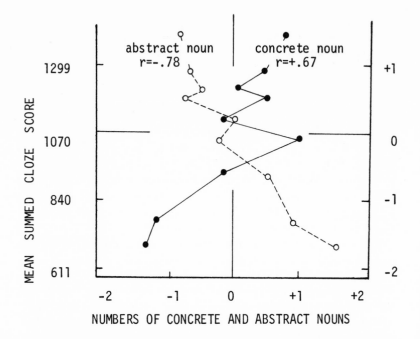

Fig. 2. Mean cloze score before reading plotted as a function of number of concrete nouns and number of abstract nouns per passage (in z-scores). Each point represents four passages.

the passage. It seems clear that simple prose contains a high proportion of concrete nouns, whereas difficult prose contains a high proportion of abstract nouns.

DISCUSSION. The most general finding is that nouns can be partitioned into subclasses that have opposite effects upon comprehensibility. It is not surprising to find that difficult prose contains more abstract nouns than less difficult prose. Writers should note, however, that abstractness is not necessarily an inalterable, inherent S-dimension. Frequently, the complexity due to abstractness is superfluous complexity; frequently, it is easy for the writer to reduce the number of abstract nouns in a passage. If a passage contains a large number of $V_{nominals}$ (*explanation*), he need only transform them to active verbs (*explain*). For instance, *The inclusion of this man is emphasis upon the importance of the group* contains three abstract nouns. It can be transformed to a version that contains none: *When I included this man, I emphasized that the group was important.* The abstractness of the first version was not due to inherent abstractness of the subject matter.

In other words, there is prose that is abstract for no better reason than that the writer chose one derivative of a verb instead of another. Much of the abstractness in scientific writing must be attributed to a reason no more profound than its tradition against "I" and "we." Perhaps the writer who eschews these two pronouns is simply being modest, but avoiding them frequently causes him to substitute a $V_{nominal}$ for its active verb form.

Proportion of Verbs

The sort of books that offer advice on clear, readable writing usually advise the practicing writer that a liberal use of verbs will make his style clearer and more forceful. In a series of experiments, King and Cofer (1960) tested the notion that the adjective-verb quotient would predict comprehensibility. Their findings were not free of conflicts, and their most general conclusion was that "the actual numbers of adjectives and of verbs are perhaps more effective variables than the ratio itself."

We have already seen that the literature permits several different definitions of content words; some definitions correlate positively with comprehensibility, others correlate negatively. We have also seen that nouns can be partitioned into subclasses that correlate positively with comprehensibility and into other subclasses that correlate negatively. Below we will examine two subclasses of verbs and a nominalized verb, and will find that verbs also can be partitioned into subclasses that have different effects upon comprehensibility.

The subclasses that were counted in each passage were:

1. V_{copula} — linking verbs such as *is*.
2. V_{full} — verbs, with the exception of copulas, that have tense markers, i.e., transitive and intransitive verbs such as *hit* and *sleep*. This category does not include the nonfinite forms (gerunds, infinitives, and participles).
3. $V_{nominal}$ — nouns derived from verbs (*explanation, knowledge*).

These words are not verbs at all, but it is interesting to examine them here because they can be substituted for verbs by applying a grammatical transformation.

RESULTS. The total for full verbs per 150-word passage ranged from 6 to 28. Figure 3 shows that the count of V_{full} is highly correlated with mean summed cloze scores ($r = .66$), but table 1 shows that V_{copula} is not ($r = .03$). If we wish to develop a predictor of comprehensibility that uses verbs, we would do well to eliminate copulas such as *is* from our definition. Linguists have noted other reasons for distinguishing *is* from the other verbs (Chomsky, 1957, p. 67).

In figure 3, note the negative correlation of $-.76$ between cloze score and $V_{nominal}$ (a class of abstract nouns that can be substituted for true verbs if the clause is grammatically transformed). The number of $V_{nominals}$ per passage ranged from 1 to 18.

DISCUSSION. The present results suggest—as have others (e.g., Coleman, 1965)—that prose having a low proportion of verbs carries a heavy load of superfluous complexity. However, the writer should not interpret these results simply as advice to invigorate his prose with verbs like *excoriate* and *fulminate*. The easiest way for him to increase the proportion of verbs is the same way he decreases the proportion of abstract nouns; he transforms $V_{nominals}$ to active verbs (e.g., he transforms *an inclusion of this is an admission that it was important* to *since she included this, she is admitting that it was important*). Such transformations obviously alter many S-dimensions correlated with comprehensibility, clause length being one of the most important. In table 1, note the high correlation (.79) between number of V_{full} and number of clauses.

The additional vigor of the verb comes not only from its stem—from its content morphemes—but also from its function morphemes. It comes from the inflectional affixes, pronouns, and auxiliary verbs that explicitly state tense, voice, mood, aspect, number, and person. The active voice of the verb plus a noun or pronoun explicitly specifies person and number. When the extra clause is added in the transformed version, the subordinate conjunction can make explicit the ideas of time, cause,

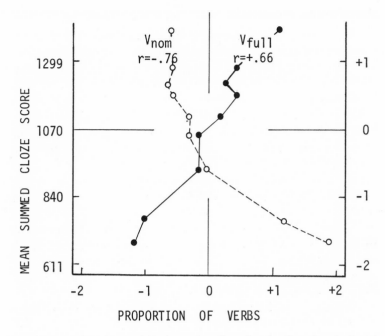

Fig. 3. Mean cloze score plotted as a function of proportion of verbs in the passage (in z-scores).

manner, condition, etc. Much more important, the finite verb is far more specific than the abstract noun. By transforming *inclusion* to *included*, tense, voice, aspect, and mood are made specific. As noted under the discussion of abstract nouns, prose can be abstract for no more profound reason than that the writer chose one derivative of a verb instead of another.

In short, proportion of verbs is a useful measure for predicting comprehensibility. On the other hand, the advice to use many verbs is not very instructive to a writer trying to improve comprehensibility. Like the rule for decreasing the number of abstract nouns, this rule can be stated far more precisely in terms of grammatical transformations. In general (Coleman, 1965), it seems that transformations using active verbs are easier to comprehend than ones using $V_{nominals}$, although length of sentence is probably an interacting variable.

Miscellaneous Proportions

Various other word-class proportions have been suggested as predictors of comprehensibility. Counts for a number of them were determined for each passage, brief comments being given below for four of them: adjectives, adverbs, pronouns, and prepositions.

ADJECTIVES. In their study of the adjective-verb quotient, King and Cofer (1960) concluded that the actual numbers of adjectives and verbs were more effective predictors than the quotient itself. We have already seen that a count of V_{full} correlates .66 with cloze scores. Two counts of adjectives were made. In the first, adjectives were defined as Adjectives, $V_{participles}$, A4 (numbers), $Noun_{adjuncts}$, A2 (predeterminers), and A3 (possessive pronouns). In the second, A2 and A3 were not counted as adjectives. According to the second count, the number of adjectives ranged from 1 to 22. Table 1 shows that both counts correlate negatively with cloze scores (−.56 and −.51). Passages with many adjectives are hard to understand.

ADVERBS. Comprehensibility decreases as adjectives increase, and we might therefore expect it to decrease as adverbs increase. But table 1 shows that number of adverbs has a positive correlation of $r = .11$ with cloze scores. It is worthwhile to subdivide adverbs to try to find the reason for this unexpected finding. Linguists (e.g., Lees, 1960) have found formal reasons for distinguishing adverbs of time and location (R, *yesterday, upstairs*), and perhaps this subclass has an unusual relation with comprehensibility. Table 1 shows that it does. Whereas adverbs of manner (Ad_{man}, *sweetly, quickly*) correlate negatively ($r = -.34$), adverbs of time and location correlate positively ($r = .25$). This positive correlation is probably due to the high frequency of occurrence of the words in this subclass.

PRONOUNS. Gray and Leary found a correlation of .476 between comprehensibility and number of pronouns. The present r was .58 (see figure 4). The number of pronouns per passage ranged from 1 to 18. It has been suggested (e.g., Miller, 1951, p. 135) that passages are easy to understand if they contain many pronouns, because pronouns usually refer to people, and

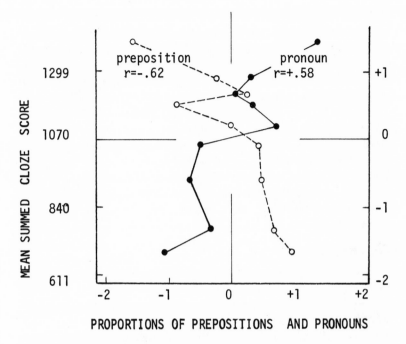

Fig. 4. Mean cloze score plotted as a function of proportion of prepositions and as a function of proportion of pronouns (in z-scores).

"people are better at reading about other people than about anything else." Perhaps. But perhaps it is also because pronouns are a form of repetition.

PREPOSITIONS. The number of prepositions per 150-word passage ranged from 3 to 26. Gray and Leary found a correlation of −.345 between comprehensibility and number of prepositions. The present r was −.62 (see figure 4). Passages that contain many prepositions are hard to understand. The relation between number of prepositions and comprehensibility is probably more complicated than the one between number of pronouns and comprehensibility. A high proportion of prepositions is usually associated with a high proportion of $V_{nominals}$ (e.g., *the reaction of the humans, a knowledge of theories*), and we have seen that this usually lowers comprehensibility. On the other hand, by altering the modification pattern we can remove the prepositions from the above examples without improving comprehensibility (*human reaction, theoretical knowledge*). As a matter of fact, this alteration would surely decrease average comprehensibility per word. This relation is probably complex enough to require study using controlled experiments.

SUMMARY. We have examined the effects of several word classes. The most important general conclusion seems to be that traditional definitions are too imprecise and too gross to yield profound insights into verbal behavior. Some definitions of a word class correlate positively with comprehensibility; others correlate negatively. The major word classes contain subclasses that correlate positively and other subclasses that correlate negatively.

Frequency of Occurrence

The preceding S-dimensions have been concerned with proportions of word classes. The present dimension and the next (volume) can be roughly grouped together under a subheading that might be called "measures of word difficulty."

Counts of word frequency appear in most readability formulas (e.g., The Lorge Readability Index, 1944). In addition, a number of controlled laboratory experiments have demonstrated the effects of word frequency upon learning and memory (e.g., Deese, 1960a). Common words are easier to learn and remember by a number of measures. On the other hand, I have computed the mean frequency of words in several passages, and in most of my counts the passages that seemed hardest to comprehend had words of highest mean frequency. A detailed analysis of the effects of word frequency seems worthwhile.

METHOD. Frequency of every word in the thirty-six passages was determined according to the L-count in *The Teachers' Wordbook* (Thorndike and Lorge, 1944). Mean frequency for all 150 words (and for content words and for function words separately) was computed for twelve passages. The twelve passages were selected to cover the range between first-grade readers and technical literature. All 5,400 words were also partitioned into five classes according to their frequency of occurrence in the L-count: 0–2 inclusive (difference of 3), 3–11 (difference of 9, 3^2), 12–92 (difference of 81, 9^2), 93–6653 (difference of 6561, 81^2), and 6654 up. Mean summed cloze score was then computed for each class. Each mean was based upon at least 64, but no more than 100 words sampled at random from all thirty-six passages. Words were repeated (e.g., the 6654+ classification contains 18 *the*s).

RESULTS. Mean L-count for the twelve passages ranged from 22,371 to 47,007 (4,972 to 10,446 occurrences per million). The rank correlation, *rho*, between mean word frequency and cloze score for the twelve passages was −.05. This *rho* does not reach traditional levels of significance, of course, but the most difficult passages had the highest mean L-counts.

Figure 5 explains this rather unexpected relation. Although

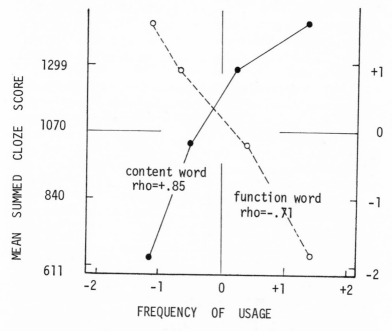

Fig. 5. Mean cloze score plotted as a function of frequency of usage. Content words and function words are plotted separately. Each point represents the mean z-score of three passages.

mean L-count of content words correlated positively with summed cloze score (*rho* for the twelve passages was .85), mean L-count of function words correlated negatively (*rho* was −.71). (It is worth emphasizing that these *rho*s based on twelve widely selected passages cannot be directly compared to the *r*s of table 1.) The negative *rho* is undoubtedly caused by the fact that dif-

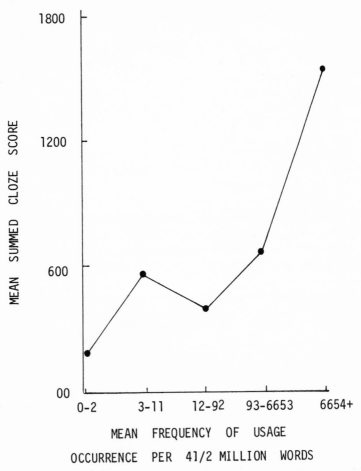

Fig. 6. Mean cloze score plotted as a function of frequency of usage. Each point represents a number of words sampled from different passages.

ficult passages contain a large number of *the*s and *of*s — two of the most frequently occurring words in English. Although these words themselves are easy to insert in cloze tests, they appear frequently in grammatical constructions such as nominalizations that are hard to understand. Thus, their surrounding words are difficult to insert correctly in cloze tests.

In figure 6, cloze scores are plotted as a function of L-count. These scores are for randomly sampled words, i.e., each point represents words selected at random from all thirty-six passages. Clearly, when the words are considered individually, the more common words are easier to insert correctly.

DISCUSSION. The above results demonstrate again — if such a demonstration is needed — that there are important reasons for distinguishing between content words and function words. Any predictor of readability based upon frequency of occurrence should probably be restricted to content words.

The frequency of content words is related to readability, and there are two ways to explain the relation. One explanation is that high frequency words have higher pre-experimental habit strength even when considered as individual units. Since the individual words have higher habit strength, response integration is easier. To use Horowitz's term (1964), they have greater "availability." The other explanation, advanced by Deese (1960b), is that a set of high-frequency words usually have pre-experimental associations with one another. Because of these pre-experimental associations with one another, the words are easier to cluster into a series. The two explanations need not be mutually exclusive, and at any rate, the present results offer little basis for preferring one to the other.

Measures of Volume

Even if passages are equated for length in words, the words themselves will differ in size: in number of letters, number of syllables, and number of morphemes. It is reasonable to expect all these measures to be related to comprehensibility. Passages with more letters will require more time to process visually. To the extent that the words are vocalized, passages with more syllables will require more time to process vocally. Passages with more meaningful units (morphemes) will require more time to process centrally.

METHOD. For all thirty-six passages, five measures of volume were obtained: number of letters, number of syllables, number of one-syllable words, number of morphemes, and number of morphemes minus inflectional morphemes. The first three measures should require no discussion. In the last two, a morpheme was defined as a word, word base, or affix. Stem-forming, suppletive, and replacive morphemes were not counted, e.g., *thermograph* (two morphemes), *were* (one morpheme), *mice* (one morpheme), *railroad* (two morphemes), *disowned* (three morphemes).

RESULTS. The number of letters per 150-word passage ranged

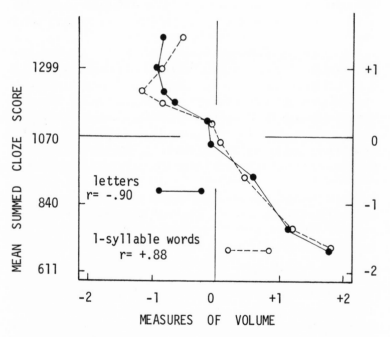

Fig. 7. Mean cloze score plotted as a function of number of letters and number of one-syllable words per passage. To facilitate comparison, the signs of the z-scores for one-syllable words has been reversed.

from 560 to 872. In figure 7, mean summed cloze scores are plotted as a function of two of the least intercorrelated S-dimensions: number of letters and number of one-syllable words. To facilitate comparison, the signs of the z-scores were reversed for the count of one-syllable words. The product-moment correlations with weighted cloze scores were surprisingly high for all measures of volume: $r = -.90$ for number of letters, $-.90$ for syllables, $+.88$ for one-syllable words, $-.88$ for morphemes, and $-.88$ for morphemes minus inflectional suffixes.

Any one of the five is a powerful predictor indeed, and one predicts about as well as the others. Passages become harder to understand as they contain more letters, syllables, or morphemes. If one is only interested in predicting comprehensibility (as in evaluating the readability of a given passage), he might as well choose the cheapest count—that of one-syllable words. Farr, Jenkins, Paterson, and England (1952) measured the time for computing the reading ease score of 100-word passages using the count of one-syllable words. It required a mean time of 82 seconds compared to 147 seconds when total number of syllables were counted, as in Flesch's formula (1949).

The problem of a person who wants to measure the readability of a given passage should be distinguished from the problem of a writer who wants to alter a passage so as to make it more comprehensible. A writer who increases the number of one-syllable words would probably have little effect on his passage's comprehensibility, or, at least, he would have less effect than a writer who reduces the number of morphemes. It simply does not seem reasonable to assume that reducing the number of letters (reducing the burden on visual processes) would improve comprehensibility as much as reducing the number of morphemes (reducing the burden on central processes plus reducing the burden on visual processes).

In other words, the writer who wishes to improve comprehensibility needs to know the independent effects of reducing morphemes, reducing syllables, and reducing number of letters. Simply because these three S-dimensions tend to be highly correlated in a representative sample of prose is no reason to be-

lieve they are inseparable. The answers to such a writer's problem
would require a controlled factorial experiment, such as has
been reported elsewhere (Coleman, 1968).

Sentence and Clause Length

The preceding two S-dimensions (word frequency and volume) can be roughly subclassed as "measures of word complexity." The present dimension and the following (number of
kernels) can be subclassed as "measures of syntactic complexity."[2] Sentence length is a measure that occurs in almost all readability formulas. It has been suggested elsewhere (Coleman,
1965) that clause length is more directly related to comprehensibility.

METHOD. An inverse measure of length was obtained by count-

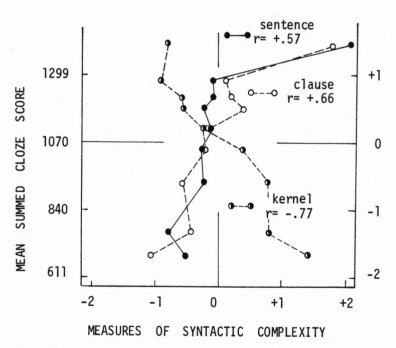

Fig. 8. Mean cloze score plotted as a function of sentences, clauses, and
kernels. Each point represents the means in z-scores for four passages.

ing the number of sentences and number of clauses in each of the thirty-six passages.

RESULTS. Clauses per passage varied from 8 to 30. In figure 8, mean weighted cloze scores are plotted as a function of number of sentences ($r = .57$), and number of clauses ($r = .66$). Note that the functions have considerable curvilinear components so that the relations may be somewhat higher than the rs suggest. The two dimensions are highly intercorrelated ($r = .67$), but number of clauses gives slightly better prediction. If one is interested only in measuring readability he might wish to use the cheaper, more economical measure – number of sentences; however, if he is a writer interested in improving comprehensibility, there are reasons for considering clause length.

DISCUSSION. It has been reported previously (Coleman, 1965) that clause length is more directly related to comprehensibility than sentence length. This study was an experimental comparison of several grammatical transformations, which concluded that "a person can process content morphemes packaged into two clauses more easily than he can process the identical morphemes packaged into a single clause."

Both clause length and sentence length are undoubtedly correlated with other determiners of syntactic complexity, but such relations will be best examined in controlled experiments. One comparison of sentences of varying clause length is provided later in the experimental section of this paper.

Number of Kernel Sentences

One of the basic notions of transformational grammars is that complex sentences are derived from simpler sentences called "kernels." For example, *John's explanation of her singing was misunderstood* is derived from simpler kernels: *she sang, John explained X, X was misunderstood*. It has been suggested that complex sentences are understood and remembered as kernels (e.g., Miller, 1962), and several experiments have supported this suggestion, at least in a general way (Coleman, 1965; Mehler, 1963; Miller, 1962). Such results predict that our 150-word passages should become more difficult to process as their number of kernels increases (e.g., the above illustrative sentence would be more difficult to process than one consisting of a single kernel: *That fellow gave the Indian the arrow*). If kernels are basic units of understanding, then clauses should become harder to understand as they include more kernels.

I doubt that complex passages would be analyzed into exactly the same kernels by any two grammarians. Probably, as in the case of dichotomizing abstract and concrete nouns, two grammarians could develop a reliable method of analysis by discussion, but it must be admitted that at present they are defined in slightly different ways. Harris (1957) tentatively identified them as having only five forms (NV, NVN, N is N, N is Adj, and N is Adv), whereas Chomsky (1957) tentatively defined them as simple active declarative sentences. More recently, Harris has noted that kernel sentences are "composed of a restricted and simple vocabulary: mostly concrete nouns and verbs and adjectives, and mostly unimorphemic words . . . it is not a word that takes an affix . . . but rather a sentence changes its form by a transformation and as part of the constants of that transformation some of the words take on affixes" (1965, p. 385).

Nevertheless, it is possible to describe a reliable count that, although it does not directly count kernels, will correlate highly with the count of kernels by most grammarians. If Harris's list of kernels is accepted, then we can count kernels by counting certain word classes, principally verbs and modifiers.

METHOD. The following word classes were counted:

1. All verbs (including gerunds, infinitives, and nominalizations, because sentences that contain nominalized verbs break into two kernels, e.g., *I like her singing* → *She is singing, I like X*).

2. All modifiers (including adjectives, adverbs, noun adjuncts, participles, numerals [A4], and adjectivalizations) with the following exceptions: (*a*) modifiers in Noun-is-modified sentences (*Sara is pretty*), (*b*) noun adjuncts that modify nominalizations (human reaction, property damage). Modifiers were counted because sentences containing modified words break into two kernels, e.g., *I see the red ball* → *I see the ball, X is red* (but see Winter, 1965). The exceptions were not counted because those kernels had already been counted in 1 above.

3. All prepositions used adjectivally or adverbally unless the

object of the preposition was a nominalized verb (*of the explanation*), or unless the prepositional phrase modified a nominalized verb (*estimate of damage*). These kernels had already been counted in 1 above. Verb participles (P) were not counted as prepositions.

4. All ellipses of any verb or modifier; e.g., *John and Mary ran* contains an ellipsis of *ran* since it breaks into two kernels, *John ran, Mary ran.*

The sum of these four word classes, although it does not directly count kernels, will correlate highly with the count given by most grammarians.

RESULTS. Kernels per 150-word passage ranged from 45 to 81. In figure 8, cloze scores are plotted as a function of the count described under Method ($r = -.77$).

DISCUSSION. The number of kernels is obviously another effective measure of syntactic complexity and can be used to refine the measure of syntactic complexity given by clause length. A 150-word passage containing few kernels is easier to understand than one containing many kernels. If the reader will examine the word classes that were summed as a kernel count, he may suspect that complexity is more affected by some of these word classes—actually the kernels they represent—than others. In other words, a more sensitive count might be made by weighting the different sorts of kernels. This weighting, however, is a problem best approached by means of controlled experiments, although some rough idea of the weighting can be gained by studying the *r*s for the word classes given in table 1.

Note that figure 8 shows a considerable increase in predictive power as one progresses from relatively gross syntactic units to more refined ones. The *r* is .57 for sentences, .66 for clauses, and $-.77$ for kernels.

Number of Different Content Words (TTR)

If the last two S-dimensions are subclassed as "descriptors of syntactic complexity," and the two before them as "descriptors of word complexity," perhaps the present dimension and next should be subclassed as "descriptors of inter-sentence complexity."

The type-token ratio (TTR) has been suggested as a predictor of comprehensibility. In one of the first studies of readability, Vogel and Washburne (1928) found the TTR to be their best indicator. Since the number of words are held constant in each of the thirty-six passages (they all contain 150 words), TTR in this investigation can be measured simply by counting the number of different words. The present count will consider content words only.

METHOD. The number of different content words were counted in each of the thirty-six passages. Actually, it would be more accurate to say that content morphemes were counted, i.e., different derivations of a word were counted as the same word (*explain, explanation*) and different inflections were counted as the same word (*girl, girls* and *ran, run*). Content words were defined as the second definition given under the discussion of *content word ratio* (page 163).

Another count was made in which synonyms of content words were not counted, i.e., any synonym was counted as a repetition of its preceding content word.

RESULTS. The number of different content words per passage ranged from 22 to 82. In figure 9, cloze scores are plotted as functions of the number of different content words. There is an obvious relation between TTR and comprehensibility. Passages with fewer different words are easier to understand. The rs in table 1 show that this relation is not increased when synonyms are considered (r for ordinary TTR $= -.64$; r for TTR considering synonyms $= -.56$). Therefore, if one is concerned only with predicting readability, he might as well restrict himself to the simpler, more objective TTR count.

Repetition

Closely related to TTR is an S-dimension that we will call "repetition." Each time a word is repeated there is a repetition, of course; however, it is reasonable to assume that the repetition of two-word sets would have a still greater effect on readability, and that the repetition of three-, four-, and higher-order sets would have progressively greater effects.

METHOD. To get an adequate sample of repeated word sets, it was necessary to consider as repetitions synonyms, pronouns, and a class of words that might be called "replacives." For instance, if a sentence in a passage was *The Cherokee chief was hunting*, then *Cherokee, Indian, brave*, and even such general words as *man* might be considered a "replacive" for chief in a later sentence such as *The man hunted deer*.

It was also necessary to consider different grammatical transformations of a sentence as repetitions. For instance, *Cherokee chief* is a two-word repetition of *chief was a Cherokee. John's explanation* is a two-word repetition of *John explained*. (For a discussion of grammatical transformations, see Chomsky, 1957; Harris, 1965; and the discussion of kernel sentences in the present paper, pages 179–181.)

WEIGHTING. A higher-order set was weighted more heavily

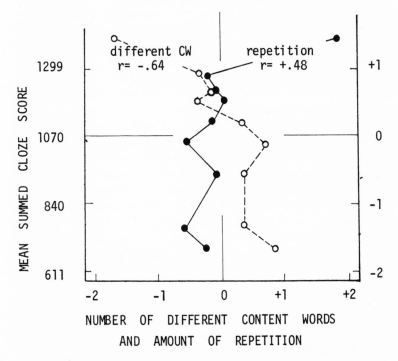

Fig. 9. Mean cloze score plotted as a function of number of different content words and as a function of amount of repetition per passage.

than a lower-order set by the following system, which is more easily illustrated than explained. The repetition of a five-word set, for example (ABCDE), was scored as 1 five-word set (ABCDE), plus 2 four-word sets (ABCD, BCDE), plus 3 three-word sets (ABC, BCD, CDE), plus 4 two-word sets (AB, BC, CD, DE), plus 5 one-word sets, giving it a total score of 15 ($1 + 2 + 3 + 4 + 5$).

RESULTS. In figure 9, cloze scores are plotted as a function of repetition.

DISCUSSION. There is an obvious relation between repetition and comprehensibility, although the function quickly reaches asymptote. In fact, all the effect for that function was probably caused by two first-grade passages. After about a sixth-grade level of difficulty, there is surprisingly little difference in amount of repetition. There are other ways to measure "repetition," and perhaps a count that would contribute to prediction over a wider range of comprehensibility could be developed, but the present count is not too promising for difficult prose. In fact, the present count ($r = .48$) is inferior to the simpler, more objective TTR ($r = -.64$).

Readability Formulas

The S-dimensions of table 1 can be combined into any number of multiple prediction equations, or readability formulas; however, the predictive power of any formula derived from such a correlation matrix will be limited. Although it may distinguish widely differing passages such as high school and grammar school prose, finer distinctions will be progressively more difficult and costly.

The rs in table 1 suggest that any measure of word complexity (letters, morphemes, or syllables) will account for about 80 percent of the predicted variance. The high intercorrelations between S-dimensions suggest that little additional variance will be predicted by adding other predictors. Therefore, it seems best to develop a formula that emphasizes economy, or ease of counting by linguistically unsophisticated raters. Similarly, because the four cloze scores are so highly intercorrelated, the present section will consider only traditional cloze scores, i.e., those obtained by deleting 20 percent of the words in a passage. Such scores being more economically obtained, this will simplify validation of the formulas.

The most easily counted S-dimension that promises high predictive power is probably the percentage of one-syllable words. If it is used as a single predictor of unweighted cloze scores, the prediction equation is:

Formula 1: Cloze % = 1.29 1-Syllable Words − 38.45

Formula 1 predicts the mean cloze score in percentage for Ss matched to the twenty original Ss, and this formula and those that follow are similar to the usual readability formulas that draw samples 100 words in length. For instance, the simplest passage contained 123 one-syllable words (82 percent of 150). Formula 1 predicts its cloze percentage to be 68.05 percent. Actually, there were 469 correct insertions, or 78 percent of the possible 600 (20 Ss × 30 deletions per test). Table 1 shows that the r between one-syllable words and cloze is .86 (actually .85923). Therefore, ignoring shrinkage, this formula will predict 73.828 percent of the variance ($r^2 = .85923^2 = .73828$).

The second most easily counted predictor is probably number of sentences per hundred words. Combining it with one-syllable words gives the following multiple prediction equation:

Formula 2: Cloze % = 1.16 1-Syl + 1.48 Sent − 37.95

If the multiple correlation (R) for this formula is squared, $R^2 = .80576$; therefore, formula 2 predicts 80.576 percent of the variance, a gain of 6.748 percent. The gain is just barely worth the cost, and adding additional predictors becomes less and less feasible economically.

The next most easily counted S-dimension is probably number of pronouns per hundred words (which does not include A3, possessive pronouns). Adding it as a predictor gives:

Formula 3: Cloze % = 1.07 1-Syl + 1.18 Sent + .76 Pron − 34.02

The multiple R^2 for formula 3 is .816. Therefore, only 1 percent additional variance is predicted by adding the pronoun count.

In formula 4, where prepositions per hundred words (which do not include T, *to*, in infinitives) are also counted, the multiple R^2 becomes .828, adding another 1 percent of predicted variance. In brief, formula 1, which requires a single count, predicts 73.8 percent of the variance, while the considerably more tedious counts of formula 4 predict 82.8 percent, a gain of only 9 percent.

Formula 4: Cloze % = 1.04 1-Syl + 1.06 Sent

+ .56 Pron − .36 Prep − 26.01

More powerful prediction equations can be derived by using different predictors, but again, the gain in predictive power is hardly worth the cost of making the more tedious counts. Consider formula 2, for instance. Instead of counting one-syllable words, number of letters might be counted; instead of counting sentences, a better predictor of syntactic complexity such as number of kernels might be counted. The multiple R^2 of these two predictors is .82100, compared to .80576 for the far more easily counted predictors of formula 2. The gain is hardly worth the cost.

In brief, the correlational data of table 1 provide enough information about the comprehensibility of English prose to derive any number of prediction equations that will predict about 80 percent of the variance when distinguishing among a wide range of passages. A number of S-dimensions, including such unexpected ones as proportion of adverbs of time and location, predict comprehensibility with surprising reliability.

However, developing a measure precise enough to distinguish between similar passages — say, alternative frames for a program — will require considerably more information than is provided by correlation matrices. In a randomly drawn sample of passages, the S-dimensions are so highly intercorrelated that it is impossible to sift out individual effects and interaction effects. A study of table 1 will reveal a number of unsuspected correlations. To develop more powerful prediction equations, experimental controls will be needed.

Cross Validation

The four readability formulas were validated by Szalay (1965). He selected seven passages that ranged from second-grade readers to professional literature. Using each of the four formulas, he predicted their expected cloze score. Then, using twenty *S*s closely matched to the original twenty by their percentile rank on the verbal section of the American College Test, he obtained actual cloze scores for the seven passages, using the same procedures that Miller and Coleman (1967) had used. As with most of the correlations in the present study, the *r*s between predicted and actual cloze scores were embarrassingly high: $r = .83$ for formula 1, .88 for formula 2, .87 for formula 3, and .89 for formula 4.

THE EXPERIMENTAL STUDIES: A RESEARCH STRATEGY FOR DEVELOPING AN EXPERIMENTAL DEFINITION OF UNDERSTANDING

Table 1 shows that the S-dimensions of prose are highly intercorrelated. To assign individual effects and plot interactions, experimental controls are needed. Experiments are usually justified as being tests of theoretically derived hypotheses, and since the following set was generated by another research strategy, it seems worthwhile to discuss that strategy.

The final goal of psychology is the combined description, prediction, explanation, and control of behavior; however, the research strategies of different scientists emphasize reaching one of the subgoals before the others. Theoretical explanation is the subgoal for most studies of complex verbal learning. Their primary purpose is to test a theoretically derived hypothesis — usually an hypothesis about a mental process underlying the overt behavior they measure. For instance, recent papers by Coleman (1965) and Mehler (1963) were described as though their only justification was the testing of an explanatory notion stated by Miller (1962), specifically the notion that complex sentences are understood in terms of their kernels. None of the experiments attempted to provide a quantitative S–R function that could form the basis for a technology of written instruction.

If a science possesses well-defined theories, refining and verifying those theories may be its most efficient strategy. Tombaugh located the planet Pluto by verifying a theoretical prediction, not by a blind search of the heavens. But in the field of complex verbal learning, there are as yet few theories that chart even roughly the relationships among its major unknowns. A Skinner-like strategy may be more efficient for sketching out a rough, preliminary chart.

If one is interested in developing a technology of written instruction, his most efficient strategy for charting the unknowns of verbal behavior might be to slight explanation for the time being and concentrate upon quantitative S–R description. Since linguistics has provided a grid of S-dimensions important to verbal behavior, a systematic way to begin would be to select a few such S-dimensions distributed at more or less equal steps across the grid and relate them to measures of behavior. Then further experiments would relate intermediate dimensions to R-measures. Once the grid is dotted with systematically located S–R functions, the gaps can be bridged by interpolation. Then we can extend the descriptive system to the other subgoals of prediction, explanation, and control. In the interim, the functions can be used as the basis for a technology of written instruction.

One way to spot dimensions at more or less equal steps across the grid is to select them from the steps involved in understanding prose. At the present preliminary stage of data collection, a gross description is all that is needed: e.g., S (a) recognizes the individual letters and packages them into words, (b) packages the words into simple sentences, (c) packages these simple sentences into more complex clauses and sentences, (d) packages these into paragraphs. These steps to understanding graduate our grid in terms general enough to include such S-dimensions as legibility and typography.

This rather gross description of understanding will serve to step off the grid in sufficient detail for preliminary data collection. For refined quantification, elaborations will be required;

i.e., as data accumulate, the grid must be graduated in finer detail by inserting steps such as ones concerned with syllables, morphemes, and tagmemes. Also, several of the steps must be relabeled as processes of analysis, particularly if the experimenter is interested in the behavior of a reader or listener. Also, different responses are of primary importance at different parts of the grid. At the beginning — at step *a* — perceptual responses such as recognition are important. Then word-for-word memorization becomes important. But by step *b*, we are already concerned with true understanding and must consider the relation of the prose to the universe it describes. Since everyone is really interested in this final response, understanding, psychology must develop a measure for it and then relate that R-measure to recognition and rote memorization. Until these R–R relations are plotted, functions that use recognition or memorization will be of slight value in quantifying the sort of behavior everyone is really interested in — education, reading, talking, listening, and the rest.

The following five experiments were selected to sprinkle with widely scattered functions one section of the grid — the section concerned with understanding. Each experiment is a developmental study that suggests an area for more detailed research, i.e., the primary purpose here is to clear a path for follow-up studies.

Let me anticipate an obvious criticism by stating explicitly that the "functions" of these five developmental studies resemble only in a gross way the precise functions of physics. I feel little motivation for collecting and describing precise, quantitative functions unless the language sample is a "usable" one, i.e., unless it represents a language population used in everyday verbal behavior. Since the sentences used in these preliminary experiments will never be encountered outside the laboratory, I see little value in describing their S–R relations except in a gross fashion. At the end of the paper, I will suggest a language population (the first four or five hundred words learned by first-graders) that is usable and small enough to yield to experimental analysis. For that sample, it will be useful to describe the functions in mathematical terminology.

The above predilection can be described in more general terms. If an experiment is to contribute to a technology of written instruction, I find four variables that must be "useful, representative" ones. These four variables must be chosen so as to make the results of the research generalizable to useful language behavior. First are the stimulus variables, or independent variables. Little need be said about them because in most current experiments they are reasonably useful and representative. Second, however, is the response, or dependent, variable. This is traditionally word-for-word memorization, and it is certainly questionable how well this represents understanding, the response we are really interested in. Third is the sampling variable of learners; and, like the weather, everyone talks about the restriction on generalizing from the usual sample of college sophomores, but no one does anything about it. Fourth is the sampling variable of the above paragraph, the sample of language materials. Here lies the critical shortcoming of most experiments in verbal learning insofar as they might be useful to a technology. Out of thousands of experiments, only a handful have used a sample of language materials that represented a usable language population. Furthermore, only a handful of experimenters formally recognized that their experiment included this sampling variable. Almost invariably they used a significance test that precluded generalizing their conclusions to any language population at all—even to an artificial one. Almost invariably they used a significance test that restricted their conclusions to the specific dozen or so items actually used in the experiment (Coleman, 1964).

Experiment I: A Measure of Understanding

At about step *b*, the packaging of words into sentences, we become interested in behavior, usually described as understanding. That is, since language provides the individual with so many techniques for paraphrasing and recoding what he reads, it is obvious that we are really interested in behavior more complicated than word-for-word memorization. The great majority of investigations of verbal learning have been restricted to word-for-word memorization, but it is not impossible to measure understanding. Gough (1965), for example, operationally defined understanding as verification. He gave S a sentence and then a picture of an event occurring in the real world. S's task was to say whether or not the sentence truly described the event.

In developing a technology of written instruction, an important step — probably the most important step for psychologists — is to develop a systematic set of R-measures at this cognitive level. The next five experiments suggest one such R-measure.[3] In each of these experiments S was assigned a task, and then tested as to how well he performed that task in the real world.

When we measure understanding, we are concerned with the relation between language and events in the real world. Obviously this relation will vary with the complexity of the assigned language and with the complexity of the universe of events that is being described. In developing a measure of understanding, it is reasonable to begin by varying the complexity of language and universe.

If one is measuring understanding by assigning S a task to perform in the real world, mathematical tasks are convenient ones for developmental studies.[4] It is easy to generate very large numbers of tasks and tests. In the next five experiments, S was assigned, as his universe, a matrix of numbers such as those in table 3. The complexity of the universe could be increased by increasing the size of the matrix. As his language, he was as-

Table 3

Miniature Language

Articles	Prep.	Pronoun	Conjun.	Verb	Noun	Adjective
a	of	it	and	divide	number	first
an	to		or	subtract	mean	second
the	by			square	row	odd
						even

Matrix

1	3
6	2

signed a miniature language such as the one in table 3. The complexity of the language could be increased by adding content words (*multiply, ratio, column, large, small*). Such languages, despite their restricted vocabulary, have most of the essential features of complete English. They permit wide variations in syntactic complexity and an infinite number of tasks such as *Square all the odd numbers, sum them, and divide by 4*.

Method

DESIGN. Two levels of complexity for the universe (2-by-2 and 3-by-3 matrices) were combined with two levels of complexity for language. Each language was represented by sentences of three lengths: eight, ten, and twelve words. This was combined with thirty undergraduate *S*s, thus yielding a 2-by-2-by-3-by-30, universe-by-language-by-length-by-*S*s design.

MATERIALS. Seventy-two sentences were generated that instructed *S* to perform an operation upon a matrix. Thirty-six of these sentences were generated from the simple language of table 3. From them, thirty-six additional sentences were generated that used a more complex language containing additional verbs (*add, multiply*), nouns (*column*), and adjectives (*top, bottom, right, left, large, small*). An example of a "simple" sentence and its "complex" counterpart is: *Divide the second row's odd number by the first row's even number* and *Multiply the second row's odd number by the right column's largest number*. Each set of thirty-six sentences had twelve eight-word sentences, twelve ten-word sentences, and twelve twelve-word sentences. All seventy-two sentences could be applied to either matrix: the 2-by-2 or the 3-by-3. Half the time they were assigned to one and half the time to the other. Each sentence was prepared for projection by a slide projector.

PRESENTATION. *S* was first given directions and enough practice slides to convince *E* that he understood the nature of his task. Projection time, which was the dependent variable, was under the control of *S*. He was instructed: "Do not leave the sentence projected for a moment longer than necessary for you to read it. The moment you finish reading it, release the button that will shut off the projector, and try to perform the operation.

If you have the slightest hunch that you understand the operation, try to perform it. Nothing will be deducted for wrong guesses.

"If you do not understand the sentence at all, project it again, but not for a moment longer than necessary for you to read it.

"I will record the total time you project the sentence on the wall."

As soon as S had performed the task correctly, another slide giving another task was inserted. S performed thirty-six such tasks in an experimental session.

Each S had two separate sessions, one for sentences written in the simple language and one for those written in the complex. That is, the thirty-six sentences for one session were all written in the simple language and the thirty-six for the other session were all written in the complex language. Half the Ss were assigned the complex language in their first session and half were assigned the simple language.

Both sizes of matrix were used in each session in a 2–3–3–2 order. The matrix to be used for a sentence was drawn on a separate page of a booklet. S turned to that page and studied the matrix for a few seconds (as long as he wanted) before he projected its sentence. There were thirty-six different matrices in a booklet, one for each sentence session.

MEASURE. Time required to understand each sentence was measured by a timer fitted to the projector that started and stopped automatically as S projected the sentence. Time was accumulated until S performed the task correctly. Then S turned to another page in his answer book, studied the matrix for a few seconds, and projected another sentence.

RESULTS. Table 4 shows that the difference between matrices was not significant ($F < 1$). The problems for the 2-by-2 matrix required 3.1075 seconds per sentence per S, while those for the 3-by-3 matrix required 3.1785.

In figure 10, mean exposure times per sentence are plotted as a function of length with level of difficulty as the parameter. Table 4 shows that all effects are significant except those due to matrices and its interactions.

DISCUSSION. The surprising finding was that the complexity

Table 4

F Table for Experiment I

Source	df	MS	F
matrices (m)	1	27.34	< 1
difficulty (d)	1	12629.39	388.69
length (1)	2	15854.19	487.94
(linear)	1	26413.56	812.92
(quadratic)	1	5294.81	162.96
m by d	1	.01	< 1
m by 1	2	15.83	< 1
d by 1	2	6050.46	186.21
m by d by 1	2	6069.33	186.79
pooled error	539	32.49	

of the universe had no measurable effect; problems concerning 3-by-3 matrices were no more difficult than those concerning 2-by-2s. This finding may not be replicated for other universes and other types of problems; nevertheless, it is somewhat surprising to find even with the present universe and problems that complexity of language is far more important than complexity of universe.

The measure, stimulus-exposure time, is less concerned with the universe than with the language. However, there are relevant measures more directly concerned with the universe, such as time to perform the operation. They would probably be more affected by complexity of the universe.

Note the strong quadratic component of figure 10. Table 4 shows that this effect is significant. As the sentences become longer and more difficult, time needed to understand them increases at an accelerated rate.

Experiment II: Content Word Ratio

As we observed in the correlational section of this paper, as words are packaged into sentences the proportion of content words affects the comprehensibility of the sentence. The technique outlined in the preceding experiment permits us to examine this S-dimension in more detail, specifically to examine its interaction with other dimensions. In experiment II, we examined its interaction with sentence length.

Method

DESIGN. Sentences were prepared in two percentages of content words (50 percent and 75 percent) and in five lengths (four-, six-, eight-, ten-, and twelve-word lengths). Sentences containing 75 percent content words were not represented in the six-word and ten-word lengths. Each sentence was learned by twelve undergraduate *S*s, thus yielding an incomplete 12-by-2-by-5, *S*s-by-percentage-by-length design.

MATERIALS, PRESENTATION, AND MEASURE. Materials, presentation, and measure resembled those of experiment I except that (*a*) there were only thirty-eight sentences, eighteen containing 75 percent content words and twenty containing 50 percent content words; (*b*) only one session was required for *S* to learn all thirty-eight sentences; (*c*) he performed all operations upon a single 2-by-2 matrix. Respective examples of sentences containing 75 percent and 50 percent content words were: *Subtract 2 from the first positive odd score, Subtract 2 from the means of the rows.*

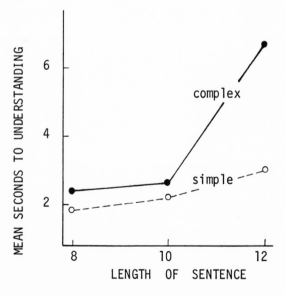

Fig. 10. Mean exposure time to understanding plotted as a function of sentence length in words for two complexities of language.

RESULTS. Mean exposure time required for understanding is given in figure 11. Stimulus exposure time was plotted as a function of length with content-word percentage as a parameter. An analysis of variance indicated that all effects including the interaction were significant beyond .01.

Tested separately, the linear component of both curves was significant beyond .001: (F = 201, df = 1–44, for the 50-percent curve and F = 68, df = 1–22 for the 75-percent curve). The quadratic component of both curves was also significant: for the 50-percent curve F = 5.4, df = 1–44, $p < .05$; for the 75-percent curve F = 7.3, df = 1–22, $p < .02$.

DISCUSSION. The results showed clearly that a sharp distinction must be made between content words and function words. The direction of the difference was not surprising, but the magnitude of the difference seemed unexpectedly large for the longer

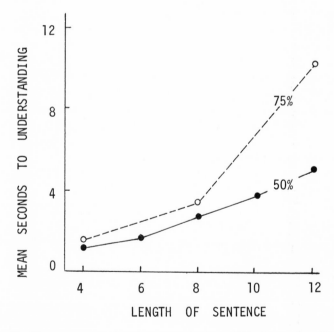

Fig. 11. Mean exposure time to understanding plotted as a function of sentence length in words for two content-word percentages.

sentences. For the twelve-word sentences, S required more than twice as much exposure time to understand the 75-percent sentences than he required to understand the 50-percent sentences.

The positive acceleration of the curves, similar to that found in experiment I, was not predicted. Before discussing implications, it is worthwhile to see if the significant quadratic effect is replicable. Experiment III was performed to retest this component.

Experiment III: Content Word Ratio

Experiment III was a replication of II except that it used a slightly different dependent variable. The same thirty-eight sentences were exposed to another twelve Ss tachistoscopically for .20 seconds. Each sentence was exposed a number of times until S could perform the operation. The measure was number of exposures to correct performance.

If plotted, the results closely resemble those of figure 11. For the different lengths the five points representing mean exposures for the 50-percent curve were 2.5, 3.1, 5.4, 6.7, and 9.3. The three points for the 75-percent curve were 2.9, 6.9, and 14.6. Both main effects, the difference between 50- and 75-percent content-word sentences and the length effect, were in the predicted direction for all twelve Ss ($p < .0003$ by a binomial test). As in experiments I and II the quadratic component was significant beyond .05 for both the 50- and 75-percent curves ($F = 4.5$, $df = 1$–44, and $F = 4.8$, $df = 1$–22). As sentences become longer and more complex, the stimulus exposure time S needs to understand them increases at an accelerated rate.

Experiment IV: Packaging Clauses into Sentences

Experiment IV lies at step c, the packaging of clauses into sentences. If the understanding of a complex sentence is considered to be a process of analysis, we might describe its understanding as requiring S to analyze the sentence into its component clauses, say C_1, C_2, and C_3. The physical characteristics of writing and speech require that C_1 be understood first. But

C_1 must be analyzed into its component tagmemes—say, T_1 and T_2—each of which must be further analyzed into its component words. That is, T_1 must be analyzed and then stored in memory while the words of T_2 are being analyzed. Then T_1 and T_2 must be stored as C_1 while similar operations are performed upon C_2, and so on. Other descriptions of understanding are possible in which understanding is considered to be a process of synthesis or a combination of analysis and synthesis.

If any such description of understanding is valid, then the hierarchical structure of a sentence should influence its inherent complexity. That is, eight words packaged into a single clause (*Multiply the odd scores by the overall mean*) are understood by a different set of operations than eight words packaged into two clauses (*Square the odd scores, and sum the squares*) or three clauses (*Square the scores, sum them, and add 2*).

These speculations suggest factorial experiments in which sentence, clause, tagmemic, and word lengths are independent variables. In experiment IV clause and sentence lengths were varied.

Method

DESIGN. Three sentence lengths (eight, ten, or twelve words) were combined with two clause lengths (sentences of either one or three clauses). Each combination was learned by thirteen Ss, thus yielding a 13-by-3-by-2, Ss-by-length-by-clauses design.

MATERIALS. The materials were two samples of thirty sentences similar to those of experiments I, II, and III. Each sample contained ten eight-word sentences, ten ten-word sentences, and ten twelve-word sentences. Each sample contained fifteen one-clause sentences and fifteen three-clause sentences. The complexity of the assigned language and the percentage of content words were controlled. S performed all operations upon the same 2-by-2 matrix. An example of a pair of sentences is *Square the odd number in the first row* and *Compute the mean, square it, and add 2*.

PRESENTATION AND MEASURE. Presentation and measure resembled those of experiments I, II, and III except that (*a*) each S had only one of the samples of thirty sentences and only a single session; (*b*) the sentences were presented in an order that systematically alternated both independent variables; (*c*) *S* performed all operations upon a single 2-by-2 matrix.

Results. In figure 12 mean exposure time to understanding is plotted as a function of length with number of clauses as the parameter. Both independent variables exert highly significant effects; all thirteen *S*s understood the one-clause sentence in a shorter mean exposure time and the length effect was in the predicted direction for all thirteen *S*s (*p* < .0002 by the binomial test).

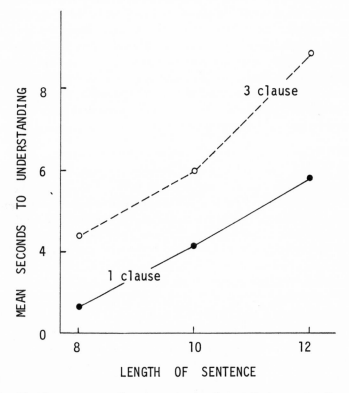

Fig. 12. Mean exposure time to understanding plotted as a function of sentence length in words. The parameter represents the number of clauses in the sentence.

The quadratic effect was in the same direction as in experiments I, II, and III, although it was not significant. However, this is not surprising considering the small number of Ss.

DISCUSSION. These results appear to contradict those of the correlational study. One of the most reliable findings of readability research is that short clauses are easier to understand than long clauses. This conflict raises the question of the difference between inherent and superfluous complexity. The independent variable in this experiment varied inherent complexity because the three-clause sentences contained more kernels than the one-clause sentences. Under those conditions, a number of words representing a single clause is easier to understand than that same number of words representing several clauses. But if inherent complexity, or number of kernels, is held constant, a set of content morphemes packaged into several clauses is easier to understand than that identical set packaged into a single clause; e.g., *When she included this, she emphasized that the group was important* is probably easier to understand than *Her inclusion of this emphasized the importance of the group* (see Coleman, 1965).

Experiment V: Depth from Pre-Experimental Vocabulary

At step d, the packaging of sentences into paragraphs, we become concerned with the relations between words that lie in different sentences. In much written instruction the student learns new notions that are defined in terms of old, familiar notions. These "notions" may be as large and complex as complete mathematical systems, or as small as a single word. For preliminary studies it was decided to restrict new notions to single words. Experiment V was an attempt to investigate the effect of adding higher-order notions defined in terms of S's pre-experimental vocabulary.

Frequently when a new term is introduced it must be defined in terms of other, lower-order new terms. For instance, a statistics instructor who defines variance as the second moment about the mean (as the average squared deviation) must first introduce the notion of a deviation from the mean. We might define depth as follows: (*a*) depth I terms that are defined in terms of the pre-experimental vocabulary; (*b*) depth II terms, whose definition includes depth I terms; and so on. Experiment V will restrict itself to depth I terms.

Method

DESIGN. Sentences introducing one, two, or three new terms were studied. Each sentence was learned by twenty-two *S*s, thus yielding a 22-by-3, *S*s-by-sentences design.

MATERIALS. Depth I terms are given: "A BAF is the square of the smallest even number. A GOL is the mean of the two smallest numbers. A MED is the sum of the two largest numbers." They were typed in a table and each *S* was allowed to study the table for five minutes before testing began. He also had the table before him throughout testing and could refer to it as he desired. Using the table, fifteen sentences were generated that instructed *S* to perform an operation upon a 2-by-2 matrix. Each sentence was twelve words in length. Five sentences each contained one new term, five sentences contained two new terms, and in the final set each contained three new terms. An example of a three-term sentence is "Add the baf to the med and then divide by the gol."

Each *S* learned all fifteen sentences, which were presented in an order that systematically alternated number of new terms. Since a considerable practice effect was expected, *S* was given ten practice slides before beginning. Otherwise, presentation closely resembled that of experiments I, II, III, and IV.

MEASURE. Response time was measured as well as stimulus exposure time. Response time was measured by a stopwatch from the time *S* turned off the projector until he solved the problem.

RESULTS. Mean response times for sentences of one, two, and three new terms were 16.26, 23.75, and 32.54 seconds. If these times are plotted as a function of number of new terms, the test of the linear component of the function is the appropriate test of significance ($p < .001$, $F = 72$, $df = 1$–42). Since the problems with three new terms required more mathematical operations, these results are to be expected.

Mean stimulus exposure time for sentences of one, two, and three new terms were 4.51, 4.83, and 5.78. The linear component is significant beyond .001 (F = 16.3, $df = 1–42$).

DISCUSSION. This experiment was clearly a preliminary one and there is little need for prolonged discussion of its results. Its purpose was to clear the way for obvious follow-up studies. For instance, one might study the most effective procedure for introducing higher-order terms: by proceeding from low to high versus proceeding from high to low.

Summary and Conclusions

The primary purpose of these five experiments was to suggest follow-up studies. They were intended to do no more than outline a small subset of the S–R functions that will be needed to develop a technology of written instruction—the subset that will be needed for an experimental analysis of understanding. It seems clear that the most formidable problem faced by an investigator following this research strategy will be due to the fact that the functions will vary for different samples of language material. Linguists have provided a good set of S-dimensions and psychologists should have little trouble in developing a meaningful set of R-measures; but so far as I know, no one has even considered the problem of defining meaningful subsets of language materials.

Obviously an investigator following this research strategy cannot collect all the S–R functions, only a tiny sample of strategically located ones. First he must outline roughly the set that will be most useful in developing a technology of written instruction. Then he must collect a sprinkling of functions systematically distributed throughout the set. If these functions are properly located, the gaps can be bridged by interpolation.

Though formidable, the task of developing a technology of written instruction is not hopelessly overambitious for present-day techniques. A single investigator could concentrate his research upon a well-defined subset of functions. At present, for instance, I am concentrating on the functions most important in predicting the learning of the language arts by first-graders (Coleman, 1968). Here, at least, we have a well-defined set of language materials, the four or five hundred most common words. The S-dimensions and R-measures are definable. I foresee no insoluble problems in collecting a respectable proportion of the needed functions.

NOTES

1. Most of this work was supported by a grant from the National Science Foundation, GB-3535. The data for the correlation studies were collected under Office of Education Contract 2599.

2. Some readability formulas (e.g., Lorge, 1944) have used number of prepositions as an indicator of syntactic complexity.

3. Another R-measure that must be developed is Information Gain (IG). In choosing between two forms of a passage, a programmer would want to compare their IG, their efficiency in transmitting information as measured by a post-test minus a pre-test. Coleman and Miller (1967) suggest one measure of IG that may have the precision needed for experimentation.

4. Alernative tasks might involve motor skills to be learned, pictures to be drawn, objects to be built, and so on.

REFERENCES

Chomsky, N. A. *Syntactic structures.* The Hague: Mouton, 1957.

Coleman, E. B. Generalizing to a language population. *Psychol. Rep.,* 1964, *14,* 219–226.

———. Learning of prose written in four grammatical transformations. *J. appl. Psychol.,* 1965, *49,* 332–341.

———. Experimental studies of readability. *Elem. Eng.,* 1968, *45,* 166–178 and 316–333.

Coleman, E. B., and Miller, G. R. A measure of information gained during prose learning. *Read. Research Quart.,* 1968, *3,* 369–386.

Deese, J. Frequency of usage and number of words in free recall: The role of association. *Psychol. Rep.,* 1960a, *7,* 337–344.

———. From the isolated unit to connected discourse. In C. N. Cofer (Ed.), *Verbal learning and verbal behavior.* New York: McGraw-Hill, 1960b.

Farr, J. N., Jenkins, J. J., Paterson, D. G., and England, A. O. Reply to Klare and Flesch re simplification of Flesch Reading Ease Formula: *J. appl. Psychol.,* 1952, *36,* 55–57.

Fillenbaum, S., Jones, L. V., and Rappaport, A. The predictability of words and their grammatical classes as a function of rate of deletion from a speech transcript. *J. verb. Learn. verb. Behav.*, 1963, *2*, 186–194.

Flesch, R. F. *The art of readable writing.* New York: Harper & Bros., 1949.

Fries, C. C. *The structure of English.* New York: Harcourt, Brace, 1952.

Gorman, A. M. Recognition memory for nouns as a function of abstractness and frequency. *J. exp. Psychol.*, 1961, *61*, 23–29.

Gough, P. B. Grammatical transformations and speed of understanding. *J. verb. Learn. verb. Behav.*, 1965, *4*, 107–111.

Gray, W. S., and Leary, B. E. *What makes a book readable?* Chicago: Univ. of Chicago Press, 1935.

Harris, Z. Co-occurrence and transformation in linguistic structure. *Language,* 1957, *33*, 283–340.

———. Transformational theory. *Language,* 1965, *41*, 363–401.

Hockett, C. F. *A course in modern linguistics.* New York: Macmillan, 1958.

Horowitz, L. M., Brown, Z. M., and Weissblatt, S. Availability and the direction of associations. *J. exp. Psychol.*, 1964, *68*, 541–549.

King, D. J., and Cofer, C. N. Exploratory studies of stories varying in the adjective-verb quotient. *J gen. Psychol.*, 1960, *62*, 199–221.

Lees, R. B. The grammar of English nominalizations. *Internat. J. Amer. Linguistics,* 1960, *26*(3) (whole part II).

Lorge, I. Predicting readability. *Teach. Coll. Rec.*, 1944, *45*, 404–419.

Mehler, G. Some effects of grammatical transformations on the recall of English sentences. *J. verb. Learn. verb. Behav.*, 1963, *2*, 346–351.

Miller, G. A. *Language and communication.* New York: McGraw-Hill, 1951.

———. Some psychological studies of grammar. *Amer. Psychologist,* 1962, *17*, 748–762.

Miller, G. R., and Coleman, E. B. A set of 36 passages calibrated for comprehensibility. *J. verb. Learn. verb. Behav.*, 1967, *6*, 851–854.

Szalay, T. Validation of the Coleman readability formulas. *Psychol. Rep.,* 1965, *17*, 965–966.

Taylor, W. R. "Cloze" readability scores as indices of individual differences in comprehension and aptitude. *J. appl. Psychol.*, 1957, *41*, 19–26.

Thorndike, E. L., and Lorge, I. *The teacher's word book.* New York: Bur. of Pub., Teach. Coll., Columbia Univ., 1944.

Vogel, M., and Washburne, C. An objective method for determining grade placement of children's reading material. *Elem. Sch. J.*, 1928, *28*, 373–381.

Winter, W. Transforms without kernels? *Language,* 1965, *41*, 484–489.

Discussion of Professor Coleman's Paper

WALTER H. MacGINITIE

Teachers College, Columbia University

Professor Coleman's paper is filled with many insights and new experimental findings. It is a substantial, thought-provoking paper, yet full of important details. I believe that I can contribute best to the purposes of this symposium by dealing primarily with three major issues as they relate to Coleman's paper. These three issues are (1) the criterion problem, (2) the nature of the materials for which comprehension difficulty is to be predicted, and (3) the nature of the subjects for whom the degree of difficulty is to be predicted. Coleman refers briefly to these three issues in the introduction to the experimental studies. I regard much of this discussion as extremely perceptive, and I would like to elaborate on certain points there that I regard as fundamental to progress in the study of written instruction.

The importance of the criterion problem has recently been underscored as a new generation of investigators has attempted to make new contributions toward scaling the difficulty of reading material. Earlier generations had progressed from simple judgments of relative difficulty to a set of passages scaled on the basis of how well children in different grades could answer questions about them. The resulting readability formulas consistently stressed the importance of sentence length and word frequency (or their substitutes) as stimulus dimensions. (See

Lorge [1949], Chall [1957], and Klare [1963] for the history of readability research.)

Much of the current work is done with the cloze procedure (Taylor, 1953) as the criterion. The cloze procedure can indeed provide a very reliable criterion. But if, as I suspect, this criterion is no more valid than a well-devised set of questions, then its higher reliability brings no solution to the basic problem.

Coleman is clearly very concerned with the criterion problem. In the present paper he reports using three criteria: cloze scores, presentation time, and response time. In other recent works (1962, 1964, 1965) he has tried other measures. This exploration of various criteria of comprehension difficulty is very helpful to other workers in the field. It would be even more helpful if the relations between some of these criteria were also studied and reported.

Coleman states that the first step in studying the complexity of prose "is to develop a set of R-measures, especially measures of the higher cognitive processes such as understanding." The very fuzziness of the term "understanding" frightens us away from it, but progress will depend on developing objective, operational response measures that go beyond verbatim learning of sentences, and that evaluate behaviors clearly related to the instructional outcomes with which we are most concerned. In the general discussion of the preceding session, Glaser enumerated the general nature of some of these criteria: transfer, posttest performance, rate of learning.

"Learning" in the context of written instruction does not generally mean the verbatim learning of sentences. The attempt to analyze what we *do* mean by "learning" in this context should have a salutary influence on education and educational research. The emphasis on understanding rather than memorization marks enlightenment in education. If we can develop an objective understanding of "understanding," the potential gains are enormous.

By such an analysis of understanding, I mean the possibility, for example, that understanding may represent a selective recoding of complex expressions into a set of simple predictions, existence statements, and "if . . . then . . ." contingencies that are indeed, in effect, memorized. Barbara Musgrave's and Jean Carl Cohen's analysis, presented at this symposium, of the equivalences between prose and list learning should be an important step in this direction.

Other measures that we might appropriately develop further as indicators of successful encounters with prose are those that Coleman has reported here and elsewhere, as well as the selection of the picture (or diagram or motion picture sequence that the prose describes), appropriateness of intonation pattern in oral reading, and response latency.

Ability to answer questions about the information in the passage has been the traditional measure of understanding. This measure at least has good face validity. We could do a lot toward standardizing and specifying the nature of the questions that are asked.

THE CRITERION PROBLEM

Let us now look specifically at the criteria of comprehensibility that Coleman has reported. In the correlation study he has developed very stable cloze scores of three different types on a set of thirty-six passages. These passages of known cloze difficulty represent in themselves a splendid contribution to work in written instruction. They will be widely used.

Of the three variations of cloze procedure used by Coleman, the maverick seems to be the third, where the subject saw only the preceding context. Even in listening, and certainly in reading, understanding is not entirely a serial processing device. Both a preceding and a following context is used to help in clarifying ambiguities and understanding hard words and murky phrases.

The close relation of the other two cloze measures is seen in the substantially perfect agreement with which they rank the thirty-two predictors. To quantify the obvious, I have computed the rank-order correlation of the absolute values of the thirty-two coefficients for the first two cloze scores. It is 0.99. The corresponding correlations of the third cloze score with each of the first two are also high, 0.96 and 0.92. On both theoretical and empirical grounds, however, it would seem more appropriate to provide a summed cloze score for just the first two cloze measures rather than for all three. There are several predictors—V_{full}, pronouns, TTR, coordinate conjunctions, and, particularly, repetitions—that have a rather different relation to the third cloze measure than to the first two.

The substantially perfect rank-order correlation between the coefficients obtained for the first two cloze measures is another indication of the great stability of the cloze criteria that Coleman has provided. It should be cautioned, however, that his high reliability is related to the extreme range of the materials. Correlations are sensitive, of course, to the heterogeneity of either variable. The thirty-six passages are said to range "from first-grade material to the most difficult technical prose." The range of cloze scores must have been correspondingly great.

Coleman comments that the correlations between the cloze scores and the thirty-two predictors are "surprisingly high." He concludes that "cloze scores are apparently a more reliable measure of a passage's comprehensibility than such measures as ratings or number of questions answered by readers." This conclusion is probably true, but it seems unwarranted as an inference from the present data. Offhand I know of no readability study based on questions answered in which such an enormous range of passage difficulty has been employed. I will argue later, in fact, that use of such a range is probably undesirable in most explorations of readability.

I also believe it is undesirable to speak consistently, as Coleman does, of summed cloze scores as "comprehensibility." We should never permit verbal labels to keep us from being constantly aware of just what task the subject is performing. In a cloze test the subject guesses at missing words and writes them in the blanks. Language is highly redundant, and subjects can often restore words successfully with only a recognition of familiar patterns of expression and no real understanding. I chose the first sentence from Coleman's paper that my eye fell upon and changed all the content words to make it foolish. The result was the sentence *It has been startled admirably that nimbus extension is more sumptuously guided to plutonium than tribal gymnastics.* Any of the underlined words is readily predictable from the rest of the sentence, though no one, I think, who successfully restored these words would claim to have understood the sentence.

This is not to say that the completion method cannot measure comprehension, but that unless the blanks are appropriately selected, much as one prepares test items, the completion method is as much or more a measure of redundancy (in the informal sense) than of comprehension (Weaver and Kingston, 1963). In fact, it might be less misleading in the long run to refer to cloze scores as measures of redundancy. (See Rankin [1959, 1965] and MacGinitie [1960] for the history and uses of the completion method and cloze procedure.)

Several of Coleman's statements and findings should be reconsidered in terms of redundancy. Where he says (page 162) that "some word classes are related to comprehensibility because they occur in syntactic constructions that are easy to comprehend," one might more parsimoniously say "some word classes are related to high cloze scores because they occur in syntactic constructions where they are highly redundant." Coleman notes that "passages with many adjectives are hard to understand," but previous investigators (Aborn, Rubenstein, and Sterling, 1959) have concluded that in the use of adjectives, writers are probably particularly idiosyncratic and careful to avoid clichés. In other words, adjectives are associated with low redundancy. To say that they are associated with low comprehensibility is an additional inference.

In addition, numerous adjectives may represent the application of embedding and deletion transformations that collapse two or more sentences into one. (See Bach [1964] for an exposition of this point.) *The white lamb is in the pen* derives from *the lamb is white* and *the lamb is in the pen*. The two-sentence form is certainly more redundant (it repeats *the lamb is*), and the cloze procedure would show it to be so. Is it more comprehensible? Quite likely, but is this because it is in two clauses or because it is more redundant?

The example I have just used is intentionally on the primary level. It is precisely at the lowest levels of difficulty that Coleman finds that the number of sentences, the number of clauses, and the number of repetitions are most predictive of difficulty (i.e., cloze scores), and I suspect that it is at these levels that numerous clauses and repetitions represent the most obvious redundancies: *The boy runs. The boy runs fast.*

Before passing on to the criterion problem as it applies to the experimental studies, I would like to urge that in one other area we should examine terminology and explanation to make sure that it is no more complicated than necessary and that it does not lead us to worry about false problems. This area is the relation of word frequency to comprehension difficulty. Coleman says:

There are two ways to explain the relation. One explanation is that high frequency words have higher pre-experimental habit strength . . . [and] response integration is easier. . . . The other explanation . . . is that a set of high frequency words usually have pre-experimental associations with one another . . . [and therefore] the words are easier to cluster into a series. [page 175]

Now, if we are speaking of redundancy — and cloze scores as the effect — then either of these explanations, especially as they would relate to response bias in completing the blanks, would be of considerable interest. But, if we are talking about understanding prose, would it not be more direct to say that more frequent words are likely to be well known, and if you know what the words mean you will be more likely to understand the sentences in which they appear? Perhaps that is too informal an account. But the gist of much of what I have said thus far is that we need to study objectively, and work at making more formal, precisely this sort of statement rather than statements that belong to some other problem.

In his experimental studies, Coleman used as his primary measure of comprehensibility the total time that the stimulus sentence had to be presented before the subject could follow the instructions it contained. I have not served as a subject under the conditions of these experiments, but it seems to me that Coleman's criterion here must be a rather direct measure of the time required to memorize the sentence. I have asked some of my friends what they would do as a subject under the conditions of the experiment. Each has assumed that his strategy would be to memorize the sentence as quickly as possible, turn out the light, and then to figure out what the sentence said for them to do. My friends and I may be quite mistaken, of course, and might resort to some other strategy in actual practice, but "time required to memorize" seems to me to be a plausible description of Coleman's criterion measure for the experiments.

Actually, for whole passages, Coleman's procedure might measure more directly the time required for the subject to comprehend the passage. With a longer passage, the subject would be less likely, I think, to try to memorize the passage verbatim during the stimulus exposure, but would probably try to recode the material. As I indicated earlier, I believe that the latter is probably closer to what we usually mean by "understanding."

THE NATURE OF THE MATERIALS

Concern for a suitable sample of language material in experiments on written instruction should be axiomatic. However, as Coleman has pointed out, "only a handful [of experiments] have used a sample of language materials that represented a usable language population" (page 190). Let us look at this issue in relation to Coleman's paper.

As he has described it, Coleman's sample of thirty-six passages used in the correlation study should represent a wide range of language materials and permit generalization to a language materials population. This may be a case of damned if you do and damned if you don't, however, for I think he has probably gone too far. That is, the factors that make instructional materials more or less difficult at one level of instruction may not be the most important factors at another level. In fact, Coleman's diagrams suggest that this is so, though there are too few points to be sure.

In his experiments, Coleman has studied short paragraphs and sentences of different complexity. These experiments are limited and exploratory, but they make an important beginning. In many respects the experiments on sentences, such as those that Coleman has reported here and in other recent publications (1962, 1964, 1965), represent a real advance in readability research. There is need for a sentence-by-sentence analysis of reading comprehension. Saying that more difficult paragraphs have fewer verbs and more pronouns really only provides clues to the underlying sources of complexity.

In the first place, we should probably focus our interest on the grammatical structure itself rather than on word classes defined by that structure. In the second place, to be of help to the writer of instructional materials, we need to make the important distinction (mentioned by Coleman at the end of his paper), between necessary sentence complexity and complexity that represents a complex way of saying something that could be said more simply. Finally, we need to know about more than average effects. Students of readability have used the mean or median values of such variables as sentence length or word frequency to characterize a whole passage in terms of that variable. Perhaps the upper quartile would be a more appropriate measure than the median. It may be that it is the one longest sentence in a paragraph that has the greatest influence on its difficulty. This comment applies also to averaging word depth within sentences.

When we know about the relation of difficulty to the structure of individual sentences, then, of course, we must study the influence of the context of other sentences and of different relations between sentences. Coleman's correlational study does provide us, for the present, with an excellent readability study and some suggested readability formulas. It is impossible to compare the usefulness of these formulas with those currently in use because of the great range of the materials and the different criterion on which Coleman's formulas are based. It is clear, however, that for materials that do cover a very wide range of difficulty, one of the simple measures of word complexity will do an excellent job of ranking the material for difficulty. Coleman suggests using the percentage of one-syllable words, since it is the measure most easily counted.

I might point out that the number of letters, which is the best of all his predictor variables, might be easier to automate. If the compositor is a computer, one could take advantage of the fact that the number of letters per hundred words is closely approximated by the number of characters in a given number of lines, minus the number of spaces in those lines, this quantity divided by the number of spaces in those lines. If the computer that is arranging the type were programmed to keep track of these matters, it could put out a continuous readability estimate of the material that is to be printed.

Where typewritten copy is involved, the estimate obtained in this way is entirely equivalent to the number of letters for a given number of words, as long as the spaces along the ragged margins are taken into account. I tried this procedure on a couple of paragraphs in Coleman's paper and found that it could be done very rapidly. On the second try (with the aid of a slide rule to figure the proportion and a ruler to measure the length of the typewritten line), counting the number of letters per hundred words (actually ninety-seven) by counting lines and spaces required less than seventy-five seconds. This compares very favorably with the average of eighty-two seconds reported by Farr, Jenkins, Paterson, and England (1952) for counting the number of one-syllable words per hundred words and looking up the corresponding reading ease score.

THE NATURE OF THE SUBJECTS

The third, and final, issue I would like to raise in discussing Coleman's paper involves the nature of the subjects for whom the degree of difficulty of the material is predicted.

Coleman quite properly laments that most work in verbal learning has been done with college sophomores as subjects. In studying the factors that make written material difficult or easy, the problem of subject selection goes far beyond the fact that third-graders find the same sentences generally harder to understand than do college sophomores. The real problem comes from the interaction between the ability of the subjects and the variables that make prose difficult. It is probably true that the same variables that are important in determining the difficulty of prose for third-graders are not altogether the same variables (at least their weights may be quite different) as those that determine the difficulty of prose for college sophomores. It is undoubtedly even more true that the factors that are important in determining the difficulty for third-graders of material written for third-graders are not the same factors that determine the difficulty for college sophomores of the prose in college textbooks.

I will give two examples of this point. The first is from Coleman's analysis of the continuum of R-dimensions involved in understanding prose. In Coleman's description some points on this continuum are: "(a) S recognizes the individual letters and packages them into words, (b) packages the words into simple sentences, (c) packages these simple sentences into more complex clauses and sentences. . . . (page 188).

For the mature reader, point (a) probably seldom exists, and even (b) may sometimes be skipped. Thus, factors that may be very influential in contributing to the difficulty of prose for children at the word perception level may be irrelevant for mature readers.

As a second example, one might note that application of embedding and deletion transformations not only produces longer and more complex clauses, but organizes the information more neatly. *The lamb is white. The lamb has a sore foot. The lamb is in the pen. The pen is behind the barn* becomes *The white lamb with the sore foot is in the pen behind the barn.* It is quite likely, it seems to me, that the longer single sentence and its equivalent individual sentences will have a much different comparative difficulty for third-graders and for college sophomores. It is conceivable, in fact, that the college sophomores might find the longer single sentence easier than the string of individual sentences, at least if embedded in a paragraph with additional information, and if difficulty is not measured by the cloze procedure, which would give undue credit for the redundancy of the string of simpler sentences.

I acknowledge with pleasure that many of the points I have made are elaborations of statements made by Coleman in his paper. I think these are important matters that need to be stressed at this time, and Coleman's paper provides us not only with some important data but with an incisive analysis of issues.

REFERENCES

Aborn, M., Rubenstein, H., and Sterling, T. D. Sources of contextual constraint upon words in sentences. *J. exp. Psychol.*, 1959, *57*, 171–180.

Bach, E. *An introduction to transformational grammars.* New York: Holt, Rinehart, & Winston, 1964.

Chall, J. S. Readability: An appraisal of research and application. *Bur. Educ. Res. Monogr.* (Ohio State Univ.), 1957, no. 34.

Coleman, E. B. Improving comprehensibility by shortening sentences. *J. appl. Psychol.*, 1962, *46*, 131–134.

———. The comprehensibility of several grammatical transformations. *J. appl. Psychol.*, 1964, *48*, 186–190.

———. Learning of prose written in four grammatical transformations. *J. appl. Psychol.*, 1965, *49*, 332–341.

Farr, J. N., Jenkins, J. J., Paterson, D. G., and England, A. O. Reply to Klare and Flesch re simplification of Flesch Reading Ease Formula. *J. appl. Psychol.*, 1952, *36*, 55–57.

Klare, G. R. *The measurement of readability.* Ames: Iowa State Univ. Press, 1963.

Lorge, I. Reading and readability. *Teach. Coll. Rec.*, 1949, *51*, 90–97.

MacGinitie, W. H. Contextual constraint in English prose. Unpublished doctoral dissertation, Columbia Univ., 1960.

Rankin, E. F. The cloze procedure—its validity and utility. In O. S. Causey and W. Eller (Eds.), Starting and improving college reading programs. *Yearb. Nat. Read. Conf.*, 1959, *8*, 131–144.

———. The cloze procedure: A survey of research. In E. L. Thurston and L. E. Hafner (Eds.), The philosophical and sociological bases of reading. *Yearb. Nat. Read. Conf.*, 1965, *14*, 133–150.

Taylor, W. L. "Cloze procedure": A new tool for measuring readability. *Journalism Quart.*, 1953, *30*, 415–433.

Weaver, W. W., and Kingston, A. J. A factor analysis of the cloze procedure and other measures of reading and language ability. *J. Commun.*, 1963, *13*, 252–261.

Experimental Analysis of Written Instruction[1]

PAUL E. JOHNSON

University of Minnesota

Written instruction is a form of language that is used to communicate concepts, skills, and attitudes in some domain of knowledge. This language, here termed a subject-matter language, is characterized by technical words, special usages for common words, and syntactic and stylistic restrictions that eliminate ambiguity. In some cases such as mathematics, this language appears almost exclusively in writing due to the fact that there are no vocal equivalents for many of its elements. A reasonable goal for the psychological study of written instruction is that it should provide descriptions of the stimulus dimensions embedded in a sample of discourse and of the manner in which these dimensions are related to measures of learning and understanding.

To begin the study of written instruction in this sense requires that we make clear the variables of the language that comprise it. The first, and perhaps most obvious, group of variables of any language are those—here termed linguistic variables—which are based upon its syntactical constraints.

LINGUISTIC VARIABLES

One source of hypotheses about the stimulus dimensions of written instruction is the description of language provided by the linguist, and recent work in psycholinguistics indicates that linguistic variables can indeed serve as independent variables in the study of verbal behavior (Jenkins, 1966). The psychologist interested in the study of written instruction cannot afford to ignore the manner in which the choice of certain parts of speech or types of sentences in an utterance is related to the comprehension of its content (e.g., Gough, 1965; Slobin, 1966). On the other hand, it is reasonable to suppose that variables such. as these are not truly at the heart of written instruction, which is constructed, after all, for communication rather than linguistic reasons. Though linguistic variables are relevant to the study of written instruction, they are variables that must be controlled if we want to achieve a description of the subject matter the instruction was formulated to communicate. The psychological problem posed by written instruction — or, for that matter, any communication that employs a subject-matter language — is essentially one of semantics rather than linguistics. But, unfortunately, the linguist has not achieved comparable understandings of the semantic system that supports or underlies a language utterance (Bloomfield, 1939; Katz and Fodor, 1963).

While recognizing the role linguistic variables play in the study of written instruction, it is the purpose of this paper to focus first upon the characteristics of the extra-linguistic variables of subject-matter language, and second upon the manner in which these variables are related to certain measures of acquisition.

Any description of the extralinguistic variables of subject-matter language must begin by considering the distinction between instruction that is formulated to communicate the articulate content of a subject matter and instruction that attempts to communicate the unspecified art of producing or creating that content (Polanyi, 1962). While instruction in the first sense has been successful in a wide variety of language contexts, instruction in the second sense has been successful almost exclusively in the personal contact of master and apprentice (Hadamard, 1945). Fruitful hypotheses about the stimulus dimensions of written instruction are likely to be based, at least initially, upon variables of the first kind, i.e., variables derived from the articulate content of subject matter as it is written down in text-books, monographs, and journals. These we shall call subject-matter variables.

SUBJECT-MATTER VARIABLES

The first requirement for using subject-matter variables in the study of written instruction is that they be described. At present there is no well-formulated description of these variables comparable to the linguists' description of linguistic variables. Probably the closest thing we have to a description of subject-matter variables is to be found in the writings of subject-matter specialists when they are attempting to characterize their discipline or one of its domains of activity (e.g., Jammer, 1957; Margenau, 1950; Theobald, 1966). Even here, the variables are often not explicitly stated and must be inferred from content analysis procedures. In fact, one approach to achieving a working description of subject-matter variables in a given sample of instruction is to analyze statistically the written communication of the domain of knowledge upon which the instruction is based. One could, of course, simply analyze the sample of instruction under consideration, but to be fruitful the system of description used in generating hypotheses about stimulus dimensions would seem to require greater generality than this.

The content analysis of written communication such as textbooks, monographs, and journals in an area of knowledge presumes some unit of analysis. Thus, for example, we might do a frequency count of key words or symbols; and this has met with some success in the past (Berelson, 1952; Lasswell and Leites, 1949; Mosteller and Wallace, 1964). On the other hand, however, we need to be sensitive to the natural units of subject-matter language. That is, it is important to determine the sense in which the formal structure of the subject matter imposes constraints upon any description of the language that communicates it (Scandura, 1966).

Apart from key words and symbols, initial possibilities for units of analysis are various kinds of groupings. While it is possible to use a linguistic unit such as the sentence in establishing these groupings (e.g., counting the words that co-occur with a given word in sentences in the language), it is likely to be more fruitful, as suggested above, to base a contingency analysis upon formal categories in the subject matter. In the case of science these may be things as specific as equations and definitions, or as general as metaphors and analogies. The usefulness of more general principles of grouping than these (e.g., de Sola Pool, 1959) will very likely depend upon the subject-matter language under consideration.

Once we have some description of the basic units employed in the written communication of a subject matter, we can ask specialists to sort and arrange these units so as to achieve additional ideas about order and structure. The problem here, of course, is the instructions under which the sortings, ratings, or other discrimination-type tasks are carried out; and initially it may be best to use relatively unconstrained instructions (e.g., sort these words, phrases, etc., into groups that reflect the structure of the subject matter). The structure imposed by these tasks as well as the distributional and sequential characteristics of the items determined by content analyses define a population of content markers. The elements of this population, together with the rules that can be written to relate them to one another, constitute a first-approximation description of subject-matter variables. Once such a description has been achieved, it is possible to ask about the sense in which its elements function as stimulus dimensions in the acquisition and understanding of instruction.

DEPENDENT VARIABLES

To study the variables of subject-matter language we need some description of dependent measures that define what it means to learn and understand this language. The specialist is once again a useful source of information. That is, one source of hypotheses about the extralinguistic knowledge required for an interpretation of written instruction is the judgment of individuals who are competent in the subject matter upon which it is based. A description of knowledge in this sense usually takes the form of behaviors and abilities that are implied by the instruction and that can be characterized by the question, "What should a person be able to do who knows X?" where X is some portion of the subject matter being described, most often of a concept or principle (Gagné, 1967). It is worth pointing out that Gagné's approach generally emphasizes the distinction between knowledge and the verbal environment in which it is communicated, and focuses upon the hierarchical dependencies between behaviors. By contrast, the approach suggested here attempts to describe the stimulus dimensions upon which such behaviors depend.

The behavioral framework used to define knowledge in the above sense can be filled out by sampling from a population of informants and by writing rules that generate the behaviors supplied by the informants. Such performance rules also specify behaviors not in the original sample. While some of these behaviors may not be judged by informants to represent the concepts under consideration, they should, nevertheless, be included in the universe of behavior that defines a knowledge of these concepts. For it is well to keep in mind that the subject-matter specialist may be unable to describe completely how his subject matter is done, much as the native speaker of a language is unable to articulate the grammar that furnishes a description of his utterances in that language.

The behaviors that the specialist takes to represent knowledge often take the form of problem-solving and discrimination tasks of one sort or another and usually, though not always, involve certain skills of subject-matter expression. In addition, tasks of this sort are generally scored correct or incorrect on the basis of subject-matter rules, i.e., content. These tasks are useful measures of acquisition to the extent that they represent what the individuals have learned from written instruction. If, however, the tasks do not represent what individuals have learned, we are left with little information except that they cannot be done successfully.

Tasks that do not have the above-mentioned properties (namely, they do not presume the skills of subject-matter expression and cannot logically be scored correct or incorrect by means of subject-matter content), are termed nonveridical tasks.

These tasks serve to establish behavioral correlates of content and can be used to determine acquisition for individuals who cannot perform the veridical tasks judged to represent a knowledge of what they have been taught. The more general rationale for the nonveridical task is based upon a concern for the quality or process underlying the behaviors that constitute knowledge (Johnson, 1968). The first stated purpose of this paper was a description of subject-matter variables. The second major purpose is to describe the nonveridical task as a dependent measure and the role that such tasks can play in the psychological study of written instruction.

THE NONVERIDICAL TASK AS A DEPENDENT MEASURE

One class of nonveridical tasks that may be useful in describing the psychological relations or structure among concepts presented in written instruction is the word-association test. Data from such tests have been used to describe associative variables in the subject matter of physics (Johnson, 1964, 1965, 1967, 1968; Rothkopf, 1967; Thurner and Johnson, 1967), sociology (Gardner and Johnson, 1968), and psychology (Verplanck, 1967).

Since these studies represent one of the first attempts to use nonveridical tasks in a systematic way in the study of subject matter, it will be instructive to treat them in some detail. Let us first consider the studies dealing with the subject matter of physics.

Initially (Johnson, 1964), the attempt was simply to determine the sense in which word associations were correlates of school experience. For this purpose, free association instructions were used (subjects were asked to write the first word that each stimulus word made them think of). Although no attempt was made to systematically sample stimulus words from written instruction, it was clear from this first study that in the course of their experience with Newtonian physics subjects learned associative relations among its concept words. Two types of associative relations were evident: (*a*) direct relations between a given stimulus word and the responses to that word, and (b) indirect relations among pairs of stimulus words. This latter type of relation is defined by the proportion of responses (across all subjects) in common between two stimulus words. In this study, both types of associative relations were found to be consistent with formal relations among concepts in the theory of Newtonian physics.

A second study in the series on physics (Johnson, 1965) employed controlled association instructions in an attempt to have subjects produce associations relevant to the domain of concepts under consideration. These instructions asked subjects to write down the first *physics* word that each stimulus word made them think of. Only direct associations were described. It was found that the frequency of equation-related associations (associations consistent with defining equations in the subject matter) was correlated with ability to solve problems based upon these equations. However, the correlation between frequency of association and problem-solving success depended upon the particular stimulus words and problems considered. In fact, it was in this study that it was first noticed that stimulus words seemed to fall into two more or less distinct classes: those words that represented concepts defined in the subject matter by their relations with other concepts — what we termed relationally defined concepts (e.g., force = mass x acceleration) — and those words that served as labels for concepts defined by environmental data (e.g., the operationally defined concepts of *mass, distance,* and *time*).[2]

A limitation of the second study was that direct comparisons could not be made between a subject's performance on the word association test and that same subject's performance on a given problem. This was due largely to the nature of the word association data; that is, since each subject gave only a single response to each stimulus word, it was not possible to conclude that the absence of a particular response to a stimulus word indicated that such a response was missing from the subject's associative hierarchy.

A third study was therefore undertaken (Johnson, 1966), this time using a multiple-response word association test. In this test subjects were asked to write as many words as they could to each stimulus word in one minute. By this time it was also apparent that some description was needed of the written instruction used to teach the subject matter. A word count was therefore performed on a portion of the subject's textbook concerned with Newtonian mechanics. The frequency of occurrence of all concept words was tabulated and stimulus words were systematically selected from the resulting frequency distribution.

The multiple-response word association test permits an additional index of the associative hierarchy for each stimulus word; namely, the average number of associations that subjects give to the word in the one minute they have for producing associations. In the language of the verbal learning researcher (Noble, 1963) this index is referred to as the "meaningfulness" of the stimulus word. Data from the third study indicated that words that occurred frequently in the written instruction of Newtonian mechanics were more meaningful than words that occurred less frequently. Moreover, all words were more meaningful for high achievers in the subject matter than they were for low achievers.

An additional test administered in this study was a similarity-rating test. Here subjects were asked to rate pairs of concept words on a seven-point rating scale, the anchors of which were the words *similar* and *dissimilar*. Response distributions to stimulus words were similar (had a large number of responses in common) for those words that were judged to represent similar concepts. The rating scale, another form of nonveridical task, was used to determine psychological dimensions of the subject matter not revealed by word association data. Once again it was found that those concepts that carried the greatest metaphorical responsibility in the subject matter (the operationally defined concepts) were responded to differently from the relationally defined concepts. This suggested that we look at the characteristics of concepts prior to subject-matter experience, particularly since most arguments for sequencing instruction are based upon the metaphors thought to be meaningful for students upon entry into a program of instruction.

The fourth study in the series on physics (Johnson, 1968) was designed to assess both word associations and similarity ratings of concept words prior to, as well as after, exposure to instruction. As in the previous study, stimulus words were selected from a frequency distribution based upon a word count of the subject's textbook. In addition to simple frequency of occurrence, the frequency with which pairs of concept words co-occurred within sentences in the textbook was also determined. The data indicated, once again, that the meaningfulness of stimulus words was related to the frequency of occurrence of these words in written instruction. However, words in the subject matter also occurred as responses prior to instruction. And, in fact, when the Thorndike-Lorge (1944) word count frequency of the stimulus words was tabulated, it was found that better than half of the words occurred with a frequency greater than fifty times per one million words of running text outside the subject matter, a relatively high frequency of occurrence.

Co-occurrence frequency did not prove to be a powerful variable, perhaps in part because the unit for this contingency analysis was not based upon the theory of the subject matter embodied in the instruction. As before, words that were associatively similar to one another were also judged to represent similar concepts, both before and after subject-matter experience. This latter finding was somewhat puzzling, and a further analysis was done for individual pairs of stimulus words. This analysis revealed that when each word in a given pair represented a relationally defined concept, associative and judged similarity were highly correlated regardless of exposure to written instruction. On the other hand, whenever an operationally defined concept was involved as one member of a pair of stimulus words, associative and judged similarity were no longer highly related. Operationally defined concepts seemed once more to have psychological properties that distinguished them from other kinds of concepts in physics.

The studies described thus far have been concerned with specific relations among concept words in Newtonian physics. A more general description of the structure of relation among a set of words, such as those which were sampled from this subject matter, can be achieved by a data reduction procedure such as factor analysis. Despite the use of this technique to describe the associative structure of certain collections of words (Deese,

1966), there is some question whether the coefficients used to index the similarity of response distributions between pairs of stimulus words are appropriate for a factor analysis (Sandborgh and Johnson, 1968; Shepard, 1962b). A better technique which makes fewer assumptions about the data is non-metric multidimensional scaling. This method is based upon recent developments in scaling by Shepard (1962a, b) and has been programmed for the computer by Kruskal (1964a, b).

In order to describe the more generalized structure of associative relation among concept words in physics, the coefficients of relation in the third study (termed relatedness coefficients), were interpreted as proximity measures and scaled according to multidimensional scaling procedures (Thurner and Johnson, 1967). These coefficients for both high and low achievers are presented in table 1. The coefficients in table 1 became the input to Kruskal's program. The configurations resulting from this scaling are presented in figures 1 and 2.

An interpretation of the configuration for the high achievers

Table 1

Median Relatedness Coefficients for High Achievers (Above Diagonal) and Low Achievers (Below Diagonal)

Stimulus words	Stimulus words													
	1	2	3	4	5	6	7	8	9	10	11	12	13	14
1. Force		25	41	24	36	32	09	11	16	34	30	20	34	21
2. Velocity	05		55	08	02	18	35	31	51	16	15	16	37	22
3. Acceleration	05	39		29	21	19	32	28	42	18	20	22	25	23
4. Mass	27	01	01		53	18	04	03	08	11	20	31	24	07
5. Weight	24	03	00	47		17	02	03	04	11	08	18	24	07
6. Work	38	06	56	07	06		26	29	13	55	40	17	24	17
7. Distance	06	18	04	01	03	13		27	36	20	08	09	16	17
8. Time	01	26	02	01	01	22	26		23	33	14	05	16	15
9. Speed	03	61	47	01	01	15	30	20		10	11	14	24	21
10. Power	36	04	01	12	11	56	01	02	02		41	15	14	17
11. Energy	26	04	03	03	02	33	01	01	01	32		23	14	23
12. Inertia	26	09	08	05	17	11	02	13	01	23	24		28	24
13. Momentum	34	29	25	17	17	16	04	07	31	11	12	47		31
14. Impulse	07	01	03	03	05	09	00	01	03	10	06	00	17	

Note: Decimals omitted.

can be made by reducing concepts to their operationally defined terms. This has been done for each of the relationally defined concepts in figure 1 and appears in table 2. Using the description of concepts in table 2, one dimension in the configuration for the high achievers can be interpreted as a *distance-time* dimension (disregarding for the moment *mass, distance, time, inertia*, and *weight*). From left to right in figure 1, the units of measurement of the concept points (gram, centimeter, and second) involve increasing multiples of centimeter and 1/second. The first portion on the left can be designated by the units of uniform motion (centimeters/second) and includes *speed, velocity, momentum*, and *impulse*. The second portion of figure 1 contains the units of accelerated motion (centimeters/second^2) and includes *acceleration* and *force*. The units of the third portion are centimeters^2/second^2, where we find the concepts of *work* and

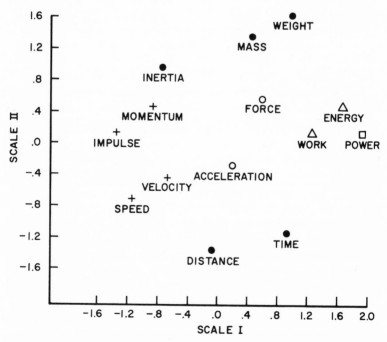

Fig. 1. Non-metric multidimensional scaling solution for high achievers.

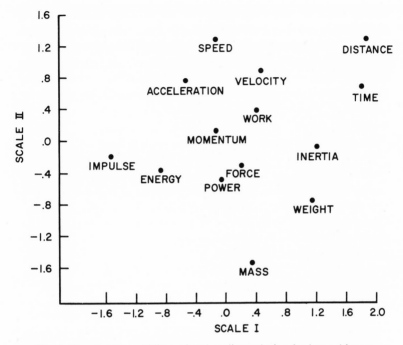

Fig. 2. Non-metric multidimensional scaling solution for low achievers.

energy. The last portion of the configuration has units of centimeter ^{2}/second ^{3} and contains the concept *power.*

The second dimension in the configuration for the high achievers is the *mass-no mass* dichotomy. All concepts at the top of the configuration are defined in terms of *mass,* all those below (*acceleration, velocity, speed, distance,* and *time*) are not. The fact that *weight* and *inertia* are defined in terms of *mass* may justify their position near *mass* at the top of figure 1.

The configuration of concepts for the low achievers in figure 2 cannot be interpreted in the same way as figure 1 because the scales themselves are arbitrary, only the relative distances among the points in the configurations being meaningful; that is, it is not possible to directly compare figures 1 and 2. In other words, the relations among concept words for the low achievers are not describable in terms of *motion* and *mass* as they were for the high achievers. This suggests as a guide for future experimentation that *motion* and *mass* may represent psychological dimensions in terms of which concepts in Newtonian physics are understood.

Although most of the work done thus far has been with physics, in part because of its well-articulated logical structure, two studies have been carried out with other subject matters.

Table 2
Reduction of Concepts to Operationally Defined Terms

Power	= Work/Time	$= \dfrac{F \times D}{T} = \dfrac{M \times A \times D}{T} = \dfrac{M \times V \times D}{T^2} = \dfrac{M \times D^2}{T^3}$
Work	= Force x Distance	$= M \times A \times D = \dfrac{M \times V \times D}{T} = \dfrac{M \times D^2}{T^2}$
Energy	= Mass x Velocity ^{2}	$= \dfrac{M \times D^2}{T^2}$
Force	= Mass x Acceleration	$= \dfrac{M \times V}{T} = \dfrac{M \times D}{T^2}$
Acceleration	= Velocity/Time	$= \dfrac{D}{T^2}$
Impulse	= Force x Time	$= M \times A \times T = \dfrac{M \times V \times T}{T} = \dfrac{M \times D}{T}$
Momentum	= Mass x Velocity	$= \dfrac{M \times D}{T}$
Velocity (speed)	= Distance/Time	$= \dfrac{D}{T}$

Note: These reductions are not precise definitions in physics, but are rather simplifications of such definitions that are taken to represent the structure of the concepts in the instruction to which subjects were exposed.

The first of these was done at Minnesota using the subject matter of sociology (Gardner and Johnson, 1968). The testing instrument was a single-response word association test. Stimulus words were chosen on the basis of their inclusion in a model of the subject matter that was used in constructing instructional materials to which subjects were exposed. Subjects were tested before and after exposure to the instructional materials, and both direct and indirect associative relations were described. Though the logical structure of sociology is less precise than physics, it was possible to find patterns of association that were consistent with relations among concepts in the instructional model for the subject matter. Perhaps more importantly in this case, it was also found that some patterns of association that had been expected did not appear. And, in fact, some relations that appeared in the associative data suggested the presence of language habits quite different from what the instructional materials were designed to teach.

In addition to this exploratory study with the subject matter of sociology, some work has been done with concepts in psychology (Verplanck, 1967). Verplanck has used the word association test as a means of assessing the acquisition of course content in introductory psychology. While this work can perhaps best be interpreted as the construction of associative norms for concept words in introductory psychology, there is some suggestion that the relations that appear in word association data also appear in essays written about the concepts. One characteristic of Verplanck's approach, or any approach to assessment that employs nonveridical tasks, is the difficulty of scoring responses. Presumably, this is done in one of two ways: either by idiosyncratic criteria or by norms that are collected from a criterion group of individuals (e.g., those who do well in the subject matter). The use of word association tests to assess subject-matter content raises an important question about the validity of such tests. A word association test, or any nonveridical task for that matter, does not, generally speaking, contain behaviors that are work samples from some larger domain of criterion behavior. That is, for the most part word association tests do not have content validity (Cronbach and Meehl, 1955). While word association data may be used to predict performance in other types of test situations, the most reasonable goal of research that employs nonveridical tasks is a description of the process underlying performance on some set of veridical or work sample tasks (i.e., construct validity).

EXPERIMENTATION

Given some description of the extralinguistic variables of subject-matter language, it is reasonable to ask how one can begin to study the roles they play in the formulation and acquisition of written instruction. That is, to what extent do subject-matter variables function as independent variables, and how are they related to categories of dependent measures such as problem solving, word association, and other behavioral correlates of content.

Before proceeding further, a word needs to be said about a variable not explicitly mentioned thus far: the subject variable. This is an important variable in any complete description of subject-matter language and the written instruction that embodies it. At the same time, however, subject matter can be viewed as a subject of empirical study in its own right. Its phenomena are real, observable, and describable; and its laws, while not always readily discernable, are nevertheless coordinate with other laws of nature. The point of view adopted here is one that emphasizes stimulus and task variables, but it is well to recognize that we continually need to describe independent and dependent variable relationships against a background level of competence.

While subject-matter variables can be used to generate the basic competence that defines the content of instruction, they are not necessarily psychological variables. As mentioned earlier, subject-matter variables are useful to the psychologist interested in studying written instruction in two respects. First, they are a source of hypotheses about the stimulus dimensions of the language used to communicate concepts, and represent psychological dimensions in this sense to the extent that generalization and discrimination take place along them. That is to say, we need to construct experimental situations in which subject-matter variables are manipulated as independent variables. If it can be shown, for example, that individuals make systematic errors of recognition or acquisition along a dimension determined by a subject-matter variable, then we have established, in part, the psychological significance of that variable (e.g., Shepard, 1958,

1962b). The second sense in which subject-matter variables are useful to the psychologist are as a source of stimulus materials that can be used with informants to establish the universe of tasks that define behaviorally what it means to know a subject matter.

One of the first problems that needs attention in the testing of subject-matter variables as psychological variables is sampling. Although psychologists have usually given considerable attention to sampling subjects, they have given much less attention to sampling stimulus materials and dependent measures. In many cases, however, particularly when language or content is involved, it is as important to be able to generalize to populations of words or other units of analysis and to measures of acquisition and understanding as it is to generalize to a population of individuals whose behavior is being described.

To sample stimulus materials in any sophisticated manner, it is necessary to have a well-defined universe of content. The traditional difficulty here has been defining the characteristics of some reasonably "natural" domain of subject matter. We may, of course, define a restricted population of materials and then choose subjects for whom this material is appropriate. Thus, in the description of general language we can limit ourselves to the first two or three hundred words that are learned by young children (Coleman, 1968). It is also possible to construct "artificial" content whose characteristics can be specified with considerable confidence (e.g., Rothkopf, 1965). While it is difficult to be sure exactly what research on the communication of such content tells us about the psychological characteristics of a more natural subject matter, it does allow us to utilize directly experimental skills and techniques from the laboratory.

In the case of subject-matter language, the population of content elements abstracted from written communication in the subject matter provides an initial set of rules and categories for generating content around which samples of written instruction can be constructed. As far as dependent measures are concerned, the universe of behaviors arrived at by presenting content stimuli to informants provides a reasonably representative index of what it means to know the subject matter — depending, of course, upon the characteristics of the sample of informants. It is important to keep in mind that there may be considerable disagreement among informants both with respect to the categories that describe a subject matter as well as with the tasks which are used to index acquisition.

Tasks such as the word association test and the rating scale can be used to determine some of the psychological properties of subject-matter variables. (For an example of the use of rating scales in establishing behavioral correlates of an abstract description of language, see Greenberg and Jenkins, 1964.) Essentially, we are asking here about the change in ratings or associations to stimulus materials as a function of stage of acquisition and the overlap between the response dimension revealed by such tasks and those provided by subject-matter informants. Acquisition and recognition tasks are appropriate, as suggested earlier, for establishing more specific dimensions of generalization. These tasks characteristically depend upon error analyses to reveal the dimensions along which stimulus or response generalization take place; and they have been used with considerable success in this respect to demonstrate the "psychological reality" of certain linguistic variables (Clifton and Odom, 1966).

The study of any subject-matter language must begin by mapping the domain of knowledge represented in the language in terms of learner responsiveness (Easley, 1966). Eventually, of course, stimulus dimensions need to be related to the universe of behaviors that define a knowledge of subject matter, both after exposure to written instruction in the laboratory setting and under conditions of more sustained exposure such as those which occur in the classroom. The fact that a population of stimulus materials, as well as of dependent measures, has been defined means that we can study acquisition both in the sense of changes in a given measure of output for several different levels or categories of input and in the sense of differences in performance on several different measures of output for given category input. This last approach may prove particularly fruitful in formulating a description of the "understanding" of subject matter as a domain of generalization (Hively, 1964).

In one sense, the experiments done to describe the relationship between the independent and dependent variables of written instruction are much like traditional psychological experiments, especially in the areas of verbal learning and psycholinguistics. In another sense, however, they are very different. In the study of instruction we cannot afford to be concerned simply with a description of the relationship between categories of independent and dependent variables. By its very nature written instruction demands that we concern ourselves with the sense in which known relationships between variables can be optimized. And it is the problem of optimization that is at the heart of any technology of written instruction.

Optimization experiments are usually characterized by their focus upon the selection and sequencing of stimulus material. Decisions about selection and sequencing are typically made to achieve criteria such as shortest possible acquisition time, widest possible range of generalization of veridical behavior, fewest number of errors, or some combination of these. In constructing sequences of material for experimental study it would be well to take account of what the psycholinguist and verbal learning researcher can tell us about the role of linguistic variables in comprehension. That is to say, before manipulating content or sequence variables of subject-matter language we need to make sure that comprehension has been achieved. Research on the hierarchical nature of veridical behaviors (e.g., Gagné and Paradise, 1961) may also be useful in generating sequencing hypotheses when the performance being optimized is complex. And, of course, some of the traditional psychological literature, particularly in the area of training research, contains what are in fact optimization studies (Glaser, 1962; Rothkopf, 1968). Even though these studies are not always formulated with an optimization model in mind (Groen and Atkinson, 1965), they are useful sources of information.

As before, a major source of hypotheses for sequencing subject-matter material is the individual who typically formulates written instruction. However, the decision an informant makes about how content should be arranged for purposes of instruction will very likely be quite different from though related to the decisions he makes in describing the content in the first place (Gardner and Johnson, 1968). Moreover, given agreement as to the content that is to be communicated, there may be considerable variation among informants as to how it should be sequenced. Thus, it is important that we once again make the specialist a sampling variable. Of course, the psychologist can use himself as informant both in describing content and when making decisions about its sequencing. But unless he also has a good knowledge of the subject matter being communicated, his own intuition is not likely to be fruitful except in highly restricted laboratory situations. Said another way, any psychological analysis of written instruction that ignores the sense in which the subject matter under consideration provides its own categories for analysis, can at best be only incomplete and, at worst, trivial.

NOTES

1. Preparation of this paper was supported in part by grants in the University of Minnesota Center for Research in Human Learning from the National Science Foundation (GS 1761), the National Institutes of Child Health and Human Development (1-HD-01136), and from the Graduate School of the University of Minnesota. This paper and the following discussion were written after the 1966 Symposium on Verbal Learning and the Technology of Written Instruction.

2. Although, in some sense, any concept in Newtonian physics can be given either an operational or relational definition, the distinction is not arbitrary but reflects patterns of usage in the subject matter (see also Johnson, 1968; Margenau, 1950).

REFERENCES

Berelson, B. *Content analysis in communication research.* Glencoe, Ill.: Free Press, 1952.

Bloomfield, L. Linguistic aspects of science. *International Encyclopedia of Unified Science*, vol. I, no. 4. Chicago: Univ. of Chicago Press, 1939.

Clifton, C., Jr., and Odom, P. Similarity relations among certain English sentence constructions. *Psychol. Monogr.*, 1966, *80*, 5 (whole no. 613), 35.

Coleman, E. B. A measure of information gained during prose learning. *Read. Research Quart.,* 1968, *3,* 369–386.

Cronbach, L., and Meehl, P. Construct validity in psychological tests. *Psychol. Bull.,* 1955, *52,* 281–302.

Deese, J. *The structure of associations in language and thought.* Baltimore: Johns Hopkins Univ. Press, 1966.

De Sola Pool, I. (Ed.), *Trends in content analysis.* Urbana: Univ. of Illinois Press, 1959.

Easley, J. A., Jr. The natural sciences and educational research—a comparison. *High Sch. J.,* 1966, *50,* 39–50.

Gagné, R. M. Curriculum research and the promotion of learning. In R. Tyler, R. M. Gagné, and M. Scriven, *Perspectives of curriculum evaluation.* Chicago: Rand McNally, 1967.

Gagné, R. M., and Paradise, N. E. Abilities and learning sets in knowledge acquisition. *Psychol. Monogr.,* 1961, *75* (whole no. 518).

Gardner, W. E., and Johnson, P. E. Evaluation of language habits in a behavioral science curriculum. *School Rev.,* 1968, *76,* 396–411.

Glaser, R. *Training research and education.* Pittsburgh: Univ. of Pittsburgh Press, 1962.

Gough, P. B. Grammatical transformation and speed of understanding. *J. verb. Learn. verb. Behav.,* 1965, *4,* 107–111.

Greenberg, J. H., and Jenkins, J. J. Studies in the psychological correlates of the sound system of American English. *Word,* 1964, *20,* 157–177.

Groen, G. J., and Atkinson, R. C. Models for optimizing the learning process. *Psychol. Bull.,* 1966, *4,* 309–320.

Hadamard, J. *The psychology of invention in the mathematical field.* Princeton: Princeton Univ. Press, 1945.

Hively, W., II. *Constructing, evaluating, and revising a program of instruction in algebra for in-service teacher training: A case history and an essay on methodology.* Minneapolis: Minnesota National Laboratory, 1964.

Jammer, M. *Concepts of force.* Cambridge: Harvard Univ. Press, 1957.

Jenkins, J. J. The role of experimentation in psycholinguistics. Invited address to the Division of Experimental Psychology of the American Psychological Association, New York, September, 1966.

Johnson, P. E. Associative meaning of concepts in physics. *J. educ. Psychol.,* 1964, *55,* 84–88.

———. Word relatedness and problem solving in high school physics. *J. educ. Psychol.,* 1965, *56,* 217–224.

————. Some psychological aspects of subject-matter structure. *J. educ. Psychol.,* 1967, *58,* 75–83.

————. On the communication of concepts in science. *J. educ. Psychol.,* 1969, *60,* 32–40.

Katz, J., and Fodor, J. The structure of semantic theory. *Language,* 1965, *39,* 170–210.

Kruskal, J. B. Multidimensional scaling by optimizing goodness of fit to a nonmetric hypothesis. *Psychometrika,* 1964a, *29,* 1–27.

————. Nonmetric multidimensional scaling: A numerical method. *Psychometrika,* 1964b, *29,* 115–129.

Lasswell, H. D., and Leites, N. *Language of politics; studies in quantitative semantics.* New York: George W. Stewart, 1949.

Margenau, H. *The nature of physical reality.* New York: McGraw-Hill, 1950.

Mosteller, F., and Wallace, D. *Inference and disputed authorship: The federalist.* Reading, Mass.: Addison-Wesley, 1964.

Mussell, B., and Johnson, P. E. Information and subject-matter structure. Paper delivered at the annual meeting of the American Educational Research Association, February, 1967.

Noble, C. Meaningfulness and familiarity. In C. N. Cofer and B. S. Musgrave (Eds.), *Verbal behavior and learning.* New York: McGraw-Hill, 1963.

Polanyi, M. *Personal knowledge.* Chicago: Univ. of Chicago Press, 1962.

Rothkopf, E. Z. Some theoretical and experimental approaches to problems in written instruction. In J. D. Krumboltz (Ed.), *Learning and the educational process.* Chicago: Rand McNally, 1965.

————. Measuring learning from connected discourse: Some results from six techniques. Paper delivered at the annual meeting of the Eastern Psychological Association, April, 1967.

————. Two scientific approaches to the management of the instruction process. In R. M. Gagné and W. J. Gephard (Eds.), *Learning research and school subjects.* Itasca, Ill.: F. E. Peacock, 1968.

Sandborgh, R. E., and Johnson, P. E. A method for the analysis of language habits in science. A paper presented at the annual meeting of the American Educational Research Association, February, 1968.

Scandura, J. Precision in research on mathematics learning: The emerging field of psychomathematics. *J. Res. sci. Teaching,* 1966, *4,* 253–274.

Shepard, R. N. Stimulus and response generalization: Tests of a model relating generalization to distance in psychological space. *J. exp. Psychol.,* 1958, *55,* 509–523.

————. The analysis of proximities: Multidimensional scaling with an unknown distance function. I. *Psychometrika,* 1962a, *27,* 125–140.

————. The analysis of proximities: Multidimensional scaling with an unknown distance function. II. *Psychometrika,* 1962b, *27,* 219–246.

Slobin, D. Grammatical transformations and sentence comprehension in childhood and adulthood. *J. verb. Learn. verb. Behav.,* 1966, *5,* 219–227.

Theobald, D. W. *The concept of energy.* London: E. & F. N. Spun, Ltd., 1966.

Thorndike, E. L., and Lorge, I. *The teacher's word book of 30,000 words.* New York: Bur. of Pub., Teach. Coll., Columbia Univ., 1944.

Thurner, R. D., and Johnson, P. E. On the configuration of subject matter. Paper delivered at the annual meeting of the American Educational Research Association, February, 1967.

Verplanck, W. Verbal associations in connected discourse: Associative and discursive concepts. Paper delivered at the annual meeting of the Eastern Psychological Association, April, 1967.

Discussion of Professor
Paul E. Johnson's Paper

JOAN L. PRENTICE

Indiana University

Dr. Johnson outlines a defensible base for investigating the psychology of written instruction. The paper deals with the question of how we should go about studying the acquisition of subject matter concepts. Distinctions between categories of variables relevant to the question are made clear. A number of points related to psycholinguistic theory and to cognitive theory come up. Four points bear closer scrutiny.

It has been suggested that linguistic variables, while not central to a study of learning from written instruction, are powerful enough to require control while the investigator engages in analysis and description of written subject matter. However, we do not yet have a sound basis for selecting linguistic control variables. If we knew enough about psycholinguistic processes to select sensible linguistic control variables, then we would be obliged to ask whether there is an interaction between linguistic structure and content structure in a comprehension task.

Linguistic variables can be differentially potent, depending on the content carried by the language. It is possible, for example, that journalistic style is most appropriate for newspapers, but that pedantic style is most communicative for professional journals. Relational and operational concepts may be optimally

238

conveyed by different language forms. Holding grammatical structure reasonably constant across content tasks does not allow the interaction question to be asked.

The formal structure unique to the subject matter under investigation is said to constrain the natural units of subject-matter language that can be derived from it. The investigator is advised to attend to these constraints. That such restrictions exist should not preclude a search for epistemological universals. A well-developed theory of written instruction should incorporate generalizations about the structure of knowledge. Discovery of epistemological universals would have direct bearing not only on subject matter subsets, but also on theories of human learning and thinking. A program for developing a theory of written instruction ought explicitly to include a search for epistemological universals.

Structure inherent in content is accounted for by positing content markers to provide structural identification of content units, plus rules that map or project the marked content units onto the subject matter structure. This proposition opens the way to a dynamic approach to content analysis. However, one note of caution should be sounded. It has been suggested that the distributional and sequential properties of content items will specify content markers. Such defining contingencies may imply a finite system of knowledge analogous to the linear operator model of grammar rejected by Chomsky. Whether the implication holds should be ascertained. If the implication does hold, the tenability of a finite state model as a model for the structure of a domain of knowledge should be examined closely.

Implicit in a theory of written instruction is the belief that we can and do learn new concepts when instances and rules are exclusively verbal. Traditional concept learning experiments are nonlinguistic, and evidence of concept mastery is veridical — identifying new instances correctly, or specifying the rule(s) by which the various positive instances are identified, and negative instances excluded. Using nonveridical tasks to assess exclusively verbal concept learning is intriguing. On what basis does the learner organize his associative hierarchy around a new word, representing, for instance, the concept *momentum?* Another interesting distinction between traditional concept acquisition studies and learning subject-matter concepts may be made. Traditional tasks pose single concept problems. Learning a subject matter requires learning multiple concepts. We should consider the possibility that some concepts are necessarily learned in sets, perhaps by a process of differentiation and interstructuring. Observing the process and product of organizing sets of concepts can help us to generate new hypotheses about the formation and organization of corresponding cognitive structures.

Some Empirical Predictors of Readability

GEORGE R. KLARE

Ohio University

"Readable" is a word that has been around a long time — since at least 1570 in written usage (Murray, 1914), and certainly longer in oral. It has, during that time, come to acquire several dictionary meanings. When used in reference to written material, the most common denotative equivalents used today are:

1. Interest-value. When such writing as a novel is said to be readable, it usually means that it is pleasant to read. Hemingway's story of the Spanish Civil War, in this sense, would be said to be more readable to a general reader than a military historian's account of the war.

2. Legibility. Readability of this second sort refers, of course, to mechanical features of handwriting or of type: whether they are clear enough so that a reader can read them efficiently. This sense was intended by Paterson and Tinker in their book, *How to Make Type Readable* (1940). Tinker, incidentally, has brought things up to date in a book called *Legibility of Print* (1963).

3. Comprehensibility. This use of the term readability refers to quality of writing that permits a reader to read and understand it readily. In this sense, critics tend to agree that Hemingway was more readable for the general reader than Faulkner.

241

It is some aspect of this third dictionary meaning that has come to be used most often when speaking of studies of the readability of connected discourse. The reason for this, in large measure, is the recently increased interest in so-called readability formulas of the sort popularized by Flesch. By way of groundwork, then, "readability," as I use it, refers to some quality in connected discourse that makes it easy to read and understand. And, incidentally, I intend to use "writing" as a general term that is interchangeable with "connected discourse" and "written material." In other words, "writing" will *not* refer to a narrowly literary production.

EMPIRICAL PREDICTORS OF READABILITY

With these preliminaries out of the way, we can look at the major question of what empirical predictors of readability there are. The chief source of information here is the group of studies made for the purpose of developing readability formulas. The classic example, in terms of typical research method, was made by Gray and Bernice Leary, and published as *What Makes a Book Readable* (1935). They collected a total of 289 possible predictors by: (1) studying previous readability work; (2) getting the opinions of approximately 100 experts, consisting of librarians, readers' advisers, publishers, and adult educators; and (3) securing reactions from 170 library patrons. The predictors were divided into four major categories: (I) Format, or Mechanical Features; (II) General Features of Organization; (III) Style of Expression and Presentation; and (IV) Content.

The probable importance of these 289 variables was then evaluated by 79 judges (like the experts above). They felt that content was about one-third of the total problem of readability, and style of expression and presentation a little under one-third; the factors of format and organization together thus constituted a little over one-third. (On this point, I later found somewhat the same thing: content overshadowed style variables in the reactions of readers of technical material.)

Gray and Leary, however, found that only the style category, containing 82 potential predictors, lent itself to quantitative analysis. The other categories could not provide very satisfactory measuring devices, since they were too subjective in nature. So, at this point, they were concerned with those *style variables, or elements of language structure,* that can serve *as predictors of ease of reading and understanding.* This is what I will mean, from now on, when speaking of "predictors of readability."

What are such usable predictors of readability? I have heard it said, and have read (somewhere) that at least 1,000 such "style" variables can be used. I have never seen a list of 1,000; I can, however, refer interested readers to Gray and Leary's list of 82. Coleman, in his excellent paper in this volume, has recently extended Gray and Leary's list to include some variables suggested by recent advances in linguistics. Bormuth (1966), in a very thorough paper, presented intercorrelations between the occurrences of 110 variables and indices of passage difficulty. Certain of these are closely related, some being the same as Gray and Leary's and Coleman's, and others being presented in terms of both form-class ratios and part-of-speech ratios.

Many of Gray and Leary's variables overlap, so the number 82 sounds bigger than it really is. For example, both "number of simple sentences" and "percentage of simple sentences" were included in the list of 82. Gray and Leary cut the list to 44, and correlated their occurrence in standard passages with the test scores of readers on the passages, and then with each other. (Coleman, in the paper cited above, used cloze scores instead of the number of questions subjects could answer on the passages. Using this criterion, he found correlations higher than those reported by Gray and Leary. Bormuth, in the paper referred to above, also used a cloze criterion and also found higher correlations than those reported by Gray and Leary for the same variables. This may have been due either to the use of the cloze measure, or to the fact that his sample passages ranged more widely in difficulty than Gray and Leary's, or both. For a discussion of this point, see MacGinitie's critique of Coleman's paper in this volume, or my 1966 critique of Bormuth's paper.)

The correlation matrix later provided data for two almost simultaneous factor analyses, one by Stolurow and Newman (1959) and one by Brinton and Danielson (1958). The former reduced the 44 variables analyzed by Gray and Leary to 23 for more convenient analysis; the latter reduced the 44 to 20. The 44 variables, though reduced from the original 82, still had considerable overlap, so the reductions to 23 and to 20 were readily possible. The two factor analyses yielded essentially the same conclusions: (1) with few exceptions, the 20 to 23 variables could be grouped roughly under two main factors, word and sentence difficulty; (2) of the two, word difficulty was relatively the more important; (3) of the remaining factors, none was clear enough to be given a name, although Brinton and Danielson suggest that a third factor had to do with stylistics, or devices, of content.

Since the work of Gray and Leary in 1935, a number of additional readability formulas have been developed (in fact, the number has approximately tripled). However, in most the formula elements used were still largely the same as those used by Gray and Leary; they were merely arranged differently. Exceptions were formulas by Morriss and Halverson (1938) and Flesch (1950, 1954, 1958) that involved "word categories," and those by Flesch (1943) and Bloomer (1959) that involved linguistic elements not previously used. These are listed in skeleton form in table 1. (Coleman has presented several new prediction equations in his paper in this volume, all using the cloze score criterion. His two most powerful and simplest factors, however, remain a word difficulty factor—percentage of one-syllable words—and a sentence difficulty factor—number of sentences per 100 words.)

How all of these new predictors would have fared had they been included in the factor analyses can only be surmised. However, certain of them, at least, would surely have been part of the word factor previously found. For example, the relation between a count of affixed morphemes (a "new" measure) and a count of syllable length (an "old" measure) has been reported to be quite close.

Up to this point, then, it seems that two major predictors of readability emerge from the studies: word difficulty and sentence difficulty. Interestingly enough, Lorge (1944) points out that the Talmudists apparently thought very nearly this same

Table 1

Uncommon Variables Used in Readability Formulas

Author(s)	Date	Variables
Morriss and Halverson	1938	Relative occurrence of: 1. Fundamental or elemental word labels 2. Simple localisms 3. Concrete word labels 4. Abstract word labels
Flesch	1943	Number of affixed morphemes in 100-word samples
Flesch	1950	Percentage of "definite" (nonabstract) words in 100-word samples
Flesch	1954	Occurrence of r count words (indicating realism, specificity, or concreteness) and e count words (indicating energy, forceful delivery, and vividness) in 100-word samples
Flesch	1958	Occurrence of words indicating "formality" vs. "popularity" in 100-word samples
Bloomer	1959	Relative occurrence of "words per modifier," and determination of sound complexity of modifiers

thing in about A.D. 900 when they made word counts and idea counts on their manuscripts. What has been added, if anything, in the thousand years since?

1. The predictors have been refined, and their use simplified.

2. The effect of the predictors on reader behavior is more precisely understood.

From this point on the discussion will concern certain aspects of these conclusions.

To begin with, I do not mean to imply that saying there are two predictors—word difficulty and sentence difficulty—tells the whole story. First of all, there are many ways of measuring each. For example, word difficulty can be measured in terms of word familiarity, word length, and initial letters of words. (See Coleman's paper in this volume for still others.) Similarly, sentence difficulty has many possible measures.

Second, I do not believe that word and sentence difficulty are the only kinds of predictors. I have tried other kinds myself:

several typographic arrangements (Klare, Nichols, and Shuford, 1957), organization (Klare, Shuford, and Nichols, 1958), stress (Klare, Mabry, and Gustafson, 1955a), and personal-interest style (words and sentences) (Klare, Mabry, and Gustafson, 1955b), for example. (A rather thorough examination of other style predictors themselves has been made by Coleman in his paper in this volume.) But rather than getting into these other predictors at the moment, I would like to stick to word and sentence difficulty. That way we can look at the effect of each more carefully. Then, if we wish, we can tie other variables to these later.

Furthermore, I believe certain human variables (i.e., abilities, experiences, and motivations) should at least be mentioned when speaking of the prediction of readability. Certainly they interact with the language predictors in ways that determine how accurate a prediction will be. And, finally, I think there are several differentiable, and easily measurable, aspects of readability that ought to be considered.

Perhaps the simplest way to handle this situation is to provide a summary table. Table 2 includes some basic variables in the language (stimulus variables) and in the reader (organism variables) that I believe contribute to some basic aspects of readability (response variables). I will discuss each of these briefly as we go, starting from reader behavior, the dependent variables.

Table 2

Some Basic Variables in the Prediction of Readability

Language (Stimulus) Variables	Human (Organism) Variables	Reading Behavior (Response Variables)
Word frequency or familiarity	Visual recognition speed	Reading efficiency
Word length	Memory span	Judgment of difficulty or acceptability
Sentence length	Educational level	
	Special reading experience	Comprehension (learning and retention)
	General motivational level	
	Set to learn	

DEPENDENT MEASURES

A number of indicators of readability have been used, including number of readers in a free-reading situation, depth of reading (into an article), and even success at the ballot box on election day (as a function of the readability of campaign speeches). But most of them can be reduced to one of three major aspects of readability.

1. Reading efficiency. This is most commonly a time measure, like number of words read per minute, but number of words read per visual fixation has also been used.

2. Judgments of difficulty or acceptability. These include preferences for one version over others, attempts at ranking, etc. There is also reason to believe that readership studies (number of readers or depth of reading in free-reading situations) should be included here.

3. Comprehension (learning and retention). Most often a comprehension test is involved, but occasionally a more traditional measure of learning or retention has been used.

With these dependent variables in mind, what effects do word and sentence difficulty have, and why? There is considerable evidence of the predictability of the word and sentence variables through studies of the validity of readability measures, although more work on the specific effect of each would be desirable (see Klare, 1963, pp. 121–156).

Using available information, let us look at word difficulty first. A basic characteristic of word difficulty appears to be frequency of occurrence of words in print. The classic American studies were those of Thorndike in his *Teacher's Wordbooks* (1921, 1932, 1944), although many other frequency studies were made here and in other countries. One trouble with frequency counts of this kind is that the values used must be population values, and cannot take account of individual differences in how frequently words have been seen. Another is the fact that there is a leveling off in the relationship (i.e., a negatively accelerated functional relationship) between frequency and such a measure as recognition speed. Still another problem, discussed by Coleman in his paper in this volume, is the finding that using the frequency of occurrence of content words is preferable to using the frequency of occurrence of all words in a passage. For a complete review of studies of word frequency that relate to readability—almost 100 were found—see Klare (1968).

Therefore, the early crude measure of frequency has been improved upon in several ways. Perhaps the most successful for readability purposes has been the use of "familiarity" counts, particularly Dale's list of 8,000 words (unpublished). Another refinement has been the use of syllable length of words in one form or another (i.e., proportion of one-syllable or multisyllable words, as well as average syllable length).

The reason that syllable measurement can be used as an index of frequency brings up one of the main reasons that frequency is important. The key is a principle (called the "law of abbreviation") usually credited to Zipf (1935), but apparently discovered by Bear independently and published earlier (1927). It is, of course, the tendency for words to become shortened as they are used more frequently.

This suggests immediately that a more readable passage should be physically shorter than a less readable one. If two passages contain 100 words, for example, that passage with the more frequent words should be measurably shorter. This was found, in fact, to be the case in passages studied by several colleagues and myself (Klare, Shuford, and Nichols, 1957). We demonstrated that the number of words read per second and the number read per visual fixation was significantly greater for the passage with the more frequent words. Was the effect *simply* due to the fact the passage was physically shorter? We checked on this by using more white space between the words in the shorter passage so that it became as long as the longer one. We found that the difference in number of words read per fixation was in fact no longer significantly different between the passages, but the number of words read per second still favored the passage with the more frequent words.

This, to sum up, seems to indicate that more frequent words are more readable because they are shorter. McGinnies, Comer, and Lacey (1952) have also demonstrated that shorter words are recognized faster in a tachistoscopic presentation. But both their study and our study indicated that there must be some other additional basis for the effect of frequency on recognition speed or reading speed. A *possibility*, at least, of what it is was demonstrated by Haseley in an unpublished M.A. thesis (1957). He used a "mask" to expose successively larger portions of single words until the words were recognized by subjects. He found a close inverse relationship between the log of the frequency of occurrence of a word and the fraction of the word necessary for recognition.

Frequency of occurrence, then, seems to aid readability by a related two-pronged effect upon visual recognition speed. The first is through a physical shortening of the word, and the second is through the fact that less of the word is necessary for recognition. This combined effect, then, shows up clearly in the reading efficiency response variable. Furthermore, the presence of frequent, as opposed to infrequent, words appears to be a major determiner of judgments of difficulty or acceptability on the part of the reader. We found, for example, tetrachoric correlation coefficients ranging from .80 to .97 for judgments of "easy to read" and "pleasant to read" in a series of studies.

Now, how could word frequency affect comprehension (in addition to reading efficiency and judgments of difficulty)? One of the observations of Thorndike and Lorge in frequency studies was that more frequently used words had more dictionary meanings, or verbal equivalents (Lorge, 1949). This, however, would seem to hinder rather than aid comprehension, through interference of possible meanings. Apparently, one reason why this does not occur (to any great extent, at least) is the distribution of meanings. As Lorge's semantic count (1949) shows, the one or two common meanings of a word usually occur a disproportionately large number of times in context. Thus, a highly frequent word will most often involve use of a highly frequent meaning, i.e., a common association.

However, frequency of words seems somewhat less closely related to comprehension than to reading efficiency in some analyses. Studies by Flesch (1943), for example, give the word variable less weight (in adult reading, at least) than the sentence variable in determining comprehension scores. (However, the factor analyses and Coleman's work contradict this, suggesting once again the need for more studies of the specific effect of the word and the sentence variables at different levels). What effect word frequency does have may well be due to increasing the efficiency of the human's very limited memory span. Perhaps, in this respect, it provides for something like Miller's "recoding" (1956), that is, it provides for more meaningful grouping for assimilation.

Whether or not the effect of shortened sentence length upon comprehension is *more* important than that of higher word frequency, it *is* clearly an important variable. It seems probable, further, that it may be acting even more directly through its effect upon the memory span than the word variable is. That is, it may well be providing for more efficient use of limited human memory.

I have included a third stimulus variable, passage redundancy. I do not have as good an empirical reason for including it as I do word and sentence variables. But defined as I wish to define it, it could be an indicator of the many readability formula predictors that are between the word and the sentence in complexity (e.g., clauses). Redundancy, in this case, refers to "the extent to which a given unit of language is determined by nearby units." A good descriptive term for my use of it is Rubenstein and Aborn's "predictability" (1958), or the extent to which each successive word in a sample of prose can be predicted.

Enough for stimulus variables. Let me turn now briefly to the remaining human variables (besides visual recognition speed and memory span, which I have already mentioned). Educational level and special reading experience seem logically to affect how readable a given passage is for a reader. The former tends to make a reader something of an expert with language generally, the latter tends to make him something of an expert with the special language of his field. One is tempted to write off these variables as, simply, further evidence of the efficacy of frequency, but they may well be somewhat more complex.

Finally, I want to take up the variable of motivation. Common sense (as well as readership studies) would say that reading matter cannot be readable unless the motivation to read is strong

enough to get a person to begin reading and to continue reading. Of greater significance at the moment, however, is the more
specific variable of a strong versus weak "set to learn" (Klare,
Shuford, and Nichols, 1957). This was our name at Illinois for
a test-induced set that had a marked effect on reading behavior.
We had noted that readers would frequently read material too
rapidly (or carelessly) to learn it adequately for experimental
purposes. Exhortations to read more carefully did not work,
but we happened to notice that if we preceded our measurements with a short preliminary passage and a clearly difficult
test, the experimental passage was learned much better. The
effect was to increase test scores, but to increase reading time
and number of fixations as well. Equally interesting, reading
efficiency and conditions of a strong set were closely related.
The rather large literature on this relationship had been inconclusive, some writers saying the relationship was high and others
low. What this shows is a rather high relationship between efficiency and comprehension measures under a strong "set to
learn," and a lower relationship under a weak "set to learn."

SUMMARY

In summary, then, it seems possible to reduce the measurement of readability to a more nearly single response variable
(speed-comprehension), just as the many potential style predictors could be reduced to word and sentence stimulus variables.
This is not to say, of course, that only one dependent variable
should be used; different aspects of readability are of concern at
different times. Similarly, it does not mean that other style predictors should not be tried. But it *does* imply that the nonstyle
predictors of format, organization, and content that Gray and
Leary did *not* study ought to be given more attention now.

There have been some studies of this sort, as I mentioned
earlier, but more are needed, despite the fact that objective
measurement and controls are difficult to apply. Having an
objective "unit of content" would, of course, make it possible to
exert a much needed measure of control when style predictors
are being studied. That is, being able to hold "what is said" con-

stant while changing "how it is said" would be very helpful. But even without such a control, investigatory studies can be done. Similarly, the "set" a reader develops, or, more easily studied, the reading directions he is given, should receive more attention. In short, it may well be more productive to look carefully at the conditions under which a few important predictors of readability are used than it is to look for more predictors of the traditional kind, as has been the case in the past.

REFERENCES

Bear, M. V. The length of words as an index of difficulty in silent reading. Unpublished master's thesis, Univ. of Chicago, 1927.

Bloomer, R. H. Level of abstraction as a function of modifier load. *J. educ. Res.*, 1959, *52*, 269–272.

Bormuth, J. R. Readability: A new approach. *Read res. quart.*, 1966, *1*, 79–132.

Brinton, J. E., and Danielson, W. A. A factor analysis of language elements affecting readability. *Journ. quart.*, 1958, *35*, 420–426.

Dale, E. Familiarity of 8,000 common words to pupils in the fourth, sixth, and eighth grades. Unpublished, but sometimes available from the Bur. of Educ. Res., Ohio State Univ., n.d.

Flesch, R. F. *Marks of readable style: A study in adult education.* New York: Bur. of Pub., Teach. Coll., Columbia Univ., 1943.

―――. Measuring the level of abstraction. *J. appl. Psychol.*, 1950, *34*, 384–390.

―――. *How to make sense.* New York: Harper & Bros., 1954.

―――. *A new way to better English.* New York: Harper & Bros., 1958.

Gray, W. S., and Leary, B. *What makes a book readable.* Chicago: Univ. of Chicago Press, 1935.

Haseley, L. The relationship between cue-value of words and their frequency of prior occurrence. Unpublished master's thesis, Ohio Univ., 1957.

Klare, G. R. *The measurement of readability.* Ames: Iowa State Univ. Press, 1963.

――― Comments on Bormuth's "Readability: A new approach." *Read. res. quart.*, 1966, *1*, 119–125.

―――. The role of word frequency in readability. *Elem. Eng. J.*, 1968, *45*, 12–22.

Klare, G. R., Mabry, J. E., and Gustafson, L. M. The relationship of patterning (underlining) to immediate retention and to acceptability of technical material. *J. appl. Psychol.*, 1955a, *49*, 40–42.

———. The relationship of human interest to immediate retention and to acceptability of technical material. *J. appl. Psychol.*, 1955b, *39*, 92–95.

Klare, G. R., Nichols, W. H., and Shuford, E. H. The relationship of typographic arrangement to the learning of technical training material. *J. appl. Psychol.*, 1957, *41*, 41–45.

Klare, G. R., Shuford, E. H., and Nichols, W. H. The relationship of style difficulty, practice, and ability to efficiency of reading and to retention. *J. appl. Psychol.*, 1957, *41*, 222–226.

———. The relation of format organization to learning. *Educ. Res. Bull.*, 1958, *37*, 39–45.

Lorge, I. Word lists as background for communication. *Teach. Coll. Rec.*, 1944, *45*, 543–552.

———. *The semantic count of the 570 commonest English words.* New York: Bur. of Pub., Teach. Coll., Columbia Univ., 1949.

MacGinitie, W. H. Discussion of Professor Coleman's paper. In Rothkopf and Johnson (Eds.). *Verbal learning research and the technology of written instruction.* New York: Teach. Coll. Press, Columbia Univ., 1971.

McGinnies, E., Comer, P. B., and Lacey, O. L. Visual recognition thresholds as a function of word length and word frequency. *J. exp. Psychol.*, 1952, *44*, 56–69.

Miller, G. A. The magical number seven, plus or minus two: Some limits on our capacity for processing information. *Psychol. Rev.*, 1956, *63*, 81–97.

Morriss, E. C., and Halverson, D. Idea analysis technique. Unpublished manuscript on file at Columbia Univ. Library, 1938.

Murray, Sir J. A. H. (Ed.). *A new English dictionary on historical principles,* vol. 8. Oxford: The Clarendon Press, 1914.

Paterson, D. G., and Tinker, M. A. *How to make type readable.* New York: Harper & Bros., 1940.

Rubenstein, H., and Aborn, M. Learning, prediction, and readability. *J. appl. Psychol.*, 1958, *42*, 28–32.

Stolurow, L. M., and Newman, J. R. A factorial analysis of objective features of printed language presumably related to reading difficulty. *J. Educ. Res.*, 1959, *52*, 243–251.

Thorndike, E. L. *The teacher's word book.* New York: Bur. of Pub., Teach. Coll., Columbia Univ., 1921.

————. *The teacher's word book of 20,000 words.* New York: Bur. of Pub., Teach. Coll., Columbia Univ., 1932.

Thorndike, E. L., and Lorge, I. *The teacher's word book of 30,000 words.* New York: Bur. of Pub., Teach. Coll., Columbia Univ., 1944.

Tinker, M. A. *Legibility of print.* Ames: Iowa State Univ. Press, 1963.

Zipf, G. K. *The psycho-biology of language.* Boston: Houghton-Mifflin, 1935.

PART III

MOTIVATIONAL AND ATTENTION-LIKE FACTORS

Learner Variables
and Learner Control of Instruction

VINCENT N. CAMPBELL

American Institutes for Research, Palo Alto

All of us have probably hoped at one time or another that some new format of instruction would be a great boon to education. Though manipulating the format is straightforward compared to inferring what is happening in the learner's head, it has been difficult to find any format improvements that are valid for a majority of educational objectives. In applied settings, individual differences and task differences remain the largest sources of variance in learning rate. This has led many of us to look for new kinds of variables, and to study the interactions among environmental, content, and learner variables.

Of all the traits and other variables ascribed to the learner, the evidence to date, and theoretical views described elsewhere (Campbell, 1963b), convince me that two variables account for most of the learner variance: (1) how hard the learner tries, and (2) how meaningful the instructional experience is from moment to moment. Meaningfulness is traditionally ascribed to instructional content, but I ascribe it to the learner because I consider meaning to be a momentary state of mind that may or may not be closely related to concurrent stimulus input. In a given environment meaningfulness varies greatly among learners, and within a learner from time to time. Meaningfulness may not be an important variable in the learning of very specific response chains, but I believe that for the vast majority of educational objectives, which are substantially cognitive, meaningfulness matters greatly. Motivation seems important for all learning tasks. The studies I will summarize examined ways to enhance meaningfulness and/or motivation. All of the studies were oriented toward maximizing the instructional effectiveness in achieving complex educational objectives, especially objectives emphasizing conceptual learning, transfer, and problem solving.

The first studies sought to maintain meaningfulness in a hierarchical learning task by insuring that the learner had mastered each basic step before going on to the next. In programmed instruction of the branching type, the learner's errors are used to evaluate whether he is ready for new objectives, or is faltering and needs a remedial loop of instruction on the same objectives. I did a series of studies (1963a) to evaluate branching, or bypassing, in which the main and final experiment, a self-instructional program on set theory, was prepared in three forms. The bypass form allowed S to skip any remedial loop if his responses to the basic step were correct. The fifteen required basic steps comprised about 15 percent of all the learning material. The long linear form permitted no bypassing, and the short linear form presented only the basic steps. A total of 780 Ss in fourth- to twelfth-grade classrooms were assigned one of the three learning methods and tested the next day on the amount learned. Test-score and learning-time means were highest with the long linear form and lowest with the short linear form. Amount learned and time spent corresponded closely to the number of program pages studied. Thus, bypassing was no more efficient than the linear methods, regardless of mathematical ability level.

It is hard to accept this result as generally valid, even though most other studies of branching have yielded similar results. Wide individual differences in what is known and what is meaningful have been amply demonstrated. There must be a way of adapting instruction to each learner's progress. Why did bypassing fail to do so? With the sets program we covered a lot of new concepts in a very short time. It may be that for concept acquisition, which requires a variety of contiguous concrete experiences (Gagné, 1965), remedial loops helped to enlarge and stabilize concepts, even though S responded correctly to the basic step introducing each concept. That is, studying new examples in the remedial loops may have been meaningful and instructive in acquiring these abstract new concepts, which might not have been true had the loops been repetitious reviews of facts instead.

Then, too, about 20 percent of the time Ss ignored the rules and bypassed after an error, or took the loop after a correct response. A pilot study had indicated that combining self-rated understanding with overt errors as joint criteria for bypassing neither added nor detracted from amount learned, so this lack of conformity to our rules is unlikely to have been important if the cause was S using his own judgment of his progress. However, if interest in the task was the main determiner of bypassing properly, low motivation may have been detrimental to the bypassing method. One way to ensure conformity is to mechanize so that branching is automatic, but this does not prevent the generally devastating effect of low motivation itself on conceptual learning.

LEARNER CONTROL OF INSTRUCTION

It occurred to us that a good general approach both to raising motivation and to adapting to each learner's changing states of mind might be to make the learner feel more responsible for his own instruction; that is, to give him the freedom to use his own judgment, and to provide him with the best alternatives from which to choose that we can think of.

Experts may know more about the subject matter and what conditions favor learning generally. But the learner seems in a better position to judge the meaningfulness of a particular experience because only he knows what he is experiencing. The meaningfulness of any single event is largely an individual matter. Of course, the learner may mistakenly overrate his own understanding as a result of getting the *wrong* meaning. Furthermore, good self-evaluation is not likely to improve learning unless the learner knows appropriate alternative study tactics and chooses among them wisely on the basis of his evaluation.

Even more important, perhaps, is the fact that the learner is always there, physically present in the learning situation where he can continuously monitor his own progress. A private tutor can do this too, perhaps better, perhaps not. Mager's pioneering work on learner control (e.g., Mager and Clark, 1963) indicated that learning was faster, even with a tutor, if the learner was allowed to structure the learning task. Even supposing that a tutor could control one student to advantage, a teacher in charge of twenty-five students cannot get to any one very often. And a programmer or textbook writer is in a far worse position for monitoring progress. In theory a computerized branching program can monitor continuously, but as yet its repertory of cues about student progress and differential responses to these cues is very narrow.

Returning to motivation, people often seem happier when they organize their own plans to pursue their own goals. Pre-school children in particular are eager and enthusiastic learners. Why does this eagerness to learn decrease steadily from year to year in school? It may be partly because students are controlled too closely. Having so little freedom and responsibility perhaps takes the fun out of school. At Summerhill School (Neill, 1960) students study only what they please, when they please, and with a high degree of freedom of expression. Neill claims that the efficiency of intrinsically motivated learning more than makes up for whatever time is spent idly.

In most early studies of self-directed learning and independent study, the learner control variable was not separated from the degree of individualization of instruction. Whitlock, Copeland, and Craig (1963) found that individual, independent study and programmed instruction were equally effective, and that both were superior to regular classroom instruction. In the few other recent studies in which individualization was held constant, learner control was found to be at least as efficient as program or teacher control, and sometimes more efficient. For example, Newman (1957) found that Ss learned the names for electrical symbols better by studying the list of pairs as they pleased than others did by following an instructor-determined sequence intended to optimize learning.

Other studies are reviewed in an article summarizing our own pilot studies on learner control (Campbell, 1964). Our pilot studies, too, suggested that learner control was at least as effective as program control for a few hours of instruction, and perhaps more effective in topics that emphasize problem solving and transfer. In topics requiring verbal memory of specifics or comprehension of discourse, learner control and program control were about equally effective.

The purpose of the following experiment was to see whether giving the learner control might show progressive effects on learning and problem-solving in a given subject matter over a period of several months, perhaps as a result of the student gradually acquiring new skills in evaluating and directing the learning process. The effects that were chiefly of interest were periodic performance during the experimental course indicating conceptual learning and transfer in the subject matter, changes in interest in the subject matter, and attitudes toward self-directed learning.

Our general approach was to compare what seemed to be the most promising integrated instructional package emphasizing learner control with what seemed to be the most effective way of teaching the same thing using substantially greater program control. Each of the two methods was intended to represent a sensible combination of instructional rules and procedures that would be feasible in nearly any school setting.

Procedure

An eight-month course in principles of global geography, which was part of the regular fourth- and fifth-grade curriculum for that school district, was chosen for the experiment because of its emphasis on transfer of principles and problem solving. The course was divided into nine units varying from two to four weeks in length. The early units taught basic principles of water, air, earth, and sun that were applied in later units dealing with life and climate in certain wind belts. The course was held for forty-five minutes each day. Specific objectives of the course were determined, and all tests and learning materials were oriented toward these objectives.

Four matched pairs of fourth- and fifth-grade classes (N = 216) took the experimental course under their regular teachers, who were given special training and assisted by the research staff. In one class of each pair study materials were arranged in an indexed file so that S could organize, evaluate, and direct his own learning. In the other class of each pair, the same total instructional resources were presented to each S as a programmed sequence over which he had little control. A given pair of learner-controlled (LC) and program-controlled (PC) classes were taught by the same two teachers, who alternated between classrooms each week. Both methods allowed the teachers to assist individuals freely. About 25 percent of the geography class time in both LC and PC classes was spent in group activities such as movies, discussions, and games. There were no homework assignments, but frequency of voluntary homework was recorded.

For all Ss the individual learning materials consisted mainly of the following mimeographed components.

1. *Objectives* of the unit were listed not as performances but as principles that concisely stated what Ss needed to understand in order to be able to answer a wide variety of questions and problems. The objectives were listed in what seemed the most logical order to learn them, and lettered A, B, C, etc. Before each objective were listed the letters of prior objectives from the same or an earlier unit that would directly contribute to understanding that objective.

2. *Practice problems* required Ss to apply the basic principles (objectives) in a variety of contexts. Correct answer keys were provided to Ss, and they understood that these problems were similar to and representative of those in the unit criterion tests, but not exactly the same problems.

3. *Short programmed segments,* requiring an average of ten to fifteen minutes to complete, explained as simply as possible the basic concepts or relations of an objective or of part of an objective. These programmed segments called for frequent participation by Ss, usually in the form of written answers or choices

among alternatives, but also including map work and actual experiments with water, air, soil, and heat. Fairly frequently a programmed segment referred Ss to a filmstrip or a reference book. Where Ss were required to respond, feedback took the form of correct answers printed in the margin of the same page, which were covered and revealed by Ss with a cardboard strip. At the end of most programmed segments there was a brief summary calling for two or three responses by Ss to indicate their understanding of the segment as a whole. No correct answers were provided in the summary, so that if Ss were not sure of their answers they were to review the segment.

The form in which the above materials were presented and the procedures for using them defined the difference between the LC and PC methods of instruction.

LEARNER-CONTROL (LC) CLASSES. At the start of each unit each LC S was given an expanding vertical cardboard file containing his mimeographed learning materials. The components described above were color coded. In the back of the file were lists of objectives for that unit and for previous hierarchically related units, a unit glossary, and a study guide that described the kinds of learning materials and tests available, and suggested ideas for planning one's own study. The remaining slots in the file were lettered A to Z, as were the objectives. Thus, for each objective there was a slot in the file that contained practice problems for that objective stapled in a single booklet, and the short programmed segment(s) for that objective, which were called "workbooks." For the later units, some of the practice problems were assembled into larger "practice tests," which each S could take any time he wanted. In addition, general classroom references, maps, and globes were available.

Each S was allowed to use his file of materials in any way he pleased, and all LC Ss were encouraged to think for themselves, to critically evaluate their own progress, and to revise their study tactics accordingly. If one approach was not working, S was to try something different. Teachers answered whatever questions Ss asked but never suggested a definite study plan, except to the extent of reminding them of some of the different resources available.

PROGRAM-CONTROL (PC) CLASSES. The same basic components of instruction were presented to each *S* in the form of a
linear programmed book, the components of which appeared
in the following order:

1. A review of the rules that *S* was to follow in studying the
program.

2. The objectives for the whole unit.

3. A brief review of prior objectives directly related to objective A of this unit.

4. Objective A.

5. The programmed segment(s) for objective A.

6. A few practice problems (1 to 6) on objective A.

7. Numbers 3 to 6 above repeated for objective B and each
objective thereafter.

8. The first few objectives of the unit repeated on a single
page. (Such groups of objectives were formed by dividing the
unit into two to four parts at natural breaking points.)

9. A group of practice problems covering this first group of
objectives.

10. Elements 8 and 9 above for each of the remaining groups
of objectives. The purpose of this segment was to give *S*s practice
at integrating related principles and at searching for the principles relevant to a particular problem.

11. The objectives for the whole unit, preceded by the instruction "Read the following summary once through carefully.
After you finish it you will take a test."

The PC *S*s were required to work straight through the program without skipping ahead, to answer all questions and to
follow all instructions in the program. With books one cannot be
sure that all *S*s do exactly as instructed, but teachers and staff
observed very few departures from the required procedure.

Criterion Measures and Results

A final criterion test was given on the last day of the unit to
all *S*s on each of the nine units of the course. Similar forms of
the test were available for *S*s to take individually earlier, and if
they passed an early test they were free to engage in enrichment
activities until the final test. Enrichment thus served as an in-

centive to reach criterion performance as soon as possible. The passing score required to get enrichment on a given unit was not constant for all *S*s. A fixed passing score would have provided little incentive for *S*s who found it either very easy or practically impossible to achieve. Passing scores were set for each *S* to match approximately (within 10 percent) his achievement on the previous unit. The only other constraint was that the mean passing score required was to be equal for the LC and PC classes of a matched pair on any given unit.

Mean scores on the unit final tests were quite similar for the LC and PC groups, differing by less than 5 percent on every unit. The LC group means were initially slightly lower but gradually gained (p < .01) during the eight months, although the trend was barely discernible, as can be seen in figure 1. The absolute level of performance (60 percent to 77 percent correct) for both groups was considered quite satisfactory in view of the difficulty of the criterion problems.

It may be argued reasonably that by equating the mean passing scores needed to get enrichment for the LC and PC groups, we experimentally prevented larger differences between the two groups in unit test means. Even if this is true, the greater efficiency of either learning method should then be revealed by differences in the mean length of time required for *S*s to pass a criterion test. But such differences were negligible according to our two indices of how fast each group approached criterion

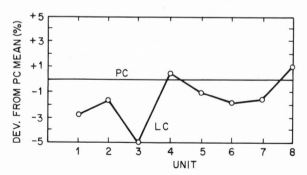

Fig. 1. LC group means on form III unit test scores (%) expressed as deviations from PC group means.

performance. One index was the percentage of Ss who passed any form of the criterion test. The other index was the number of days each S spent on a unit before passing a criterion test.

There was a marked and consistent difference ($p < .001$) between LC and PC groups in the frequency of voluntary homework. Figure 2 shows the difference in terms of the mean percentage of days on which an S took work home for the sequence of eight units. The PC Ss took work home about twice as often during the first half of the course, but the difference diminished during the last half of the course. If homework time could be added to study time, the LC group might appear to learn more efficiently by having achieved the same level of test performance after less studying. However, there was no measure of number of hours spent studying at home, and no basis for determining how substantial an effect homework had on test performance.

In addition to the unit tests, three other criterion tests confirmed the almost equivalent performance of the LC and PC groups. One was a brief general geography test given just before and after the course, on which both groups gained about 36 percent on the nonchance test score scale. Another was a one-hour test covering the whole course that was given about five months after the course ended. Parts of the test differentiated the skills of remembering principles, applying principles, locating relevant principles, and combinations of these skills. There

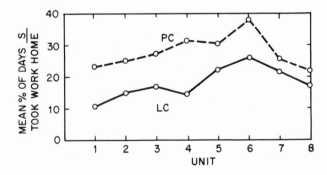

Fig. 2. Mean % of days on each unit on which work was taken home under LC and PC methods.

was no appreciable difference between groups on any part of the test.

The ninth and final unit of the course was a test unit on which both LC and PC classes were given the same treatment; that is, both were given a less structured set of learning materials, including practice problems and a list of objectives. All Ss could organize and study the materials in any way they pleased. Thus, it was a learner-controlled situation, but somewhat different from the LC method of the first eight units. On this unit any broad generalizable skills of self-direction acquired by LC Ss during the first eight units should have been revealed. But the final test means on this unit were nearly identical for the LC and PC groups. If any self-directing skills were acquired by the LC Ss they may have been rather specific to the format in which the first eight units were cast. Examination of other criteria of performance on the ninth unit corroborated the test score results.

CHANGES IN MOTIVATION. Two attitudinal measures were derived from a questionnaire given before and again near the end of the course: interest in learning about geography, and preference for directing one's own study rather than depending on the teacher to do it. On both of these variables the LC Ss gained significantly more ($p < .05$) between pre- and post-testing than did the PC Ss. The LC group showed a mean increase in interest in geography, while the PC group showed a slight mean decrease in interest in geography. Both groups gained in preference for self-direction, but the LC group gained significantly more than the PC group.

The finding that giving learners more control gave them a taste for more control, as well as a greater interest in the topic, suggests that learner control might in the long run enhance learning by better maintaining motivation to learn. However, projecting into the future the gradual gain in test performance of the LC group relative to the PC group (figure 1), it might be years before there was an important difference. Then, too, no longer-term gain would be expected if the LC group's gradual gain was caused by the diminishing difference between groups in frequency of voluntary homework (figure 2). Changes in homework and in interest are both more plausible explanations of the gradual LC gain than is the growth of self-direction skills, in view of the findings of equivalent performance on the unstructured final unit in which both LC and PC groups were highly self-directed. Perhaps acquisition of broadly useful skills such as planning, organizing, and searching that generalize to many new situations requires more individual coaching than was available to our Ss; and perhaps it requires a more variable set of learning resources and conditions, such as might be provided by learner control of the whole curriculum for many years, rather than by a single course that has uniform conditions of control.

Considering that the LC and PC methods were about equally effective on the achievement criteria, it may be that the conditions common to the two treatments were more important than the conditions that differentiated them. That is, for both groups the objectives were clearly identified and the hierarchical relations among them were explicitly shown. The elements of instruction were carefully prepared and linked with their proper objectives. Practice problems and program responses provided ample opportunity for all Ss to evaluate their own progress. If their progress did not satisfy them they could restudy completed materials or seek help from teachers and parents. These commonalities may have mattered more than who controlled the decisions as to how to use the various printed components of instruction.

On the other hand, control of the learning process may be important, too. Equivalent performance can mean that the independent variables do not matter, but it can also mean that the two learning methods compared were evenly balanced with regard to good and bad features.

I suggest that what is needed is not any fixed level of learner control, but rather a decision system that allocates some decisions to the student, some decisions to the teacher, and perhaps makes some decisions automatically. The system would be constructed on the basis of research (not yet done) indicating which kinds of decisions are made best by which decision-makers. For example, in the teaching of a concept it might work out that the learner decides best whether a given illustration has been meaningfully presented, that the teacher can best diagnose a learner's particular misunderstanding and try to remedy it, and that a computer program can decide best how many illustrations a certain learner needs in order to master the concept (perhaps by comparing his performance to the performance of previous learners). Of course, the decision-allocating system might need to be changed from time to time as teachers are trained differently, students learn better study skills, and computerized control systems improve.

I have the impression that freedom to choose one's own learning objectives is a lot more motivating than freedom to decide only *how* one will reach the objectives. In our experiments Ss had no choice in *what* they were to learn, only in how they would go about it. The course's specific objectives were ours, not the students'. Choosing one's own goals may well be a key factor in augmenting learning through learner control. Giving each student a say in the choice of objectives is an important feature of a computer-based educational center that we are planning.

Letting each learner choose what to learn creates a problem for educational researchers, of course. It is difficult to compare the learning rates of students who have different learning objectives. But that is largely a limitation of our present professional mode of single experiments, each having unique learning objectives and criterion tests. I think the time is coming when carefully developed learning objectives and their corresponding criterion tests will be accessible in standard form throughout the country, so that effectiveness of learning procedures can be compared by retrieving the performance data accumulated by other researchers and schools where students have chosen the same objectives and taken the same tests. Such standard objectives and tests would be periodically updated, of course, but there would be enough stability over time to permit comparison and evaluation of educational methods.

In order to assess the progress of American education, instruments are being prepared to measure the achievement by large sociological groups of those specific objectives that scholars, educators, and thoughtful laymen agree are important (Tyler, 1966). Part of our contribution to this effort has been to prepare

objectives and measures in the field of citizenship (Campbell and
Nichols, 1968). The rather high degree of consensus we have
achieved as to what objectives are most important in the con-
troversial area of citizenship is quite encouraging for the future
prospect of making available to researchers and schools sets of
objectives in all areas of achievement from which teachers and
students could choose to serve nearly all their educational needs.

LEARNER VARIABLES IN RELATION TO RESPONSE MODE AND FEEDBACK VARIABLES IN PROGRAMMED INSTRUCTION

A good deal of research has been done in comparing response
modes, or feedback conditions, in programmed instruction. The
results have varied, but in general no clear advantage has been
shown for a particular response mode or type of feedback. Various recent projects at the American Institutes for Research,
Palo Alto, have sought orderly explanation by relating response
and feedback variables to characteristics of the learners and to
the detailed process of learning.

Lloyd Brooks has constructed an apparatus that records the
time interval between stimulus and response, time spent writing,
and time spent studying feedback for programmed instructional
materials. Among his findings are that in using Holland and
Skinner's *The Analysis of Behavior* (1961), the time spent in the
actual mechanics of writing out answers to some early portions
of this program was about 40 percent of total learning time.
Subtracting this writing time out, Ss who wrote out answers
spent about the same amount of time reading and thinking as
did Ss who did not write their answers. However, "writers"
spent proportionately more time on difficult frames and less
time on easy ones than did "thinkers." Such adjustment of study
time to difficulty seems like a good thing, especially in view of a
finding by Hamilton and Brooks (1965), with another program,
that reviewing frames having long latencies increased post-test
performance more than reviewing frames having short latencies.
Achievement with the Holland and Skinner program was higher
for writers than for thinkers, but other advantageous response

modes are to be sought that avoid a 40 percent increase in learn-ing time (Brooks, 1965, 1966).

Interpreting the response mode results in terms of processes within the learner, and an advantage of *S* having to commit himself to an answer may be that the greater ego involvement helps maintain attention for the otherwise poorly motivated learner. On the other hand, the set for writing answers may focus *S*'s attention on the first answer that crosses threshold rather than on a relevant thought.

Another question concerning public commitment to written answers is whether the testlike atmosphere can produce anxiety to a disrupting degree in some highly motivated learners. There is evidence from a recent study by Peggie Campeau (1965) that immediate feedback may somewhat allay the test anxiety asso-ciated with write-in programs. She found that anxious girls learned more from a write-in program if answers were supplied immediately, while nonanxious girls did as well with no feed-back. No such interaction was found with boys.

Another study, by Nancy Hamilton (1965), revealed a new twist in interactions between ability of the learner and learning method. It was a study of programmed response mode in initial learning and review. The response modes were "writing" and "just reading." She found that with general learning materials (as opposed to paired-associates), high-ability learners did as well with a reading-only mode throughout, whereas low-ability *S*s learned very little by any mode. By contrast, medium-ability *S*s learned more if the response mode during review was different from that during initial learning. Order did not matter; writing-then-reading and reading-then-writing were both superior to writing throughout or reading throughout.

LEARNING SKILL REPERTORIES

I would like to end this description of our work with learner variables by suggesting that something may be gained by ascrib-ing to the school-age or adult learner a repertory of learning skills with varying probabilities being elicited by any given learn-ing situation. Skills such as holding in mind simultaneously two or three key elements in a problem or principle; searching for relevant information in one's memory or in the environment; avoiding distractions; adapting reading rate to depth, complexity of unfamiliarity of the ideas; testing hypotheses; and so on. What makes one learner more able than another may be a larger repertory of skills to draw on, keener development of each skill, or a better strategy for selecting skills appropriate to each part of the learning task.

The effectiveness of a learning method may depend mainly on whether the learning skills it tends to elicit from S are appropriate to the objective of the moment. Our finding that giving the learner maximum control over study method is at least as effective as whatever fixed program we tried could be interpreted in this framework as follows: Our well-intentioned fixed program may elicit some appropriate learning skills, but just as often it prevents the learner from drawing on his full repertory of skills by telling him to do X when his own skill-selecting strategy evolved through years of learning suggests that the best tactic at the moment is Y or Z.

What seem to be needed are not so much rules for programming learning in general, but strategies (be they the learner's, the educational planner's, or both) which adapt learning conditions to kinds of learning objectives. Gagné (1965) has attempted a comprehensive framework of this sort, and two other recent projects represent effort in this direction. Briggs (1965, 1967) outlined methods for analyzing objectives in order to prescribe combinations of instructional media and optimal sequencing. Markle (1967) constructed a training course in first aid in which the medium of instruction was designed to match the type of objective, and the amount and content of instruction were empirically modified on the basis of the performance of learners from the target population, on whom materials and tests were tried continually throughout the development process.

REFERENCES

Briggs, L. J. *Sequencing of instruction in relation to hierarchies of competence.* Palo Alto: American Institutes for Research (AIR-G3-10/67-FR), 1967.

Briggs, L. J., Campeau, P., Gagné, R., and May, M. *Instructional media: A procedure for the design of multi-media instruction, a critical review of research, and suggestions for future research.* Palo Alto: American Institutes for Research (AIR-E57-10/65-FR), 1965.

Brooks, L. *Shaping faster question answering.* Palo Alto: American Institutes for Research (AIR-C28-6/65-TR), 1965.

————. Personal communication, 1966.

Campbell, V. Bypassing as a way of adapting self-instruction programs to individual differences. *J. educ. Psychol.,* 1963a, *54*, 337–345.

————. *Learning: From R-M theory to educational planning.* Palo Alto: American Institutes for Research (AIR-D10-11/63-TRb), 1963b.

————. Self-direction and programed instruction for five different types of learning objectives. *Psychol. in the Sch.,* 1964, *1*, 348–359.

Campbell, V., and Nichols, D. National assessment of citizenship education. *Social Education,* March, 1968, *32*, no. 3, 279–281.

Campeau, P. *Level of anxiety and presence or absence of feedback in programed instruction.* Palo Alto: American Institutes for Research (AIR-D96-2/65-FR), 1965.

Gagné, R. M. *The conditions of learning.* New York: Holt, Rinehart & Winston, 1965.

Hamilton, N. R. *Increasing long-term retention of knowledge: Experiment 1.* Palo Alto: American Institutes for Research (AIR-D49-7/65-SR [1]), 1965.

Hamilton, N. R., and Brooks, L. O. Personal communication, 1965.

Holland, J. G., and Skinner, B. F. *The analysis of behavior.* New York: McGraw-Hill, 1961.

Mager, R., and Clark, C. Explorations in student-controlled instruction. *Psychol. Rep.,* 1963, *13*, 71–76.

Markle, D. G. *Development of a first aid training course.* Palo Alto: American Institutes for Research (AIR-E81-4/67-FR), 1967.

Neill, A. S. *Summerhill.* New York: Hart, 1960.

Newman, S. E. Student vs. instructor design of study method. *J. educ. Psychol.,* 1957, *48*, 328–333.

Tyler, R. W. Let's clear the air on assessing education. *Nation's Schools,* 1966, *77*, 68–70.

Whitlock, G., Copeland, L., and Craig, A. Programming vs. independent study in learning elementary statistics. *Psychol. Rep.,* 1963, *12*, 171–174.

Discussion of Professor Campbell's Paper

H. W. GUSTAFSON

Bell Telephone Laboratories

It is easy to see from Campbell's survey of recent and ongoing research why A.I.R. enjoys the reputation of a leading contributor to the state of the art in programmed instruction. Time obviously will not allow detailed examination of all the studies mentioned; consequently, I shall limit my comments to the two investigations described in the main body of the paper: the experiments dealing with bypassing and learner control of instruction.

In abbreviated form, my interpretation of these two studies runs as follows. Campbell twice experimented with nonlinear methods of self-instruction and found them no more effective or efficient than linear programs covering the same content. In principle, however, one would have expected the nonlinear approaches to show up more favorably, either because they ought to have proved inherently more motivating or because, ostensibly, they were adaptive to individual differences and, therefore, should have made the instruction more meaningful. It is the increased motivation or meaningfulness, or both, that presumably should have resulted in better performance.

The focal question, it seems to me, is why this did not happen. There must be a faulty link in the argument somewhere. Either the nonlinear techniques failed to improve motivation; or they were not adaptive to individual differences; or adaptivity did not yield greater meaningfulness; or enhanced motivation and meaningfulness did not pay off in achievement; or, finally, either the data are defective, or have been erroneously evaluated.

Assuming that Campbell's powers of analysis are, like those of the rest of us, fallible on occasion, it is not improbable that some sort of case could be made on every one of the foregoing counts. I am somewhat dubious, for one thing, about the conceptual link between adaptivity and increased meaningfulness. In the bypassing study, particularly, it is not at all apparent why we should expect the branching version of the program to be more meaningful than the long linear version. Why should a learner find it less meaningful to see all the remedial loops than to see only part of them? Taken at face value, the data would seem to suggest the contrary, as Campbell acknowledges. This is not to disavow the existence of a fundamental relationship between adaptivity and meaningfulness, but in the present instance the connection is operationally obscure, and I would have preferred to hear it spelled out in further detail.

In any case, the issue I want to pursue is not that one, but rather the presumption that the nonlinear methods were adaptive to individual differences. The methods may have been adaptive, but there are reasons, I believe, to suspect that they were not. In developing this thesis, I should like to look first at the bypassing study.

THE ROLE OF DIAGNOSTIC TESTS IN BRANCHING PROGRAMS

The key to the efficiency of any bypassing program—and of branching programs generally—is the set of diagnostic tests used to control the branching process. The ideal diagnostic test at any branching node is one just barely difficult enough to guarantee that the student adequately comprehends the material to which the test pertains. (The modifier "adequately" is used advisedly; I shall return to this below.) If the difficulty of the test is increased a single j.n.d. beyond this optimum level, the learner is likely to be subjected to remedial instruction he does not need and thereby take more time to complete the program than he should. If, on the other hand, the test is made too easy, the student is likely to move ahead to new material before he is prepared, thus finishing the program faster but learning less than he otherwise would. In either situation the bypassing procedure is not adaptive to the needs of the individual and may be even maladaptive.

In the event the diagnostic tests have the wrong difficulty for a given student, the *degree* of adaptivity, or maladaptivity, will be determined primarily by the quality of the mainstream instruction [1] (if any) that leads up to the tests. From the standpoint of final performance, the worst combination would be bad mainstream instruction followed by easy tests. Here the student might always require remedial teaching but never get it. With respect to study time, the opposite combination would be least productive (i.e., good mainstream instruction followed by excessively hard tests). Here the learner might always be forced through remedial material needlessly. A mixture of bad mainstream instruction with easy tests and good instruction with difficult tests can readily eventuate in a bypassing program both less effective and less efficient than the same program without branching.

For the sake of emphasis, let me restate this idea slightly differently. I am saying that contrary to common belief, it is not invariably advisable for a student to branch to a remedial sequence when he fails a diagnostic test or to skip the remedial sequence when he passes the test. It depends on the test. If the test is easy and the student fails it, remedial instruction is plainly appropriate. But if the test is hard — harder than necessary to demonstrate adequate comprehension of the subject matter — failure may or may not indicate a need for remediation. Conversely, the passing of an excessively easy test does not ensure that the learner has understood. Hence, bypassing may or may not be the suitable action to take. Furthermore, the difficulty level of a diagnostic test interacts perversely with the quality of the associated mainstream instruction. A test of inappropriate difficulty cannot under any circumstances provide accurate diagnosis, but the ill effects of incorrect diagnosis can be either mitigated or exacerbated by the instruction that precedes it.

I submit that the unspectacular performance of Campbell's bypassing program—and of branching programs historically—is owed in all likelihood to diagnostic questions of inappropriate difficulty, possibly coupled with mainstream instruction of inappropriate quality. Additional experimentation with the course is indicated where the diagnostic tests and mainstream instruction are systematically manipulated in an effort to maximize program adaptivity. The development of an empirical procedure for increasing program adaptivity through successive course revisions would constitute a significant contribution to the technology of instruction.

Predictive Validity

The notions of test difficulty and quality of instruction, as applied to branching programs, are much more complicated than I may have made them sound. An extensive treatment of these concepts would be out of order, but a word or two of clarification seems mandatory.

What I mean by the "difficulty" of a diagnostic test is not merely the fraction of students passing the test, but a subtler psychometric property that is best understood and defined in terms of predictive validity. In an ideal branching program, each diagnostic test would be a perfect predictor of that subset of terminal performance purportedly fostered by the instructional material immediately related to the test. *Ipso facto,* any test possessing this characteristic must possess precisely the correct difficulty, regardless of the exact sense in which the latter term is taken. Perfect prediction, in short, implies a perfect level of difficulty. Thus, the concept of predictive validity subsumes the concept of test difficulty intended herein and, more to the point, strikes all the way to the theoretical heart of the matter. In the majority of practical applications, however, it is not feasible to make a direct attack on the measurement of predictive validity. Very often the only workable tactic is to juggle the "difficulties" of the diagnostic tests (as determined, in classical fashion, by the proportion of students passing) while trusting to the validity of the tests on the basis of item content.[2]

The empirical assessment of predictive validity is impeded, in practice, by several obstacles, the most formidable of which is a general inability to break the terminal performance of the learner into separately measurable portions associated one to one with individual sections of the instructional program. Except in the dullest of subject matters, mappings from instructional text to criterion examination are rarely one to one, but many to many. Each segment of instruction usually helps to foster many elements of terminal performance, and each element of end performance in turn is shaped by many instructional segments. As long as this condition holds, it is hard to concoct a reasonable procedure for evaluating the predictive validity of any single diagnostic test.

Other Methodological Problems

Another awkward problem is that both the predictive validity of a diagnostic test and the quality of the mainstream instruction preceding it are likely to vary as a function of the path the individual learner takes in getting there. In general, each student arriving at a given step in a branching program has been prepared for the step in a manner different from all other students. This would not matter in the case of a completely adaptive program, but in real life it undoubtedly does matter, and any satisfactory formulation of the concepts of predictive validity and instructional quality must somehow take account of the problem.

Predictive validity and instructional quality also will vary as a function of the instructional objectives and the standards imposed as to what constitutes adequate achievement. If the same program is used in both the fourth grade and the twelfth grade, as in Campbell's study, we can scarcely hope to obtain the same level of final performance from the two populations. This is what I was getting at earlier in saying that the diagnostic tests should be just difficult enough to assure us that the student "adequately" comprehends. In most subjects, clearly, an adequate level of comprehension for a fourth-grader would hardly be adequate for a senior in high school. It follows that if different target populations are anticipated, then different sets of diagnostic tests are necessary. And if different diagnostic questions are employed, the mainstream instruction probably ought to be different, too.

According to Campbell's report (1963) on bypassing, his branching program actually had adverse effects on performance when administered to pupils in the fourth and sixth grades. The fourth- and sixth-graders who took the bypass version apparently learned less than if they had studied an ordinary linear program for the same length of time. My guess is that they found most of the diagnostic questions excessively hard and were frequently branched into remedial loops that, in view of the limited capacity of these students to master the subject matter, added nothing to their understanding. If the diagnostic questions had been easier and the pupils had bypassed more of the remedial loops, I suspect they would have learned just as much — which is to say, practically nothing — but would have done so in considerably less time.

Before leaving the topic of diagnostic tests, one more methodological problem should be mentioned which, though recognized by Campbell, is sometimes overlooked. We want the diagnostic questions in a branching program to have the property that if a student gets them right, he is certain, within errors of measurement, to perform adequately on the criterion examination. This does not imply, however, that performance on the diagnostic tests should be correlated highly with achievement on the criterion examination. For whenever a student fails a diagnostic test he receives remedial instruction that, hopefully, equips him just as well for the criterion examination as his fellow learner who bypasses. As noted by Shettel, Clapp, and Klaus (1963), if the remedial loops and the diagnostic questions are perfect, the post-training correlation between diagnostic tests and criterion examination should be effectively zero. In an experimental design like Campbell's, therefore, the diagnostic tests should correlate highly with the criterion examination only in the case of those students who take the short linear program lacking remedial loops. This correlation then becomes an approximate

index of predictive validity. As for the long linear version of the
program, I do not know what magnitude of correlation ought to
be anticipated and, doubt, moreover, whether existing test
theory could help us much in making a prediction.

Elsewhere, Campbell (1963) reports correlations of about .50
for the short linear program (for the eighth, tenth, and twelfth
grades) and says these indicated a "substantial" degree of validity. The coefficients are computed between total score on all
diagnostic tests and total criterion score. I hate to quarrel over
an adjective, but it seems clear that predictive validities of .50,
if substantial, are not substantial enough to provide a sound
basis for controlling the branching process, since a predictive
validity of .50 can readily yield incorrect diagnosis in 25 percent
of the cases. To be sure, the coefficients cited by Campbell are
at best rough estimates of the "true" predictive validities of the
individual diagnostic tests, but the data offer no grounds between the diagnostic and criterion tests for believing that the
true individual validities would be any higher.

In summary, it takes good diagnostic tests to make a branching program adaptive to individual differences. But the concept
of test goodness is complex and operationally elusive. By blend-
ing test theory with instructional research more intimately than
heretofore, the study of branching methods has unintentionally
opened up a challenging and almost wholly unexplored domain
of psychometric inquiry. Until some light is cast on that domain,
I see little chance of progress in understanding how branching
programs work.

LEARNER CONTROL OF INSTRUCTION

Turning from the bypassing study, I should like now to introduce two questions about the second of Campbell's investigations, the one comparing a linear program with learner-
controlled instruction. The first question has to do with the
mechanism underlying the differential change in attitude between control and experimental groups. Did this difference
arise out of differential behavior by the two groups during the
learning process, or from mental and emotional effects that may
be attributed to the feeling that one is, or is not, master of his

own fate? In other words, do the data tell us that attitudes can be altered as a function of the way instructional sequences are arranged, or is the observed result a consequence of giving the self-guided learner a feeling of increased responsibility?

I raise this question not only because the substantive issue is important, but also to point up the fact that the paper furnishes little information regarding the patterns of learning behavior evidenced by the members of the experimental group. From the data presented we do not know how the learning strategies of the students differed under the two instructional treatments, or, apart from the relative frequency of voluntary homework, even that they did differ in any significant way. The students working under self-direction had access to the same learning resources supplied in the linear program, and it is conceivable that many self-directed learners adopted strategies equivalent or identical to those in the linear program. One would be led to conclude, if this were the case, that the differential attitude change was owed chiefly to affective influences.

Whatever may have produced the attitude difference, we are more or less compelled to assume that the finding reflects superior motivation on the part of the experimental group. Yet this better-motivated group performed no more proficiently than the rest of the students. This seems a trifle startling and leads directly to the second question: Why not?

The answer proffered will come as no surprise. I think it likely that the learner-controlled approach, as compared to the linear program, was on the whole maladaptive to individual differences. That is, the learning strategy elected by the average individual in the experimental group was probably less effective than the linear program would have been. If this is true, the maladaptivity of learner control could well have canceled out any advantage deriving from superior motivation.

The preceding conjecture is predicated on some admittedly free-ranging speculation concerning the observed differential frequency of voluntary homework. My guess is that the students taking the linear program quickly perceived the volume of labor that lay before them and realized they could not complete the course on schedule without doing homework. (Besides eliciting more homework, incidentally, this perception may have placed the control group under feelings of pressure that they found distasteful. If so, their loss of interest in geography accompanied by increased preference for self-direction would be readily understandable.) The experimental group, on the other hand, not seeing a clearly delineated path of study ahead, may have been slower to recognize the necessity for homework, and for the less able students, at any rate, this would have made the method of self-direction maladaptive.

This line of thought is conjectural, as I said, and need not be taken too seriously. It does serve, nevertheless, to illustrate my thesis, namely, that nonlinear instruction, whether implemented by branching or by learner control, can be just as easily maladaptive as adaptive. There is no *a priori* reason to suppose that nonlinear approaches to teaching, merely because they are nonlinear, are likely to accommodate themselves to individual differences. However, both of Campbell's experiments appear strongly flavored with the opposite assumption, and I cannot help but regard this as a damaging conceptual flaw.

CONCLUSIONS

In view of the possibility that the techniques of bypassing and learner control both were maladaptive, we cannot with any degree of assurance ascribe the findings of either study to particular causes. Consequently, although the data are in many ways suggestive, the results are inconclusive and, in my opinion, frankly, not terribly informative. I infer, moreover, that Campbell must concur in this assessment, in light of his imaginative leap from a generally negative outcome to the conclusion that an even greater amount of learner control is desirable.

The only way to acquire insight into the effects of nonlinear instructional methods is, evidently, to catalogue and analyze the specific learning behavior of individual students exposed to such approaches. This demands that in the future we obtain longitudinal case histories and scrutinize the data with a far more watchful eye to individual differences than we have exhibited in the past. I envision more intensive application of clinical forms of analysis to individual data, coupled with more widespread utilization of statistical methods for group data along the lines of Q-techniques and multiple regression. An interesting example of the latter kind of analysis using multiple correlation has appeared in connection with a study of self-directed learning involving the identification of computer-generated sounds (Swets *et al.*, 1966). Despite the fact that concern for individual differences is distinctly alien to the modern tradition of experimental psychology, I am convinced that psychologists have no alternative if they want to play a part in advancing the technology of adaptive programming.

In closing, I ought at least to pay lip service to a request by our symposium director that the discussants of "practical" papers try to relate their remarks to "the best current knowledge of verbal learning processes." As things stand, however, the black art of adaptive programming seems so far removed from the refined science of verbal learning that if there is a connection between the two, it regrettably escapes me. Perhaps someone else can clarify the relationship.

NOTES

1. The mainstream is the common core of instruction received by all students, regardless of branching. In Campbell's program the mainstream consisted of the fifteen basic steps.

2. At the time of the symposium I avoided the term "predictive validity" and instead tried to rely exclusively on "test difficulty." This led inevitably to misunderstanding, so I subsequently added the present section and also changed the terminology in several places later on. In talking about the tests in branching programs, I like the coined word "diagnostivity" better than "predictive validity," but have not ventured to employ it here.

REFERENCES

Campbell, V. N. Bypassing as a way of adapting self-instruction programs to individual differences. *J. educ. Psychol.*, 1963, *54*, 337–345.

Shettel, H. H., Clapp, D. J., and Klaus, D. J. *The application of a by-pass technique to programmed instruction for managerial training.* Pittsburgh: American Institutes for Research (AIR-C74-7/63-FR), July, 1963.

Swets, J. A., Harris, J. R., McElroy, L. S., and Rudloe, H. Computer-aided instruction in perceptual identification. *Behav. Sci.*, 1966, *11*, 98–104.

Experiments on Mathemagenic Behavior and the Technology of Written Instruction

ERNST Z. ROTHKOPF

Bell Telephone Laboratories

I want to review in brief a conceptual framework that has evolved in our laboratory. It is a conception of how people learn from written material, whether it be connected discourse printed in a book or nonsense syllables typed on the tape of a memory drum. This conceptual framework has been described elsewhere (Rothkopf, 1963, 1965). I will therefore limit myself here to a brief discussion of its character. I also hope to describe results from some of the research that has been stimulated by the conceptual model.

TWO-PROCESS MODEL OF LEARNING

The conceptual framework that we have been using assumes that learning from written material has to be understood in terms of *two* distinct processes. The first of these comprises inspection and study activities on the part of the subject. I have also called these "mathemagenic behaviors" (Rothkopf, 1965). The second process is substantive learning, i.e., the acquisition of subject-matter skills. The manner in which the first process takes place determines the course of the second process. Mathemagenic behaviors play a critically important role in determining what substantive matter can be learned.

The nature of the dependency of substantive learning on mathemagenic behavior can be understood in terms of the distinction between nominal and effective stimulation (see Underwood, 1963; Rothkopf, 1957). The nominal stimuli include the written letters, words, and sentences that confront the student. Effective stimuli are the actual results of this confrontation. Substantive learning is determined (or at least limited) by the nature of effective stimulation. Effective stimulation, in turn, depends critically on the character of mathemagenic behaviors because mathemagenic behaviors essentially involve the translation of nominal into effective stimuli. The need for some translation from the nominal written stimulus display to effective stimulation such as perhaps subvocal speech is quite obvious in a theoretical account of how humans learn from written material. It is clear that it is not possible to learn anything educationally important from a written passage without some sort of activity on the part of the subject. Students must "study." They must "read."

In the folk myths of schooling, accounts of study activities are commonly couched in motivational terms or in terms of incentives. It is also frequently believed that these dispositions to study are relatively stable characteristics of the student. In the conceptual framework that I am describing, mathemagenic behaviors are viewed largely as habit systems that can be readily altered by environmental events.

It is assumed that mathemagenic behaviors can be and are constantly modified during "study" by learning and other processes. An important hypothesis in this connection is that learned changes in mathemagenic behaviors are governed by fundamental mechanics that are different from substantive learning. Substantive learning resembles classical conditioning; learned changes in mathemagenic behavior bear some resemblance to instrumental conditioning.

Mathemagenic behaviors have attributes such as stimulus control, topography, and persistence. Each of these attributes are modifiable by environmental events, i.e., mathemagenic behaviors include instrumental responses that are shaped by contingencies of the study situation. Learned changes in mathe-

magenic behaviors bring about different modes of translation of
the nominal stimuli and hence different patterns of effective
stimulation. Since the effective stimuli determine what can be
learned, the reshaping of mathemagenic behaviors brings about
changes in the character of substantive learning.

Substantive learning, on the other hand, resembles the classical conditioning paradigm, at least in the sense that temporal
contiguity among terms is a necessary and perhaps sufficient
condition for learning associations among these terms. Please
note that I am not concerned, at present, with whether this
conception of substantive verbal learning provides an adequate
account of how humans talk or understand, whatever that may
mean. Rather, I am only assuming that contiguity is necessary
for certain interesting learned performance changes to occur.
The classical conditioning situation provides a useful metaphor
because it is plausible to think of each of the printed or written
letters or words as "previously conditioned" stimuli which play
the same role as *unconditioned stimuli* in the classical conditioning
experiment (see Rothkopf, 1963). When a suitable translation
takes place, the written materials induce a chain of internal
responding that, in turn, may be a sufficient condition for substantive learning. The mathemagenic behaviors determine the
nature of the translation. Therefore, they determine the nature
of the chain of internal responding and what is learned. (It
should be noted that the resemblances between verbal learning and classical conditioning processes has been pointed out
before, e.g., Cook and Kendler, 1956.)

REPETITION INTERVAL DATA

The present analysis of human learning into two distinct but
interdependent processes departs from current thought on
verbal learning mainly in greater emphasis on the importance
of S's activities during study. Historically, these activities became
of particular interest to me during some work on the effect of
repetition of paired associates that were presented within well-
formed English sentences (Rothkopf and Coke, 1963, 1966).
We found that a given sentence presented exactly two times in

immediate succession produced much lower performance on a subsequent retention test than two presentations with other sentences interposed between the two exposures. Similar observations had also been reported by Greeno (1964).

One interpretation of the dependence of learning on the spacing between two repetitions is a kind of mental chemistry. This type of account, to use a crude metaphor, treats a trial as if it produced some kind of deposit. Two trials, in quick succession, leave less deposit behind than two more widely spaced practice events. An example of this view can be seen in a paper by Estes (1955). It appears to be assumed in theories of this kind that learning is the inescapable consequence of bombardment by environmental particles, and that stimulus specifications are all important predictors, not of what *can* be learned, but of what *will* be learned.

We chose, instead, to interpret the repetition data in terms of the attentive activities on the part of the subjects. This interpretation was prompted by the observation that the depressing effect of immediate repetition on any associated pair was more pronounced if *all* the items in the experimental list were repeated immediately than if only some were. The experimental facts were consistent with the view that subjects learned not only about our experimental sentences (i.e., substantive learning), but also that a second kind of learning took place in which the inspection activities of the Ss were shaped by the practice procedures.

The differences between immediate and delayed repetition were found to be particularly strong when the second presentation consisted of a testlike event, e.g., when the required response term was predictable at the time of the initial presentation of the sentence. This could be interpreted to mean that the experimental procedure was disposing the subject to respond from immediate memory during the testlike event. In our experimental context this meant shaping Ss to rely on cues that were not consistent with the training objectives. Consequently, in the post-training test, Ss found that they hadn't learned what was required for high performance.

The evidence from the experiment on repetition interval

indicated that *Ss'* activities during study were quite important in determining what substantive learning took place.

Because I am a little frivolous, I called the study activities in which the subject was engaged during practice *mathemagenic behavior*. It was a useful word to invent. It avoided circumlocutions and made it easier to stress the distinction between learned changes in study behavior, on the one hand, and the learning that resulted from study on the other. *Mathemagenic* is a handy adjective. It comes from the Greek words *mathemain*, "that which is learned" and *gineisthos*, "to be born." Mathemagenic behavior is behavior that gives birth to learning. I have also used the term "inspection behavior" (Rothkopf, 1963) to refer to mathemagenic activities.

In light of the insights gained during our work on repetition interval (Rothkopf and Coke, 1963, 1966), we came to believe that the most important research task was to gain some understanding of the factors that control mathemagenic behavior. In view of the weak measurement techniques that were available, this seemed a difficult objective. But it promised insights into the human learning process which were likely to bear on practical problems in instruction. If we understood how to maintain effective mathemagenic behaviors, substantial student achievement could be attainable, even with badly designed experimental materials.

MATHEMAGENIC BEHAVIOR AND TESTLIKE EVENTS

One of the first factors that suggested itself as an important determinant for mathemagenic behaviors was the character of testlike events. There were several reasons for this interest. Testlike events are probably the most common form of intercourse between teacher and student; they are also a prominent feature of programmed instruction. The anticipation method which has been extensively studied in the verbal learning laboratory is a testlike event, and so is the test phase of the method of simultaneous presentation, i.e., the stimulated recall method.

We therefore conducted a series of interrelated experiments

on the effects of testlike events on mathemagenic behaviors. Some of these have been reported before. I want to summarize some of the results we have obtained because they provided the major empirical source for my conjectures about the character of mathemagenic activities.

General Method

In these experiments *Ss* were asked to study a very long prose passage (5,000 to 9,000 words). Throughout the experimental passage, at regular intervals, we interspersed questions and observed whether these questions affected mathemagenic behavior.

Here are some more details about the experimental procedure. On being seated in the experimental chamber, *S* was given a loose-leaf notebook. This notebook contained all the materials that *S* needed for the experiment, except for the criterion test by which we measured what he learned. General directions about the experiment, specific directions about what *S* was to do at various phases of the experiment, the experimental text, and the experimental questions were all contained within this loose-leaf binder. A large digital clock was on display in the experimental chamber so *S* could record the time he started and finished each page. A sketch of the experimental question–feedback arrangement is shown in figure 1. The questions, printed on distinctively colored pink paper, were held in the notebook by binder rings. The left edge of each question slip was hidden by a three-inch cardboard mask that had been fashioned from file folders. In experimental treatments in which *S* was given feedback as to the correct answers after responding, he tore the question slip out of the notebook. The correct answer was found on the left margin of the question slip. Ordinarily, it was hidden by the cardboard mask. After checking his answer, *S* inserted the question slip into a ballot-like box standing at his work station. In treatments in which answers to the questions were not provided, *S* simply tore the question slip out after having responded and then inserted it into the ballot box.

Our formulation was so crude that it allowed only two possible states of mathemagenic behavior: the state in which mathe-

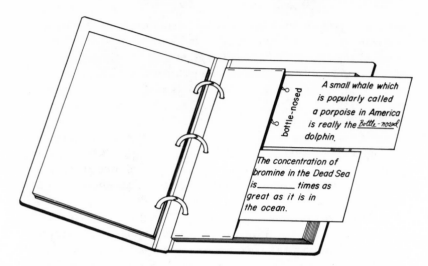

Fig. 1. Typical arrangement for placing experimental questions in the loose-leaf notebook containing the training material. A response has been made to the top question and S has torn the question slip from the ring binding. The correct answer is now seen in the left margin. The correct answer to the lower question is still hidden by the cardboard mask.

magenic behavior is consistent with training objectives, and the state in which it is not. The state produced by any given treatment was inferred from performance on a retention test administered to S after he finished reading. This method of measurement posed serious problems in inference, because it was well known that testlike events were directly instructive, that is, they produced learned changes in future performance on the test items. It was therefore possible that any facilitation observed on the retention test was due to the direct instructive effect of these test-like events rather than their influence on mathemagenic behavior. We used the following stratagem to take care of this difficulty. The 9,000-word passage was divided into twelve three-page zones. For each of these three-page zones we constructed a number of questions, dividing each into two equal subsets such that there is no direct transfer of training between subset A and subset B. This can readily be done in a passage that is topically uniform but has weak sequential or hierarchal organization.

Zero direct transfer between subsets A and B was empirically verified by having Ss master subset A, and then testing them on subset B and demonstrating that no gains in subset B performance resulted from training on subset A. The experimental logic was that if the knowledge required to answer questions from subset A did not produce direct transfer of training to performance on questions in subset B, but exposure to subset A during training somehow improved performance on subset B in the final examination, then this effect was *not* due to the direct instructional effect of subset A questions but rather to their effects on mathemagenic behaviors.

It has been the practice in nearly all our experiments on the relationship between testlike events and learning to measure not only the effect of questions on mathemagenic behaviors, but also the direct instructive effects of question. The latter effects were measured by testing Ss on the material on which the experimental questions were based, i.e., subset A. This was always done *after* the test on subset B items had been completed.

QUESTIONS BEFORE VS. QUESTIONS AFTER

Using the general procedures described above, a series of studies were carried out in my laboratory on the role of questions during reading. Here is a summary of what we found. If the testlike event occurred *before* reading the material to which the questions were relevant, then they only had direct instructive consequences. Their effect on mathemagenic behavior, on the other hand, was not substantially different from no question at all. If the questions were presented just *after* the zone to which they were relevant, then post-test performance indicated a marked elevating effect due to mathemagenic as well as direct instructional components (Rothkopf, 1966). We were able to rule out the possibility that differences between questions just before and just after were due to distraction-like phenomena. Questions presented just before reading do not inhibit learning because S "looks for the answers" to the question that has been asked.

The finding that questions about material that has just been read facilitate the development of effective mathemagenic behaviors is consistent with the view that mathemagenic behaviors are adaptive. One interpretation is that S engages in a set of mathemagenic activities while being exposed to a particular three-page zone of text, z. If the substantive skills that are required through these activities are sufficient for S successfully to answer the questions that follow zone z, then mathemagenic activities similar to those that occurred in zone z will take place during exposure to zone $z + 1$. Conversely, if performance on the question that followed zone z was not satisfactory, then the mathemagenic activities in the subsequent zone are likely to be modified. As this process of test and modification continues from zone to zone, mathemagenic behaviors are likely to change until they consistently produce substantive skills that are sufficient to handle the type of question used in the experiment.

TOPOGRAPHY

The manner by which questions produce mathemagenic behaviors that are consistent with high criterion test performance can be interpreted to mean that short-answer questions shape the topography of the mathemagenic activities. This can result in what appears to be general facilitation of learning. It can also result in increased learning for specific subportions of a given text. We have observed, for example, that by biasing the set of experimental questions to which Ss were exposed, we could produce mathemagenic behaviors that facilitated test performance on specific classes of knowledge.

By illustration, if the experimental questions uniformly require quantitative answers or proper names, then more knowledge about quantities and names are acquired during the course of study. Such results from a recent study (Rothkopf and Bisbicos, 1967) are illustrated in figure 2. The plot shows the proportion of correct responses on retention test questions that required measures (M) or names (N) for answers. Performance on test items derived from the first eighteen pages of the experimental text has been plotted separately from performance on items derived from the second eighteen pages. The treatments in which questions followed the relevant text segments and also involved some questions requiring M- and N-type answers during study (SAMX and SAMN in figure 2) produced

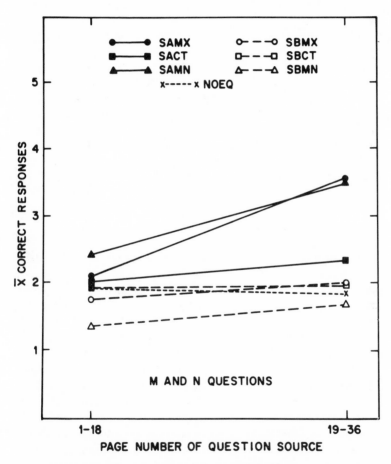

Fig. 2. Performance on measure (M) and name (N) questions on a retention test as function of the location of the question source in the experimental text. Treatment codes are explained in the text.

better performance on M or N items in the test. This advantage increased as study progressed.

Facilitated M or N learning that was attributable to mathemagenic effects was not observed in connection with treatments involving M or N questions embedded in the text just before the relevant segments (SBMX, SBMN) or in treatments without M or N questions (i.e., SACT, SBCT, or NOEQ). Facilitated learning of special subsets of the instructional material appeared to take place without deterioration in the learning of other classes of material within the text.

These results do not lend themselves easily to glib mentalistic accounts, such as that the questions inform *S* as to the intentions of the experimenter. Questions presented before reading should have been equally informative, but it should be noted that the experimental effect I have just described was obtained only when questions *followed* the relevant text segment. It was not obtained when questions preceded the portions of the text from which they were drawn. These results were obtained in two experiments (Rothkopf, 1966; Rothkopf and Bisbicos, 1967).

KNOWLEDGE OF RESULTS

Another one of the findings from our experiments was that feedback of correct answers after *S*s responded to the questions did not matter very much as far as mathemagenic behaviors were concerned. This suggests that in our experimental situation *S*s were able to determine success or lack of success on the experimental questions even without being tendered the correct answer after responding. This seems very reasonable, particularly for *S*s who could not make any response at all. Feedback was, however, quite important with respect to the direct instructive effect of questions, that is, it facilitated performance on test questions that were directly relevant to the material on which the experimental questions were based (Rothkopf, 1966).

Let me summarize these findings. Experimental questions inserted into a passage at regular, fairly short intervals, and relevant to materials that have just been read, can have a general facilitative effect on what is learned from the passage. This general facilitative effect goes broadly beyond the questions that the subject was actually asked. I interpret these findings to mean that questions shape studying activities, that is, that they shape what I have called mathemagenic behaviors. The shaping takes place because mathemagenic behaviors are adaptive and tend toward forms that will increase the likelihood of successful performance on the experimental questions. This shaping takes place even when formal knowledge of results has not been provided because *S* has his own indicator of success or lack of success. The direct instructive result of questions, however, is strongly increased by providing knowledge of results after *S* has responded to the experimental question.

DETERIORATION OF MATHEMAGENIC BEHAVIORS

It seems useful to understand not only factors that will produce effective mathemagenic activities but also the condition that will cause mathemagenic behaviors to deteriorate. The law of minimum learning on the effect of immediate repetition suggests one such class of conditions.

Recently, some observations on the effects of massed exposure on prose learning suggested that the diminishing effectiveness of massed practice (i.e., the classical learning curve) may be interpreted in terms of modifications of mathemagenic activities. The results of a study by Rothkopf (1968) indicated that the shape of the negatively accelerated learning curve may, at least in part, be due to the extinction or deterioration of mathemagenic behaviors. In that study, *S*s read a 1,500-word passage on leather-making either zero, one, two, or four times. If multiple exposures were indicated for *S*, he read the passage repeatedly in quick succession. Approximately ten minutes after the last reading, he was tested for learning by the completion method (i.e., the cloze procedure), in which only substantive words were deleted. A plot of the proportion of correct responses on this test as a function of the number of exposures to the text indicated a classical negatively accelerated curve.

Two accounts suggested themselves for the diminishing learning return per exposure. One hypothesis about the diminishing learning gains at each successive exposure was that it resulted from decreasing inspection time; Ss spent less time per page on each successive reading. This decrease in inspection time as a function of the number of exposures is a phenomenon that bears an interesting but complex relationship to mathemagenic activities; it has been observed in several experiments. However, decrease in inspection time was not a sufficient explanation of the flattening of the learning curve, because it could be shown that the amount of learning gain per unit of study time decreased steadily with each exposure.

The alternative account for diminishing learning gains is, of course, the hypothesis that gains at any practice trial are proportional to the difference between the performance level that has been attained and some theoretical maximum (e.g., Hull, 1943, pp. 102–123; Estes, 1950). One of the consequences of such a model is that learning curves for items of various levels of difficulty should differ markedly from each other in slope. This prediction was tested by subdividing the 123 items of the *Leather* completion test according to p_0, the initial guessing difficulty (i.e., the percentage of correct responses for Ss who did not see the passage prior to the completion test). Four different levels were used: $p_0 = 0(N = 45)$, $0 < p_0 < 0.2(N = 29)$, $0.2 < p_0 < 0.4$, $(N = 18)$, $p_0 > 0.4(N = 31)$. The proportion of correct completion responses as a function of the number of inspections prior to testing is shown for these four categories of items in figure 3. The four curves were nearly parallel. Each of the four classes of items gained, on the average, about the same number of correct responses per exposure. Our data, therefore, did *not* support the interpretation that there was a slowing of the learning rate in terms of approach to a common theoretical maximum constraint for all items such as "mastery."

The additional assumption that theoretical maxima differ for various deletions in the passage, however, may serve to bring the proportionality hypothesis in line with the data. This is not an unreasonable assumption, since it is well known that there are large differences in ambiguity among various syntactic and semantic constructions (e.g., Aborn, Rubinstein, and Sterling, 1959; Coleman, 1965). The failure of the first two hypotheses

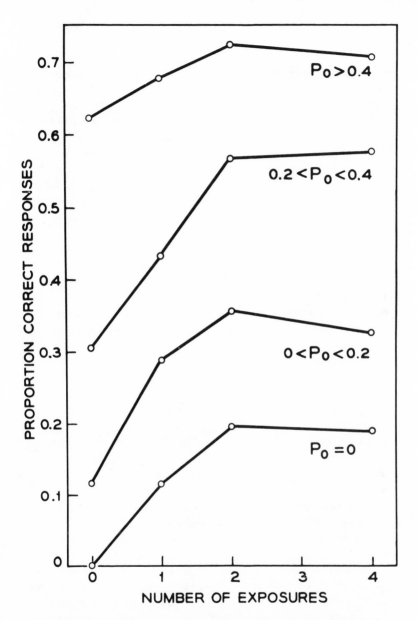

Fig. 3. Proportion of correct responses on a post-training completion test as function of number of exposures to the experimental passage. The data has been plotted separately for test items of various pre-exposure guessing probabilities (P_0).

left open the possibility that the negatively accelerated learning curve was due to modification or extinction of mathemagenic behaviors as a function of repeated or prolonged inspection. The decline in inspection time, according to this interpretation, is an indicator of the successive changes in mathemagenic behaviors. The fact that the amount of learning gain per unit inspection time was also decreasing as a function of exposures may mean, in addition, that the effective quality of mathemagenic behaviors was deteriorating as a function of repeated exposure.

PRACTICAL APPLICATIONS

The many imperfections in the theory of mathemagenic behaviors and the empirical greenness of the concept makes prescription for practice a hazardous enterprise. But the data and the theory, crude as they may be, indicate some practical directions that should be explored. They also suggest a few interesting and unanswered questions.

Adjunct Questions as Aids to Learning

Adjunct questions may aid learning, but they may also seriously interfere with it. This follows from the conception of mathemagenic behaviors as an adaptive process that is greatly influenced by testlike events.

Facilitation can be expected when the knowledges that are needed to successfully answer the adjunct questions are also representative of the knowledges that will support performance on the criterion test. It is assumed, in turn, that the criterion test is representative of the terminal behaviors that are the aims of instruction.

The notion that the knowledges that support performance on the adjunct questions are representative of the knowledges that support the criterion test is a fairly complex and difficult conception. It presupposes dimensions along which knowledges that support the terminal behaviors can be characterized. Representativeness would imply suitable sampling in terms of these dimensions. Discovering and describing these dimensions is technically extremely difficult (perhaps impossible) although intuitively appealing. However, some effort has been made in this direction (see P. Johnson, this volume). At present, a workable though limited alternative approach may be to make up a very large set of questions from specifications of terminal behaviors and to select adjunct question-by-sampling without bias from this set.

Certain biases in the knowledge required to answer adjunct questions may shape inappropriate mathemagenic behaviors. These behaviors are called inappropriate because they produce substantive learning that is inconsistent with the instructional goals. This may happen when the information required by the adjunct questions becomes too predictable (see Rothkopf, 1965), or when the location of this information in the written text promotes incomplete inspection. The latter has been observed in an interesting experiment by Anderson and Faust (1967). In this study *S* encountered a written question at the end of each paragraph. The sentence in the paragraph that carried the answer to the experimental question was distinguishable either because of fixed location in the paragraph sequence or because one of the words was underlined. It was found under those conditions that *S*s learned less from the remaining sentences of the paragraph. This was particularly pronounced among faster readers.

In considering whether adjunct questions will be useful, it is important to reflect on the rather overly flexible but useful concept of the topography of mathemagenic behaviors. Different topographies of mathemagenic behaviors result in different translations of the nominal stimuli. Although we have no working indicators of translation at present — except perhaps inspection time — translation, at least in principle, has observable consequences.

One way to think about topography is in terms of "perfect" translations of each sentence of a passage. It is thus possible to think of the topography of mathemagenic behaviors as associated with the probability that sentences in the passage will have a perfect translation. Topography is related both to the level of this probability over all sentences and differences in this probability among various identifiable subclasses of sentences.

From an instructional point of view, it becomes advantageous to shape inequalities in probabilities of translation of various classes of sentences when the written instructional material have *not* been edited to suit the specific instructional purpose for which they are being used. For example, a passage about gasoline engines may include information about *maintenance* and *repair* as well as *function*. If the instructional objectives involve only *function*, then it is to S's advantage to maximize translation of *function* sentences in the passage. To the extent that S's capacity for perfect translation is limited, it may also be an adaptive mathemagenic topography to reduce the translation of *repairs* and *maintenance* sentences.

The practical question is how such topographies should be achieved. It seems important to first ask what is the distribution in the passage of sentences that are relevant to the instructional objectives. If relevant sentences are neatly clustered, then the most practical instructive step would be either to limit reading assignment to relevant portions or to make appropriate editorial changes. If the relevant sentences are scattered, then topographic cuing offers some possibility for the control of mathemagenic behaviors (e.g., Hershberger and Terry, 1965). But this method requires editorial effort — although the required instructional editing is probably easier to do than manuscript revision. The technique, however, is mechanically bothersome, and there is little empirical evidence to suggest that it produces results that are worth the trouble.

Will directions to S help? Is it useful to provide hortatory messages? Probably! There is some experimental evidence that such messages facilitate learning somewhat (Rothkopf, 1966), and such devices cost little. It is not known, however, how long the facilitating effects of hortatory directions retain their potency.

Typographical cuing, such as underlining and color, controls mathemagenic behaviors because it makes use of stimulus displays that attract attention on the printed page. Directions to read carefully and other similar hortatory messages have the status of *previously conditioned* stimuli that elicit mathemagenic maneuvers that only sometimes have useful consequences for *S*, e.g., reading more slowly. The study behaviors under the control of these devices appear to be of a very general character, as are those under the control of verbal directions such as "Remember this!" It is not very well known how useful the intention to remember (or to forget) really is.

Questions delivered after reading a relevant text segment appear to promise a somewhat more flexible technique for adjusting *S*s' mathemagenic behaviors to instructional objectives. The limits of this technique are not well known. How soon will questions lose their ability to shape mathemagenic behaviors? What characteristics of the testlike event are necessary for the shaping process? Are questions equally useful with students of diverse socioeconomic background? How important are the frequency and regularity of spacing adjunct questions? These and other related questions require extensive additional experimentation.

There are probably a number of other methods for increasing the likelihood that sentences in an instructional passage will be effectively translated. Among these are techniques that will stimulate and structure the search. Searching for information in a passage has a kind of immediacy that would stimulate translation. Such translation may be sufficient for the growth of appropriate learned structures even though the information for which the student is directed to search is not directly related to the course objectives. The practical trick is to formulate a search objective (i.e., appropriate directions to initiate the search activities) that will maximize the translation of sentences relevant to the instructional objectives.

It is important to understand what techniques will tend to produce effective mathemagenic behaviors. But it should be kept in mind that the experimental investigation of such techniques will reveal little if *S*s in the experiment display vigorous and effective mathemagenic activities without special treatment. This sometimes happens in laboratory situations that are unusual and appear challenging to *S*s.

Besides trying to understand what procedures produce effective mathemagenic activities, it would also be useful to find out more about the conditions that cause mathemagenic activities to deteriorate. The effect of repetition and/or recent exposure has been referred to earlier in this paper. Text characteristics must also play a very considerable role here, but very little exact information is available as to the factors in text that produce deterioration of effective study activities.

NOTE

1. The distinction between nominal and effective stimulus occurred quite early in the history of psychology, but has been commonly neglected in theories of learning. Hull is one of the few exceptions. He recognized the problem when he distinguished between the stimulus object (S) and the afferent consequences of stimulation (s) in his book *Principles of Behavior* (1943, p. 47). The distinction was incorporated into Hull's postulate structure by adopting Hovland's practice (1937) of plotting stimulus generalization curves with j.n.d.'s on the abscissa rather than some physical measure of stimulus differences. More recently, a similar technique has been used in the study of human learning by Rothkopf (1957). The most influential recent writer on the nominal-effective stimulus distinction has been Underwood (1963).

REFERENCES

Aborn, M., Rubinstein, H., and Sterling, T. D. Sources of contextual constraint upon words in sentences. *J. exp. Psychol.*, 1959, 57, 171–180.

Anderson, R. C., and Faust, G. W. The effects of strong formal prompts in programmed instruction. *Amer. Educ. Res. J.*, 1967, 4, 345–352.

Coleman, E. On understanding prose: Some determiners of its complexity. Unpublished report, New Mexico State Univ., 1965.

Cook, J. O., and Kendler, T. S. A theoretical model to explain some paired-associate learning data. In G. Finch and F. Cameron (Eds.), *Symposium on Air Force human engineering, personnel, and training research*. Washington, D.C.: National Academy of Science–National Research Council, pub. no. 455, 1956, 90–98.

Estes, W. K. Towards a statistical theory of learning. *Psychol. Rev.*, 1950, 57, 94–107.

———. Statistical theory of distributional phenomena in learning. *Psychol. Rev.*, 1955, 62, 369–377.

Greeno, J. G. Paired-associate learning with massed and distributed repetitions of items. *J. exper. Psychol.*, 1964, *67*, 268–295.

Hershberger, W. A., and Terry, D. F. Typographical cuing in conventional and programmed texts. *J. appl. Psychol.*, 1965, *49*, 55–60.

Hovland, C. I. The generalization of conditioned responses: I. The sensory generalization of conditioned responses with varying frequency of tone. *J. gen. Psychol.*, 1937, *17*, 125–148.

Hull, C. L. *Principles of behavior.* New York: Appleton-Century-Crofts, 1943.

Rothkopf, E. Z. Some conjectures about inspection behavior in learning from written sentences and the response mode problem in programmed self-instruction. *J. progmd. Instruct.*, 1963, *2*, 31–46.

———. Some theoretical and experimental approaches to problems in written instruction. In J. D. Krumboltz (Ed.), *Learning and the educational process.* Chicago: Rand McNally, 1965, 193–221.

———. Learning from written material: An exploration of the control of inspection behavior by test-like events. *Amer. Educ. Res. J.*, 1966, *3*, 241–249.

Rothkopf, E. Z., and Bisbicos, E. E. Selective facilitative effects of interspersed questions on learning from written materials. *J. educ. Psychol.*, 1967, *58*, 56–61.

Rothkopf, E. Z., and Coke, E. U. Repetition interval and rehearsal method in learning equivalences from written sentences. *J. verb. Learn. verb. Behav.*, 1963, *2*, 406–416.

———. Variations in phrasing, repetition interval, and the recall of sentence materials. *J. verb. Learn. verb. Behav.*, 1966, *5*, 86–91.

Underwood, B. J. Stimulus selection in verbal learning. In C. N. Cofer and B. S. Musgrave (Eds.), *Verbal behavior and learning.* New York: McGraw-Hill, 1963.

PART IV

AN ADDENDUM FROM COMPUTER TECHNOLOGY

The Computer in the Technology of Written Instruction

MAX V. MATHEWS

Bell Telephone Laboratories

Instructional programs are particularly good examples for computer text processing. I recently wrote an experimental program to teach Fortran computer programming to Bell Labs personnel, a program that not only taught Fortran but also taught how to use our computation system. However, the change of technology was so rapid that before the program was completed it was essentially obsolete. Instructional programs take a long time to write, to test, and to publish. Anything computers could do to mechanize the publication process and make it easier for these programs to be modified would be very valuable. Probably ease of modification is even more important to the original publication speed.

These considerations led me to develop some computer editing and mechanical publication procedures. It also led me into some broader problems of the whole question of how computers will be more involved in the area of technical communication. Programmed instruction isn't the only thing being pushed hard by technology today; the rate at which our whole civilization can go forward soon will be limited by communications or human learning rates.

We will start by discussing our particular computer text-

307

editing and image-drawing program, and proceed to a few more general remarks about facilitating various kinds of communication with computers.

ALPHANUMERIC MATERIAL

A diagram of our text-editing program is shown in figure 1. One originates a document on a typewriter. The typewriter characters go into a computer where they can be stored in the memory on either magnetic tape or magnetic disc files. At the command of the typewriter they can either be written out on another typewriter or, in what is a more interesting form of out-

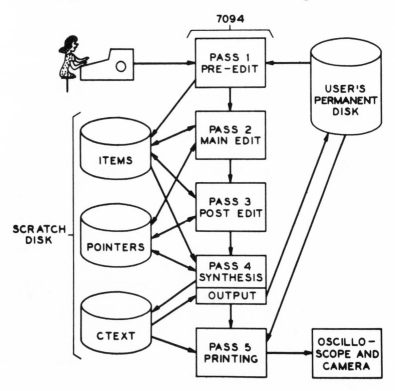

Fig. 1. Block diagram of the MACE system for computer editing and printing of text.

put, produced on a cathode ray tube that is photographed and replicated by a printing press.

What are some of the features that we think are desirable in this particular form of editing? Clearly it should be human engineered, and often people's interaction with computers are not. This requirement means essentially two things. First, the input device should be a good typewriter, as good as a secretary's machine and better than a teletypewriter or keyboard on a card punch. Second, the repertoire of editing instructions available to the user should be both appropriate to a secretary and reasonably flexible so that many things can be done. These are our two objectives.

We did not attempt the large job of developing a special typewriter, but simply selected a commercially available model and connected it to our computer. It was an IBM Selectric with golf ball font, which we hope is almost as good as a secretary's typewriter. The editing instructions were under our control, all editing instructions being identified and separated from the text by prefacing them with one particular symbol, which the computer recognized. Thus, they were able to be intermixed with the text in any order the user desired. A list of available instructions is given in figure 2. However, we will not discuss the full repertoire.

An example of a manuscript as it was typed, complete with corrections, is shown in figure 3. On it are instructions for doing the things one normally does on a typewriter, such as backspace and type over errors, roll the carriage back and cross out characters, and roll the carriage back and type over characters. One was also able to throw out a line, a paragraph, or an even larger unit. One was also able to incorporate previously typed material into new documents. This incorporation was very important in that existing documents were able to be modified. And though the modifications had to be proofread, the rest was reproduced exactly as it was. Repagination and justification were automatic.

The computer was also able to prepare a proof manuscript in which the lines were numbered as references for further editing. Format control was operated in two modes, one honoring carriage returns on the input, the other producing both right- and

CLASS I

[E xxx/	Erase item xxx.
[E xxx,yyy,zzz/	Erase line yyy of item xxx.
[E xxx,yyy,zzz/	Erase lines yyy through zzz of item xxx.
[I xxx,yyy/...insertion.../	Insert the text between the slashes after line yyy of itemxxx.
[O xxx,yyy/...substitution.../	Overwrite line yyy of item xxx with the text between the slashes.
[S xxx,yyy/ expression A (substitution) expression B/	
[S xxx/ expression A (insertion)/	
[C xxx,yyy/carriage return.../carriage return	Correct line yyy of item xxx on a character by character basis.
[U xxx,yyy/carriage return.../carriage return	Underline specified characters in line yyy of item xxx.
[R FILE, Text, N,www,xxx/	Read request.
[G FILE, Text,www,xxx/	Galley proof request.
[T FILE, Text,www,xxx/	Type final copy.
[F	Fixed format.
[J	Normal mode (justify).
[P	Paragraph (used in normal mode).
[X www,xxx/	Randomize the order of items www through xxx.
[M www,xxx,n/	Multiprocess items www through xxx using routine PROC n.

CLASS II

[v n/	Space vertically n times
[h n/	Space horizontally n times.
[m a,b/	Margins: a spaces on left, b spaces on right
[p	Go to new page.
[l n/	Type on every nth line
[e (x,n)...(y,m)/	Equate character x to symbol number n, etc. (to extend character set)

Fig. 2. A list of editing commands available in the MACE system.

left-hand justification. Examples of proof text and output text are shown in figures 4 and 5.

Other editorial commands included global changes that replaced all instances of a given word. A number of instructions referred to output format (e.g., whether to generate proof or final copy, whether to use a fixed format or justified format). We even included an instruction to randomize the order of the words in a text for the benefit of programmed instruction research.

```
(MEMO)(DESCRIPTION)
[1 10/[F
II.  Description of System
Objectives/ [U#,#/
The purpose of this system is three-fold:
(1) to allow for input and correction of typewritten text;
(2) store material for future editing and/or processing;
(3) to provide high quality typographical output.
[0#,1/II.  Description/
[112/[JThe significance of such a system lies primarily in point
two for although typists and poofreaders can prepare manuscripts
and t-ype-typesetters  can produce aesthetically pleasing copy,
no one relishes the task of altering previously prepared material.
[C 12,-2/                /
Consequently, the ability to store text in a form that can
be easily updated represents a great convenience.  Therefore,
the aim of this project has been to develop a system of
editing in which the user can provide input to a computer
by a device which is familiar and easy to use.  [S#/and p(r)/
[1 14/Furthermore, the [E#/The corrections themselves
constitute input.  [S12,2/point (●"(2)" )for/
[19.5  E10,8/[010,2/II.  Description/
[1 11.5 [S12,8/venience.([P       )There/
[1 20  [R MEMO,DESCRIPTION,-1,6,8
[1 25  [RMEMO,DESCRIPTION,100,28.5/
[1 30  [R MEMO,MANUAL,0,0,0/
```

Fig. 3. An example of input typing to the MACE system showing both text and editing commands.

FILE- MEMO   STANDARD TEXT · DESCRIPTION············   07/12/65 21:59:12

10.00 [F

    IL Description

    Objectives

    The purpose of this system is three-fold:

    (1) to allow for input and correction of typewritten text;

    (2) store material for future editing and/or processing;

    (3) to provide high quality typographical output.

12.00 [JThe significance of such a system lies primarily in point (2) for

    although typists and proofreaders can prepare manuscripts and typesetters can produce

    aesthetically pleasing copy, no one relishes the task of altering previously prepared

    material. Consequently, the ability to store text in a form that can be easily updated

    represents a great convenience.[P

        Therefore, the aim of this project has been to develop a system of editing in which

    the user can provide input to a computer by a device which is familiar and easy to use.

14.00 The corrections themselves constitute input.

Fig. 4. Example of "galley" proof from the MACE computer editing program.

IL Description
Objectives
The purpose of this system is three-fold:
(1) to allow for input and correction of typewritten text;
(2) store material for future editing and/or processing;
(3) to provide high quality typographical output.

The significance of such a system lies primarily in point (2) for although typists and proofreaders can prepare manuscripts and typesetters can produce aesthetically pleasing copy, no one relishes the task of altering previously prepared material. Consequently, the ability to store text in a form that can be easily updated represents a great convenience.
    Therefore, the aim of this project has been to develop a system of editing in which the user can provide input to a computer by a device which is familiar and easy to use. The corrections themselves constitute input.

Fig. 5. Example of justified final copy from the MACE computer editing program.

COMBINING GRAPHIC
AND ALPHANUMERIC MATERIAL

So far we have discussed only alphanumeric material that can be typed on a typewriter or printed on a press. Now let us consider an overlooked problem of combining graphic and alphanumeric material. In almost any written material or instructional material, the graphics are very important. They can also be handled by computers. Moreover, some of the most significant computer advances are occurring in the graphics field.

There are two ways of dealing with graphics. The oldest is the TV mode, in which an image is scanned with a zigzag scan and the brightness of the image at every point is recorded. It suffers from two limitations. One is the enormous channel capacity required to transmit a picture or memory size to store the picture. The other is that currently existing equipment does not have sufficient resolution. TV sets are all right for cartoons but not for prolonged reading of text.

Alternative graphic image generation schemes are still very much in a research basis, but we will describe them. Consider the face of a TV tube (as shown on figure 6) as a sort of blackboard on which the computer will write. A blackboard, in order to be appropriate for a computer, must be quantized into addressable positions in both x and y. The number of addressable positions varies from 1,000 to 16,000, depending on the quality of the tube. The computer simply places points at any one of x or y positions or draws straight lines between any two of the positions. All images are constructed from these two elementary building blocks by means of the computer program itself.

Why is this process of great interest and why does it have more potential than the TV process? The answer is that very complicated images can be generated from a moderate amount of digital information, and that the image generation process itself is entirely under the control of a computer program based on the information in the memory of the computer, which makes this inherently a very flexible process. This same computer can draw a very wide range of things. The letters in a text and the illustrations can be produced in just the same way. The best way

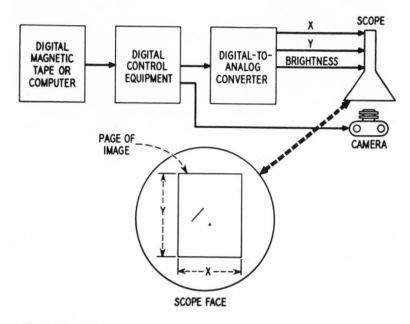

Fig. 6. Block diagram of microfilm output for a digital computer showing
page layout and Cartesian plotting principle.

of appreciating the potentialities is to look at a few samples
shown in figures 7–12. All were made on the same device, a
Stromberg-Carlson 4020 microfilm printer, which is essentially
what is shown in figure 6. Most of these pictures are produced
in the normal course of our scientific consultations; they have
very little to do with instruction, but are quite illustrative of the
range of things that can be done.

Figure 7 is a map showing a communication network. Figure
8 is a plot of some satellite radiation data. The picture has several thousand points plotted on it. The computer can prepare
this very well, but a draftsman would be hopelessly bored. One
can look at this plot and get a very good idea about the extent of
the radiation without examining the individual points, but if
one looked at the listing of the numbers represented by the individual points he would get no idea of the pattern.

Figure 9 illustrates a general graphing routine for which the computer can draw not only curves, but also the coordinate system. In addition, it can label the axes, print a title and subtitle, and label the curves with numbers. The program is flexible enough to prepare graphs for publication automatically. At the moment we would like better quality, but the next generation of microfilm printers should provide it.

Figure 10 is the pattern for an electric circuit. The actual circuit will be fabricated from the pattern by methods of photography and deposition. Hence, computers are almost in a position of being able to draw themselves.

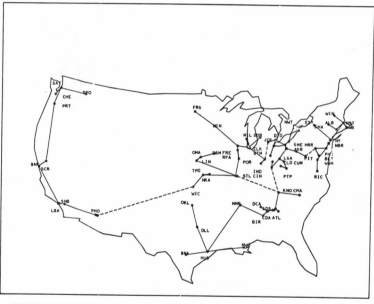

Fig. 7. A map of the United States drawn on a computer microfilm output device.

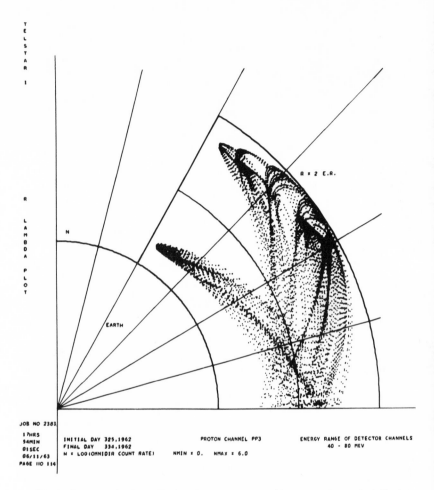

Fig. 8. Plot of satellite radiation data preprepared by computer and plotted on a microfilm output device.

Figure 11 shows five views of a recognizable object. It was represented in the computer as a bunch of spheres. To get a view we merely had to specify the direction in which to view the object. Hidden lines were calculated automatically.

Figure 12 is an example of an alphabet drawn on the cathode ray tube. Patterns for these particular letters do not exist in any

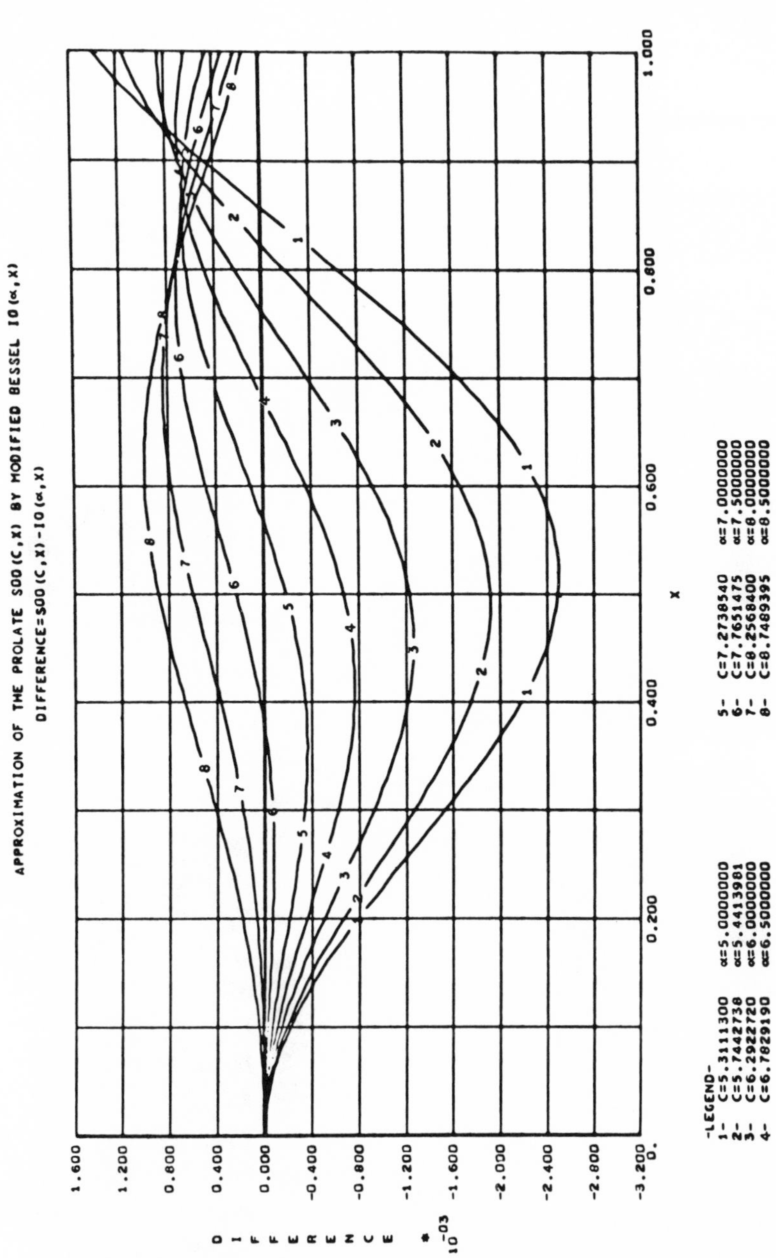

Fig. 9. Example of general graphing program, T plot, which provides a convenient graphical output for computers.

Fig. 10. Example of the mask for a thin
film-deposited circuit, which has been
drawn by a computer on a microfilm output device.

Fig. 11. Mickey Mouse as seen by the computer from various directions and drawn on a microfilm output device.

analog form, rather, each letter is drawn as a number of short straight lines by the process we have discussed. In this particular case, an average of twenty-five lines is involved for each letter. One can overdraw a line to make a heavier resulting line or add serifs to the letters. One can also make shapely letters and can have an upper and lower case alphabet (which many computers lack). Since the shape of each letter is simply a group of digits in the memory of the computer, one can have different fonts, Greek letters, and mathematical signs. Finally, since these

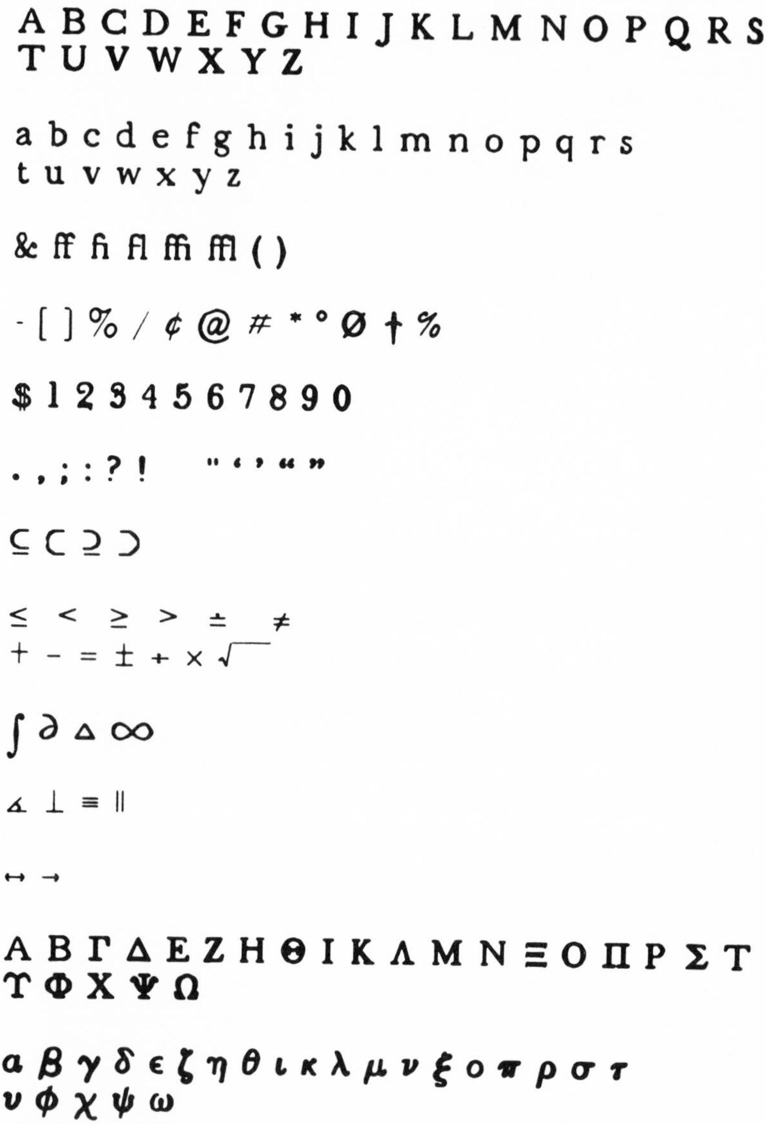

A B C D E F G H I J K L M N O P Q R S
T U V W X Y Z

a b c d e f g h i j k l m n o p q r s
t u v w x y z

& ff fi fl ffi ffl ( )

· [ ] % / ¢ @ # * ° Ø † ‰

$ 1 2 3 4 5 6 7 8 9 0

. , ; : ? !   " ' " "

⊆ ⊂ ⊇ ⊃

≤ < ≥ > ≐ ≠
+ − = ± ÷ × √‾

∫ ∂ △ ∞

∡ ⊥ ≡ ‖

↔ →

A B Γ Δ E Z H Θ I K Λ M N Ξ O Π P Σ T
Υ Φ X Ψ Ω

α β γ δ ε ζ η θ ι κ λ μ ν ξ ο π ρ σ τ
υ φ χ ψ ω

Fig. 12. Font of computer-drawn letters available on the microfilm output
device.

letters are produced in the same way as all the other images we have shown, they can easily be combined with pictures either as labels on the picture or as graphics incorporated into text.

SOME CONSIDERATIONS OF HUMAN-COMPUTER COMMUNICATIONS

We will say no more about our specific computer editing and image-generation programs, but will conclude with some more general considerations of human-computer communications.

The programs we have discussed so far have used computers in a conventional, batch-processing mode. It is becoming easier to interact directly with a computer via a typewriter console. However, interacting with computers is not a panacea. Some important factors to consider are (1) the mode of presentation to the person, (2) the transmission requirements that go between the person and the computer, and (3) the memory capacity of the computer.

The mode of presentation that one can currently buy off the shelf comes in the form of either a teletypewriter or an electric typewriter. Typing is a reasonable mode of communication; the machine can receive as fast as people can react. Reading the output of an active electrically controlled typewriter is annoying. The rate of typing is much too slow and the movement of keys or carriage is distracting. Before computers are really to be effective instructional tools, some better mode of communication will have to be developed. Perhaps one solution may be to use a typewriter input and a cathode ray tube output. Its effectiveness is not yet evaluated, but will depend upon how easily people can read cathode ray tubes. It does have the advantage that pictures can be drawn on the tube as well as in the text.

For transmission, we distinguish between teletype rates of about 10 characters per second which are well matched to typewriters, but not people; telephone rates which with the right equipment can transmit 500 characters per second and can easily drive a reasonable effective display tube; and coaxial cables which can easily handle 500,000 or more characters per second and can drive a TV-type display tube.

One cannot make a clear statement about the cost of these channels, except that coaxial cables are very expensive for long distances. On the other hand, they are perfectly feasible for a few miles. The main point is not to overlook transmission costs when considering an instructional network.

Memories can be discussed in terms of time, size, and dollars. One method of storing information is the magnetic core, which is the standard rapid-access memory of most computers. Here one can get a given piece of information in microseconds. It is feasible to store perhaps 20 million bits of information for about one cent per bit per year. Clearly, one cannot store many volumes of instructional material in this way.

A second, slower but larger, memory is the magnetic discs. These devices are similar to phonograph records except that recording is magnetic. Arms move back and forth to any particular point on the disc. The length of time to get at a particular bit of information really depends upon how fast one can move this arm, the speed of which is in the neighborhood of one-tenth of a second. Such memories, holding 10^8 bits, are reasonable in size and cost about one-hundredth of a cent per bit per year, or a hundred times cheaper than core memory. Both discs and cores are available now.

Experimental memories, which are now being developed, include storage on small film-sheets which are kept in cells. This is a semipermanent storage—one must rewrite and replace a a whole film sheet to change anything on it. Access time may be a few seconds, it holds up to 10^{12} bits, and costs 10^{-4} cents per bit per year. Thus, a book with 10^6 bits could be stored for one dollar per year. Such low costs and large sizes are essential if practical amounts of instructional material are to be processed by computers.

PART V

GENERAL DISCUSSION

In Search of Useful Variables: Some Methodological Considerations

LAWRENCE M. STOLUROW

Harvard University

There are a number of issues that have recurred in this symposium. One is the familiar scientific vs. technological approach, which has some implications that might be worth pointing out.

The first of these implications concerns research strategy. Depending on whether one is committed to a scientific or technological orientation to problems, one uses different strategies to develop his research. In learning prose, this distinction has implications for the way studies originate. With the so-called scientific orientation it has become customary, though not necessary, to begin with a theoretical construct from the psychology of learning, linguistics, or psycholinguistics. It is the interest in a construct that determines the variables to be considered when a search is made of prose materials for features and conditions that fit criteria associated with the construct. If a study begins with a psychological construct, then the search is for linguistic characteristics that fit the requirements of the psychological construct. On the other hand, if it begins with a linguistic construct, then the search is for the psychological characteristics that appear to relate to the linguistic construct.

The next step is either to assume that or determine whether variations found in language are consistent with the requirements of the variable and the construct to which it relates. If it is a psychological construct, such as interference or facilitation, then the linguistic variables (e.g., the number of meanings a word has) are chosen because it is suspected that they will produce interference or facilitation under different conditions.

To many psychologically oriented researchers, language is another interesting or convenient vehicle for the study of theoretical constructs and problems. The fact that language is used for these studies is not crucial, and interest in results often depends more on the relevance of language to psychological theory than to linguistics. The selection of materials for these studies is based upon the impression that the language fits the requirements of the construct being tested. In this approach, the psychological fit is more important than is the preservation of natural conditions. Consequently, if something has to give in designing a study, it generally is the reality, or naturalness, of the language rather than the criteria that define the variables. Therefore, the language materials actually used may be atypical or unusual. For example, paralogues might be used in place of selected real words, or only simple sentences may be used throughout a 1,000-word passage to keep it uniform.) In short, liberties might be taken with the language used to meet the requirements of the psychological construct. The reverse also may be the case if the interest is in a linguistic construct.

It is a happy, but nevertheless usual, coincidence when natural prose meets the requirements of a psychological construct, or when the psychological construct meets the requirements of the linguistic construct. But since one does not always map upon the other, studies often require that something give. For this reason, I refer to this approach as the hypothetical-reconstructive approach. Using it, the investigator starts with a hypothesis about a construct and the factors that relate to it. The hypothesis and the construct determine what the investigator looks for in prose. For example, if the psychological investigator is interested in interference theory, then he may think about this construct in the following way. Interference can vary depending upon the level of drive, or motivation, whenever the stimulus is associated with a number of different responses. This means that in relation to the construct of interference the number of available responses is a factor in determining the amount of interference that results as drive level varies. With this in mind, a choice of variables is possible for a study. If language is to be the vehicle, then the investigator will probably look at the number of meanings associated with each one of a set of words as the index of the number of different responses a learner is likely to have available when he learns prose that uses these words. He will then determine how different levels of drive are to be introduced.

From this type of analysis an experiment can be developed. Since many different experimental designs are possible, the one selected will be the one that is most interesting or that has the best chance of success. For example, the drive may be held constant and the words in a 1,000-word passage varied so as to produce differences in the amount of interference. Or the words may be kept constant and the drive level varied. This example illustrates how an investigator looks for variations in characteristics of the material so that he can design a study involving some interesting variations from the point of view of his hypothesis. The variations are chosen because it appears from logical implication that the performance of students will vary in a measurable way. Furthermore, the data would lend support to the hypothesis or provide a basis for its refutation. If, however, the prose fails to provide the variations needed to meet the requirements of the construct, then some liberties might be taken to construct the required set of conditions. This means that prose would be reconstructed to meet the requirements of the construct. Then, if supporting data are obtained, the construct is assumed to be useful in studying language. However, the distortions made to meet the experimental requirements limit the degree to which the results to this subset of the language can be generalized.

A frequently used alternative approach is to start by examining language to see what interesting variables might be identified. The variables of interest are those that raise a question or in some way present an explanatory problem. The next step is to infer an explanation. For example, suppose it is noted that people respond differently to different kinds of utterances.

To some utterances they take immediate overt action; to others they say something. This observation may lead to a question about the psychological factors that make this possible. This could suggest that features of the utterances such as their structure might be the critical cues. It may be observed that the question *How do you feel?* invariably elicits an oral response, and that *Place the thermometer in your mouth* is a request that results in overt action. Further examination may reveal that statements such as *People who stay in bed with a cold frequently recover faster* simply elicits an attention response. Though the basis for correct performance in relation to such utterances might require discrimination on the part of the learner, it is not obvious which critical cues permit him to discriminate reliably. The next step, then, is to see if the stimulus basis for discrimination can be identified. It is often the case that a search is made for data that, when found, suggest that the analysis is insufficient or logically incorrect. In short, the hypothesis is tested in terms of what data exist that relate to its implications. Frequently, the data used to test in this way are not exactly what one needs. Therefore, the next step is to conduct a study. If this is done, then the data generated by the study will determine the validity of the analysis.

With the first approach mentioned, the theory determines the nature of the prose and the conditions used to study it. With the second approach features of the language determine the basis of a search for an existing theory that is adequate to account for correct performance. If an adequate theory is not found, then a theory is extended to handle these problems. While these alternative strategies are not really based upon a valid distinction between science and technology, they frequently are identified as one or the other when, in fact, both are scientific approaches to problems.

More important to the study of learning prose is the potential problem these two approaches present to the development of the field. If the first one were to become the dominant strategy, I see two difficulties. First, psychological learning theory is too limited in its own development to provide sufficient explanation and guidance to someone interested in learning prose. Therefore, if the hypothetico-reconstructive approach were to be the dominant strategy, then a number of interesting things might not be done that should be. Second, when learning theory is used it concentrates the limited available research effort on one problem (or at best a few) to which it can be applied at its present stage of development. It would seem desirable for learning theories to be stretched to cover more and more of the learning problems we find around us. I do not mean to use the word "stretch" in its more negative sense, but rather to say that we need to extend and develop the breadth of theoretical coverage beyond what we have. Many will argue this point in favor of the need for greater refinement of the existing concepts. In the final analysis the approach taken will probably depend upon the personality characteristics of the investigator. However, my own preference is to see us take the latter approach, although its potential dangers may lead us into "dust bowl empiricism."

In Martin's paper[1] presenting Yngve's parsing procedure, there is a theory of the way individuals cope with sentences. This, in my view, is an illustration of the second, or analytical-experimental, approach. Parsing can be thought of as a way of establishing the associative grain of prose, and the learner can be said to be discriminating not only specific strings, but also classes or types of strings that may or may not correspond to a parsing analysis. Presumably, the individual learns to extract from these strings characteristics that are reliably related to the way in which he should behave toward them. Whether he actually uses the same labels that the linguist uses is doubtful for most users of the language, but this does not mean that he does not have a label or a unique response that he could use as a label.

In a sense, parsing is a form of task analysis. One question is whose task it describes. It can describe the behavior of the individual who is generating language or the individual who is trying to learn from the language. It would seem that the author's task is different from the learner's. As a task-analytic procedure parsing seems to be quite useful. Though Yngve's procedure assigns numbers and presumably generates reliable data about the grain of prose, the problem is with its validity. At a minimum level we can get a fix on validity simply by seeing if sentences with different Yngve numbers result in different behaviors on the part of persons who were asked to generate prose, or of persons who were asked to learn prose that has different parsing values.

A related implication that comes to mind is the study of intra-list interference in learning verbatim prose. Starting with Ebbinhaus, about 1896, there has been an experimental interest in determining the nature of the associations formed when word strings are learned. The data from strings of nonsense syllables showed that the learner formed remote associations as well as adjacent ones. This led to the theory that made use of excitatory and inhibitory gradients to predict that the point of maximum interference would appear just to the right of the center term in a serial learning curve (see Noble and Fuchs, 1959). A plot of the interference data is a bow-shaped intraserial interference curve; it has been shown to obtain for prose as well as for serial lists of nonsense syllables.

The Yngve analysis gives us a very different model to use in looking for interference effects. In fact, it says that there may be more than one point of maximum interference in a sentence. In this model the degree of imbedding is the factor that determines the extent of the interference. The maximum point, if there is one, might appear almost anywhere, for it would depend upon the structure of the sentence. It is important and useful to distinguish among the word groupings, for they determine the adjacent and remote associations that would exist during learning. The most critical data are those obtained during learning. It also would seem that the method of presenting prose would make a difference in the pattern of adjacent and remote associations. If sentences were presented to the learner one word at a time, then the learner would be forced to develop associations in a manner consistent with the serial learning model. On the other hand, if they were presented all at once but for brief periods, then the learner could use grouping skills, which could result in association patterns that relate to the parsing analysis. The one-word-at-a-time method seems to bias the results toward the intraserial interference model. The analysis of what individuals presumably do in analyzing sentences is, in fact, a hypothesis or theory that needs to be testable by empirical study. Also, we need to know if people group words when they compose sentences, when they learn from sentences, and when they learn sentences verbatim. There is good reason to distinguish among these three processes: composition (oral or written), learning *of* prose, and learning *from* prose.

We need techniques that allow us to locate the natural breaks (groupings) in word strings that individuals impose upon sentences. Some techniques already exist that might, with further testing, be useful for this purpose. For instance, individuals can be asked to real aloud, and records can be made of these readings. The records would yield data on the natural breaks that random readers impose upon sentences. Through the use of selected materials that have been parsed, one can determine whether the Yngve method of grouping predicts the parses, but a different study is needed to determine if the Yngve method predicts the composition of prose, a more difficult task. More easily accomplished is the study of learning from prose. However, it is clear that we need to identify the breaks that occur while the person is composing sentences. These breaks have different implications from those that occur when sentences are used for learning.

Furthermore, it is conceivable that the sequence of words in a sentence is not necessarily related to the way in which the internal processing of information, which ultimately results in language behavior, occurs.

Language habits are sufficiently well developed in most individuals rather early in life, so that the basic language characteristics we call grammar, or syntax, are produced by processes that are probably relatively automatic. The distinction between composition of prose and learning of and from prose suggests that there are also other processes that may involve different activities. Memorizing prose and reading prose may involve very different processes; consequently the units used by the individual may not always be the same. We need models for each of these types of behavior and we need to make predictions about what will happen under different conditions. For example, we need to develop theories about verbatim memory that make predictions about where sentences will fragment over time, and where substitutions will occur. Substantive learning and memory seem to be easier than verbatim memory, judging from the number of repetitions required for learning. Similarly, immediate and delayed retention seem to have different characteristics, and models for each would probably deal with processes involved in information storage and retrieval. However, while it is likely that these processes have some relationship to those involved in composing sentences, it does not necessarily follow that this is the case. An individual composing prose may generate a large number of sentences from one or two kernel ideas. Not only whole sentences but groups of sentences may actually be produced in a relatively automatic manner. But the composition process, at least at some stages, for some authors, with some ideas, probably is a multistep process. It is conceivable that the units processed in storage and retrieval are kernels that cue grammatical skills employed in composition. In short, we may be dealing with a two-stage process: the retrieval of key terms and the cuing of grammatical skills.

It is also conceivable that new research techniques could be designed, or existing ones adapted, for studying the units used by individuals in retrieval, so that the two processes could be studied. It may be possible to pose a research question to identify the controlling stimulus and criterion response. For example, this could be done by deleting parts of the material and determining whether the criterion response in fact occurs. The "black-out" procedure used by Holland[2] is one that relates to this approach rather nicely. The "cloze" procedure also seems to be potentially useful if rational rules replace the rule of random deletion. For prose that is being learned verbatim, a rule should be sought to determine which words to black out. When the rule results in the deletion of material that actually makes the student's response either different from that which was expected or highly unreliable, then it can be assumed that a controlling stimulus has been affected. Through further adjustments in what is blacked out, the nature of the controlling stimulus can be determined more precisely. From this back-and-forth, or delete-and-try, approach, using different students each time and some rationale to guide the process, it should be possible to derive useful data supporting concepts that also stand up when cross-validated.

One can use a stimulus-and-response analysis of the task of learning from prose if the concepts are defined in some operational way. Here, a set of distinctions among the functions that the different parts of the materials perform may be useful in selectively blacking out words or word strings. Among stimulus functions we can distinguish between words called *cues, elicitors,* and *reinforcers* or *confirmers.* The same word in different sentences could be associated with each of these three functions. It is not the word itself but rather its use that is important. Different classes of usage present different learning problems. With cues, for example, one is concerned with the problem of discrimination. With elicitors one is concerned with their reliability in producing a response. An elicitor, or prompt, must dependably produce the desired behavior. The cues with which one works are ultimately determined by the nature of the subject matter, since the semantics of the content area determine the terminology that is critical. Elicitors, on the other hand, are used for a particular purpose. With respect to responses, one is concerned with the nature of the molar, or final, response and with its progressive development from smaller units. This is generally achieved through the use of elicitors.

This brings us to some questions that are seldom raised, namely, questions of task engineering. Here we are dealing with the problem of response synthesis, or "shaping." Included in this concept are questions of sequencing and of how we organize, or put together materials (e.g., cues and elicitors) so that, at the end, the individual conforms to some pattern of performance that is assumed adequate or sufficient for the instructional objective. Generally, the criterion for the adequacy of a student's performance varies with his level of development and with his place in the course (early vs. late).

In task engineering we start with few theoretical concepts. The experimental conditions are distinguished by operational definitions, and we proceed inductively, hoping to arrive at broader concepts, or theories, regarding the nature of the teaching-learning process. The process of engineering starts with the terminal behavior and works back to the point at which the learner would be expected to begin. In effect, one examines the process of learning over a finite span defined by the initial and terminal points, which are basically arbitrary. Generally, the basis for selecting the points is built into the culture of the subject matter and current school practices. To this extent, these are natural units. We should also recognize that this approach is deeply imbedded in thinking and working with the learning of concepts and skills *from* prose. It is not an approach that is derived directly from the learning *of* prose, although that, too, could be the terminal behavior. There is nothing in the approach that rules out memorization but, generally, when that is the objective, more practice is required. Substantive learning appears to take place sooner than verbatim learning.

With substantive learning a larger number of questions arise, particularly with respect to sequencing. We are concerned with the way one organizes materials for different individuals. I call the process *attribute modulation,* because the teacher's task is to modulate attributes of the materials in ways that uniquely fit the needs of the student. Studies of organizing rules such as the class-descriptive cue rule and the more general rules of asynchrony are operationalized approaches to attribute modulation that seem to have worked (Stolurow, 1956; Detambel and Stolurow, 1956; Wulff and Stolurow, 1957).

As Dr. Glaser has said, we need to have the conditions sufficiently specified for defining the terminal performance. We need to know that the student can do x under condition y. We also need to know what the objective is that we are trying to optimize. I find it convenient to refer to this dimension of our objective as the psychological dimension, for which I identify three requirements. They are; rapid learning, good retention, and good transfer. Existing data suggest that these are not perfectly correlated when we relate indices of each obtained under a variety of learning conditions. Some conditions, for example, tend to produce the highest rates of learning but do not lead to the best retention. Others produce high retention but poor transfer (e.g., see Cartwright, 1962).

A number of the questions raised by earlier speakers relate to questions which stem from a so-called technological approach. For example, the research to which Dr. Lumsdaine alluded was done under a contract sponsored by the Air Force. In that work we accomplished task analyses of technical materials and described the associative relationships to be established by training in the terms used by Dr. Goss. We found one-to-one, many-to-one, one-to-many, and many-to-many associative pairings, all of which were derived from an examination of technical tasks in the manner I described as the hypothetico-reconstructive approach. We then submitted the materials to investigation (e.g., Stolurow, Hodgson, and Silva, 1956; Stolurow and Bergum, 1958; Wulff and Stolurow, 1957). These studies were concerned not only with the learning of complex associative sets, but also with the effects of "sharing" and "overlapping" (Stolurow, Detambel, and Newman, 1956). These effects were looked at in terms of transfer, but the transfer was of a special type, which we called "association reversal" (see Stolurow, Hodgson and Silva, 1956).

An example of this type of transfer is learning to translate from French into English after having learned the reverse. What was initially learned was that the stimulus term (or subject of a sentence) becomes the response term (or predicate) in the transfer task. We were most interested in what would happen in association reversal when the patterns of associative relationships were complex, e.g., one to many, many to one, or many to many. In other words, the learner was given a set of terms to associate with one response (many to one), a stimulus term to associate with a set of responses (one to many), or several stimulus terms to associate with several response terms (many to many). The last is what happens in troubleshooting, or fault-finding, where symptoms may be defined by information on dials, but can be, and typically are, described in verbal form in both the text and the classroom. The responses also refer to behavior in the sense of actual repair activities, but these, too, are described verbally in the text or the class. In effect, the verbal learning serves as a mediating mechanism. Having learned the sets of relationships between descriptors of symptoms and of courses, the student then relates each to appropriate events in a working situation.

With the many-to-many paradigms of association, the relationships involve sharing and overlapping connections among the stimulus and response elements. The stimulus responses and elements are the natural language labels that would be provided the individual to identify stimuli and responses. They are the terms he would be expected to use when asked to say what he would do if he were actually troubleshooting. The prose is highly denotative. The stimulus terms describe cursor positions on dials he will work with, while the response terms describe the parts he would look at and their condition (e.g., broken valve).

The procedure for "reconstruction" as it was followed in these studies was to analyze what the person needed to know to perform the task. Then these relationships were analyzed on an antecedent-consequent basis in terms of their temporal order of occurrence on the job. This produced the paradigms of associative sharing and overlapping. For example, the verbal stimulus element "high fuel flow" was shared by a number of different responses, all of which the individual had to learn if he was to become competent as a troubleshooter. The associative paradigms were treated as multiple stimulus-response sets rather than simple one-to-one pairs when materials were reconstructed from the analysis (see Stolurow and Bergum, 1958; Wulff and Stolurow, 1957).

When generalized in this way, paired associates become paired sets of associates. We found that paired columnar presentation, without the structural words of prose, aided learning (see figure 2). Also, when we presented materials in one direction of association and then another (see tasks I and II in figure 3), we found that there was high positive transfer when the associative paradigms were one to two (condition 9 in figure 3), but that transfer became highly negative when the associative paradigms were of the many-to-many type (condition 5). The results of one study using these paradigms are summarized in figure 4. All the paradigms in figure 3 were learned by all stu-

dents as a control measure. These data indicate that when terms
are associated with one another in a one-to-two relationship
involving only sharing, the reverse direction of association can
be learned more readily than the original direction. They also
indicate that as the pattern of relationship gets more complex in
terms of sharing and overlapping, learning the "backward"
direction of association is more difficult than learning the "forward" direction. To reverse the direction of association can be
looked at as a transfer condition that varies from positive and
facilitating to negative and interfering, depending upon the
complexity of the associative relationships among the terms.
There is apparently a very powerful interference effect produced by association overlapping. It seems that the amount of

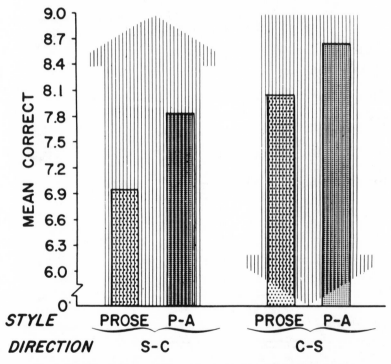

Fig. 1. Symptom-cause relationships in Lesson "5" and Lesson "9."

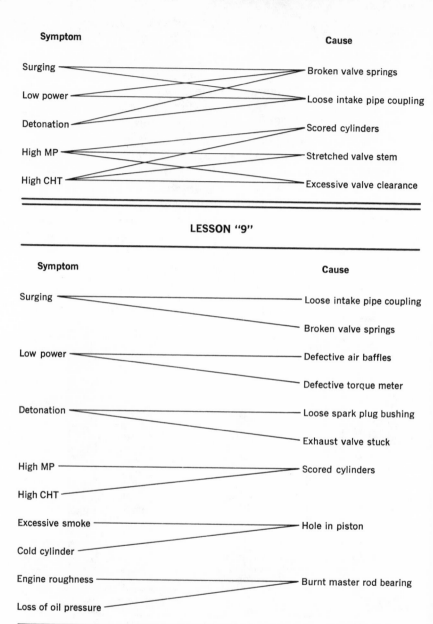

Fig. 2. Means of correct responses for groups given various combinations of style and direction of association.

Paradigms of Interrelationships of S-Terms and R-Terms for the Six Conditions Employed in Two Experiments*

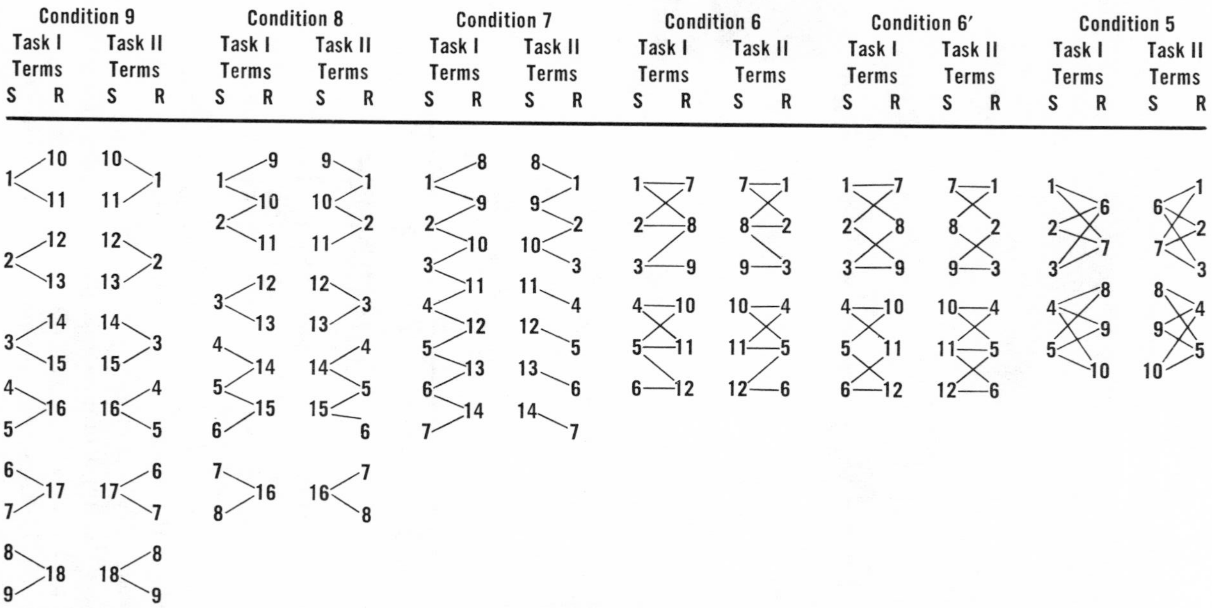

Fig. 3. The ratio of S-terms to linkages in going from condition 9 to condition 5 is .75, .67, .58, .50, .50, and .42, respectively. This is an objective measure of S and R sharing. Condition 6 and condition 6′ do not differ from each other in the amount of sharing but do differ in the amount of overlapping of connections each contains. Condition 6′ has four overlapping linkages, whereas condition 6 has only two.

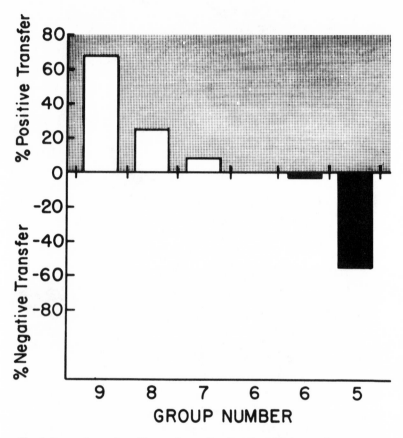

Fig. 4. Percentage of positive and negative transfer with increasing amounts of S and R sharing — experiment II. The numbers on the abscissa refer to the several experimental conditions outlined in table 1.

sharing is somewhat less potent than the number of overlapping terms. Since the number of associates was kept constant, it seems reasonable to assume that the amounts of overlap and sharing are the important factors that determine the changes in transfer under association reversal.

This kind of analysis of prose material to develop a hypothesis with implications for learning and transfer is very similar to what Barbara Musgrave and Jean Cohen described. We started with textual materials used by students and simply analyzed them to see what learning problems might be produced by their structure and the way they are used. In addition, we deleted noncritical parts of the conventional prose to make up "P-A" tabulations (without the dotted lines) to see what effect a "blackout" procedure would have. We use "P-A" to represent paired sets of associates, and compared the original prose with the reconstructed material presented as a paired-columnar presentation to see if the isolation of the relationships would help the learner. While sentences are the usual way of conveying verbal information to a learner, the paired-columnar format could make the critical verbal relationships salient. This might be a useful device to facilitate learning from prose. In this situation we found the paired-columnar presentation superior to the prose (see Figure 1). This suggests that in learning from prose — as contrasted with learning of prose — the grammatically required material for composing sentences may not be necessary and, in fact, may be a negative factor when the nature of the relationships in the contingency statements (if . . . then . . .) are clear. It is assumed that the subjects introduced their own language to express the materials presented to them in the paired-columnar arrangement.

I mentioned this research for a number of reasons. One is to illustrate the approaches described. Another is that on a couple of occasions during the symposium it seemed that a case was being made for the consistent advantage of the presence of grammatical structure in presenting to students prose materials from which they were to learn. The data in the study Bergum and I made indicate that there are conditions in which the inclusion of the structural elements can be a disadvantage. This may occur only when the terms to be related fit a complex associative paradigm involving sharing and overlapping, but even so it does suggest that at least one limiting condition exists for the generalization.

Another kind of data, opposite to some of the points made, that I think might be extrapolated from learning from prose should also be mentioned because they require reconsideration of a widely held position. The data came from a situation in which we added stimulus materials to those required and got more efficient learning. Let me describe the situation.

The study was developed from a reconstruction based upon a task analysis of faultfinding, or troubleshooting (Stolurow, 1956). In the task, the learner has a panel in front of him on which there is a set of locations identifiable in terms of a row and column position. We can call the panel a matrix; it has three columns and six rows, or eighteen cells, all covered by a flap. The learner's problem was to look at each symptom presented to him on a 3 x 5 card and to associate it with a cell in the matrix. In effect, he was to learn eighteen paired associates. The card information was a verbal description of a symptom. The learner read each card and then lifted a flap that represented a possible trouble spot on this panel. Five conditions were used. In one, the panel was completely uniform in color so that all the cell flaps were black. This was condition 1C (one color). It was the basic condition for learning. In this condition, the student had all the information he needed for learning, since each card (or stimulus) was uniquely related to a cell. For example, all the individual had to remember was that he was to go to row A, column 3, for card J.

We used four other conditions to see if learning might be facilitated. One was the use of colors as diacritical signs. For example, in condition 2C two colors were randomly assigned to cells so that the matrix was now coded with half red and half blue patches on flaps, but the colors were not in correspondence with either row or column arrangements; rather, they were scattered. We also used three, six, and nine different colors to get the five different conditions. For all of them, the colors were randomly assigned to cell positions. As more diacritical signs were used, we found that learning was improved. The rationale was that the colors, while unnecessary, provided the individual with a class-descriptive cue. This is a cue common to some, but not all, of the elements of a set to be learned. It was our hypothesis that the colors permitted the student to break the task down into subtasks. Adding color was not an added burden; in fact, it was just the opposite. If the effect of color is thought of in the sense of adding information, then color acted to permit the individual to associate a color with a set of terms and thereby reduce the size of the set of possibilities that he had to consider when he looked at a card. The colors became a basis for breaking the total task down into subsets.

Possibly some of the characteristics talked about in the analysis of grammatical material serve as signs of this type. Structural features of the language may provide the learner with useful cues in segmenting prose to make it easier to learn. In other words, some structural characteristics may provide the learner with a basis for grouping, or clustering materials into subsets, that he otherwise would have to learn as a larger set. They could reduce the number of elements with which he has to cope at any point in time. This possibility in relation to what was said previously about paired arrangements for sets of associates is consistent in its emphasis upon the desirability of salience and subtasking, but raises the question of how structural features of prose are to be used to have the desired facilitating effect.

The question of psychological objectives is the last one I want to discuss. It has two aspects that are quite interesting in terms of some preliminary data we have obtained. One deals with the fact, mentioned earlier, that measures do not all vary in the same way. The point here is that the educator has to decide what is most important: rapid learning, better retention, or superior transfer. He has to commit himself to a psychological objective as well as to content objectives. Different prose structures and different ways of presenting verbal materials play a part in determining which objectives are achieved. Some structural forms may facilitate learning but not promote retention or transfer. We need studies of the relationships between structural characteristics of prose and its learnability, retentivity, and transferability.

Another dimension to this problem is illustrated by aptitude correlates of learning from prose when only the sequence of the instructional material is manipulated. We find evidence of an interaction that Dr. Glaser mentioned. In other words, a characteristic of individuals may be related to their terminal performance when one sequence of frames is used, but this same characteristic may not be correlated with terminal performance when a different sequence is used. This means that the performance objectives were accomplished for some students with one sequence and for others with a different sequence. This was found with a program teaching elementary students concepts in arithmetic, in which the students learned quantitative concepts from prose. The results indicate that some sequential structures, or organization of the verbal instructional material, make the verbal aptitude of students predictive of terminal performance, while others do not. In other words, the correlation of their learning scores with their language aptitude (one of the prediction variables used) drops to zero with one sequence, but is significantly high and positively related to final performance with another. These data were obtained with students who were within a range of some thirty I.Q. points of each other in general intellectual ability. The same general result was obtained in another study (Stolurow, 1967). The sequences that exist within a set of frames determine the ease or difficulty with which students learn. The ease of learning a particular sequence depends upon the student's aptitude profile.

In another study (summarized in Stolurow, 1967), we compared two notation systems for teaching logic. One was the Peano-Russell system, which is the more traditional form of notation illustrated in the expression PQ, meaning P and Q. The other was the Polish notation system in which the same expression is written as KPQ, where K is the operator standing for "and." Scores from a set of aptitude tests (verbal, quantitative, and inference) were related to learning scores when each of these notation systems was used with a different group of college students. The programs were identical in sequence, treatment of concepts, coverage of truth tables, and related points of the propositional logic course. With the Peano-Russell notation we found that the three aptitude measures correlated significantly with terminal performance. With the Polish notation system none of these aptitude tests correlated significantly.

This suggests the hypothesis that what was happening to change the predictability of performance was due to the symbol processing engaged in by the students. The symbol system that one processes while learning has conventions associated with it that require the learner to do things with the symbols in order to relate them to his existing meaning system. The Polish notation system requires the student to engage in transformations of symbols so he can make sense out of expressions. With the Peano-Russell notation system, fewer transformations are required. The hypothesis is that the student is using very different processing skills, depending on whether he learns the same concepts from the Peano-Russell expressions or the Polish ones.

These data also raise serious questions about the validity of the aptitude tests, for one could infer from the data provided by the group that studied with the Peano-Russell notation that the aptitude tests were predicting the learning of logical concepts. However, the group that studied with the Polish notation were also learning logical concepts. The aptitude tests did not relate to the learning that could be called propositional logic. The data suggest that the processing skills elicited by a specific set of symbols account for the performance scores that correlate with the aptitude tests. Knowledge of logic, or the logical concepts that were learned by both groups, are what we usually think of as the content of the course. If we continue to think this way, then the aptitude tests are not valid for the general prediction of the ability to acquire knowledge, since they only predict performance under certain instructional conditions.

This interpretation raises some questions that relate to the theory of parsing that one uses to describe what a person does in generating or analyzing a sentence or a logical proposition. Parsing is a form of symbolic processing, and it is involved in the extraction of meaning from expressions in symbolic logic. The hypothesis just discussed suggests that any form of expression in a natural language that is used to convey meaning to a student is going to require a set of processing skills, of which parsing skills may be a subset. With two structurally different, but linguistically equivalent, statements, it can be inferred that the student has to do different things in order to elicit meaningful associations. If this analogy is correct, then perhaps the correlation of aptitude with learning scores can give us some indication of the skills involved in learning from each of the differently structured materials. The transformation processes an individual is required to use when presented with sentences in different forms will depend upon his habitual processing skills. When the same words are presented in different sequences as determined by different transformation rules, it can be inferred that the learner has to transform some of these into another form with which he is more familiar. When that is required, he has to use different skills to learn.

Two approaches to research seem to have promise. In one, the aptitude correlates of learning from different forms of expression are determined. Another would be to have individuals express in their own words a concept, process, or instruction. The resulting statements would reveal how they transform the material and the extent to which there is any transformational consistency.

NOTES

1. The reference is to a talk at the symposium by Dr. Edwin Martin (University of Michigan), which will be published elsewhere.

2. The reference is to a talk at the symposium by Dr. James Holland (University of Pittsburgh), which will be published elsewhere.

REFERENCES

Cartwright, G. P. Two types of programmed instruction for mentally retarded adolescents. Unpublished master's thesis, Univ. of Illinois, 1962.

Detambel, M. H., and Stolurow, L. M. Stimulus sequence and concept learning. *J. exp. Psychol.*, 1956, *51*(1), 34–40.

Noble, C. E., and Fuchs, J. E. Serial errors in human learning: A test of the McCrary-Hunter Hypothesis. *Science,* 1959, *129* (570–571).

Stolurow, L. M. Utilization of class-descriptive cues in the learning of technical information—studies in task engineering. In G. Finch and F. Cameron (Eds.), *Symposium on Air Force human engineering, personnel and training research*. Washington, D.C.: National Academy of Sciences–National Research Council, pub. no. 455, 1956, 248–266.

—— A computer assisted instructional system in theory and research. In D. Unwin and J. Leedham (Eds.), *Aspects of educational technology*. London: Methuen & Co. Ltd., 1967. (The Proceedings of the Programmed Learning Conference, Loughborough, England, April 15–18, 1966.)

Stolurow, L. M., and Bergum, B. Learning diagnostic information — effects of direction of association and of prose vs. paired-associates presentation. In G. Finch and F. Cameron (Eds.), *Symposium on Air Force human engineering, personnel and training research*. Washington, D.C.: National Academy of Sciences–National Research Council, pub. no. 516, 1958, 69–84.

Stolurow, L. M., Detambel, M. H., and Newman, J. R. Transfer effects of "association reversal" under several conditions of stimulus and response "sharing." *American Psychologist*, 1956, *11*, 485. (Abstract of paper presented at 28th Annual Meeting of the Midwestern Psychological Association, St. Louis, and deposited with the ADI Auxiliary Publications Project, Photoduplication Service, Library of Congress, Washington, D.C., doc. no. 5004.)

Stolurow, L. M., Hodgson, T. F., and Silva, J. Transfer and retroaction effects of "association reversal" and "familiarization" training in trouble-shooting. *Psychol. Monogr.*, 1956, *70* (12, whole no. 419).

Wulff, J. J., and Stolurow, L. M. The role of class-descriptive cues in paired-associates learning. *J. exp. Psychol.*, 1957, *53*, 199–206.

Comments Relating to the Design of Written Instruction

ROBERT GLASER

University of Pittsburgh

My assigned role is to examine the problem of the *application* of knowledge of verbal learning and to indicate the kind of information that is required for the development and evaluation of instructional materials. In order to do this, it is necessary to introduce a framework for thinking about instructional materials and interweave into this schema some of the things that went on in this symposium.

REQUIREMENTS IN THE DESIGN OF INSTRUCTIONAL MATERIALS

A first requirement in the design of instructional materials is *analysis of the subject-matter domain.* This analysis takes place on two levels: (*a*) in terms of the structure of the discipline as given to us by subject-matter experts, and (*b*) in terms of the kinds of tasks involved, as the psychologist needs to look at them. Presumably, there are different learning phenomena involved in different kinds of tasks. Thus, an initial problem in the preparation of written instructions is to know what is being learned. Once this is determined, stimulus materials and appropriate response requirements can be set up for the learner.

348

A second kind of information required for instructional design is specification of *the kind of performance to be optimized;* this provides performance criteria. This information obviously influences the instructional situation. What are the criteria: a high score on a test, the difference between a pre-test and a post-test score, transfer of training, and/or retention? The tactics of instruction differ depending upon what is to be optimized.

A third kind of information is *the entering repertoire of the learner,* that is, the kind of behavior that the learner brings to the instructional situation. The interaction between entering behavior and instructional variables is often ignored; frequently, it is controlled out for experimental purposes by standardized nonsense materials or similarly constrained tasks. In order to take account of this interaction, it is necessary to measure the performance of the learner prior to instruction in order to obtain his baseline performance characteristics. Behavioral change, then, can be interpreted from this baseline.

INSTRUCTIONAL TREATMENT
AND EDUCATIONAL CHANGE

Having specified, to some extent, the nature of the subject matter, the learning criteria to be optimized, and the entering repertoire of the learner, the subsequent instructional task is to go from entering behavior to the required subject-matter competence. This brings up consideration of the independent variables of educational change: the instructional treatment. The problem here is somewhat different from the manipulation of independent variables in the usual laboratory learning experiment, because with instructional treatment variables the attempt is made not so much to describe learning as to *prescribe* it. Such prescription needs to be made on the basis of the entering repertoire of the subject and information about his learning history. The use of learner history requires that instructional materials be dynamic enough so that they are responsive to learner performance; instructional materials should change, depending upon the way in which the learner goes through a learning sequence. This adaptation to the learner may be broken down into two aspects: (a) the long-term habits of the subject, such as aptitudes and sets that he brings to the learning situation; and (b) the shorter-run behavior (e.g., short-runs of responses over five minutes, an hour, or a week) consisting of measures of latency, error runs, number of trials, amount of reinforcement, aspects of VTE, and so forth. Short-term histories can provide a basis from which predictions can be made from one instructional prescription to the next.

The Problem of Task Analysis

Many of the papers presented in this symposium touch upon the necessity for the analysis of subject matter—the task-analysis problem. When a psychologist who has carried out verbal learning experiments thinks about written instructions, he comes up against the fact that he now has to handle a real-life task. This presents a special problem because for all his experimental life he has been designing particular tasks for the laboratory and, hence, knows their characteristics. Now, however, he is required to use "real" tasks for experimentation. He then realizes that this poses a special problem because he has no familiar techniques for analyzing task properties. Along these lines, Chomsky and his students have been confronting psychologists who study verbal learning with real-life tasks and are forcing the consideration of tasks with certain complexities. This raises the question of how real tasks can be analyzed and classified so that their properties are laid out for experimental study. A relevant example is Eleanor Gibson's article (1965) on reading, in which she makes the distinction between *what* is to be learned (a job for the psychologist to be concerned with first) and *how* it is learned. Gibson devotes experimental time to analyzing the nature and structure of the task prior to manipulating variables that influence the learning of the task.

In the present symposium, Goss and Musgrave consider the analysis of tasks using paired-associate list learning techniques. As I interpret their efforts, they are interested in determining whether they can use the techniques in which they are so proficient as a means of analyzing real-life tasks. Goss, particularly, hopes that this is a paired-associate world, and works under the assumption that what we know about the paired-associate model can be applied to much of the behavior involved in using written instructions. This remains to be seen and, perhaps, is a significant risk; but he, armed with his model, is proceeding from his knowledge of list learning and paired-associate techniques to real-world tasks.

It is also possible to proceed from the real-world tasks by a sort of task analysis and to generate the models with which you have to operate. Musgrave functions a little in this latter way. She is interested in having subjects generate lists and tables from written material and plans to study the data obtained. The student-generated table can be an interesting variable to study. Some kind of theory can be elaborated on how the student derives tables from written materials and what the potential variables that influence the nature of the table generated are. By controlling the nature of the written passage, one might be able to predict the kind of table a student would make in learning to memorize a written passage. This kind of investigation has been reported by Seibel (1965).

Glanzer and Newman, especially the latter, are also concerned with the characteristics of tasks, and the way in which a task is to be analyzed. The work presented by Johnson on the analysis of response probabilities supports the task analysis notion in a somewhat different way. It shows how the structure of the subject-matter domain results in certain stimulus-selection tendencies, related, of course, to the question of what it is that needs to be learned.

The Influence of Individual Differences on Learning

The entering repertoire of the subject obviously is related to the question of how individual differences influence learning. Newman points to the importance of studying the way in which the learner instructs himself and how the learner complicates things and does not handle them in paired-associate form. Rothkopf suggests that learning goes on in support of the criteria that the subject knows he is trying to optimize. Such data point to the necessity of examining in detail the individual difference x treatment interactions in learning studies. It will be difficult to generate effective written instructions unless we are more secure about individual difference effects. One way of studying individual differences is to determine behavioral baselines by detailed assessment of response-related characteristics of the subject prior to conducting an experiment.

The Importance of Behavioral Measurement

Coleman's paper and the paper presented by Klare are concerned with the stimulus properties of prose materials that influence behavior. This again points to the necessary endeavor of task analysis. However, these papers suggest another emphasis to be made in considering the design of written instruction. It is necessary to ask, not only about the characteristics of the behavior we are interested in producing in the reader, but also about how this behavior can be measured. We should not be too ready to use the handy ways available, like the cloze procedure or associative strength measures; we should be more disciplined and specify what kind of behavior we are interested in producing in the learner, proceed to try to obtain this behavior, and then measure it appropriately. (It is also possible that if we state the experimental problem as the use of some kind of written materials to produce certain kinds of behaviors in subjects, the answer may be a form of instructions that does not look like prose at all. It may be nonprose or tables of some sort.) Coleman's miniature language procedure suggests the development of standard prose setups and standard measurements for them. These can consist of passages that sample subject-matter domains and textual and verbal constraints, which can influence these miniature situations. This would help counteract the trend in experimental psychology that results in a diversity of nonstandard experimental situations that make experiments noninterchangeable and resist uniform interpretation.

An intriguing kind of experimentation is "responsive" prose manipulation. I am not sure how this can be done, but it seems possible to get a subject to read some prose, to ask some questions about it, and then make up the next prose passage in accordance with his performance on the previous passage, keeping in mind the kind of behavior you want eventually to attain. I am suggesting that prose can be designed on the basis of a subject's responses to a just immediate passage in order to shape his behavior toward criterion performance.

RELEVANT CONSIDERATIONS FOR WRITTEN INSTRUCTION

Overall, in research and development on the problem of written instruction, the following considerations seem relevant:

The Properties of Task Competence

In analyzing the properties of the task performance, a distinction should probably be made between *content* repertoire and *component* repertoire. Content repertoire is a function of the nature and structure of the subject matter (whether it is arithmetic, logic, or a spoken language), and the technical terms and concepts involved. Component repertoire refers to the classes of behavior, as psychologists think of behavior, involved in working with the subject-matter content. Thinking in terms of a component repertoire requires that questions be asked about the stimulus-response relationships involved in the subject matter. For example, is there a point-to-point correspondence between the stimulus and response as there might be in following simple directions, or is a more mediated, thematic response involved? Analysis of the component repertoire permits the investigator to look at what has been found in psychological research about the variables that influence the learning of tasks with such component characteristics.

With particular reference to written instruction, a further distinction can be made between content and function. *Function* refers to the fact that, in addition to content information, written instructions sometimes tell the learner what he is to learn and direct his attention in a certain way, to certain aspects of the stimulus situation and to particular ways of selecting stimuli. They also serve as a stimulus for recall, directing the learner to call up previous knowledge, as well as establishing a learning set or a way of thinking about the content. The function of written instructions, as contrasted to their content, seems to be an important aspect for study.

In analyzing task competence, the dimensions of generalization are of interest. There are certain dimensions of the content along which we may wish the student to generalize his learning. For example, we may be concerned with generalization to different language populations, generalizations that are going to result in concept formation and in transfer to different response modes.

Pre-experimental Behavior (Entering Repertoire)

As has already been said, this is the behavior that the student brings to the written instructions. The student may have already learned certain aspects of task competence, and the designer of the instructions needs to know whether he is to adapt to various levels of initial competence. Another aspect of pre-experimental behavior is prerequisite knowledge and skill; these are the knowledges and skills that the written instructions assume in order for learning to proceed. The presence or absence of certain prerequisite behaviors will facilitate or inhibit what the subject gets out of the written passage. These prerequisite behaviors involve, for example, previously acquired problem-solving sets and those learning predispositions that the English language forces upon individuals living in an English-speaking society.

Acquiring Task Competence

The problem here is how to get from pre-experimental behavior to task competence. How this is accomplished depends, of course, upon the kind of learning and the kind of behavior involved. Some gross considerations can be suggested:

1. Does learning the task involve primarily response learning and the establishment of new forms of response? In this case, learning might proceed by the matching and alignment of properties of the learner's responses with the response properties defined as competence, a kind of successive approximation or shaping process.

2. On the other hand, does learning the task primarily involve establishing stimulus control over already learned responses? In this case, the subject must learn to discriminate certain stimuli in the environment and to have these stimuli set the occasion for old responses. This kind of learning is distinguished by the fact that competent responses are being transferred to new stimuli, as, for example, in second-language learning.

3. Very evident in proficient verbal behavior is the fact that the expert becomes less and less dependent upon environmental support, and displays much self-sustaining behavior. Two questions for investigation in the design of written instructions are how to establish increasingly minimal environmental and textual support, and how to maintain competence by maintaining this self-sustaining behavior. Written instructional materials will be different if we are trying to set up new forms of response, or trying to establish stimulus control over old forms of response, or attempting to maintain proficient behavior.

Finally, the distinction made earlier between the "description" and "prescription" of learning should be reemphasized. While adequate scientific description permits prescription, the tactics for doing the work of each enterprise differ. As carried out, the study of verbal learning seems to require experiments designed to establish functional relationships and to test theories. The design of written instructions requires specification of the behavioral change desired in the learner and the arrangement of the instructional environment in order to produce the behavior specified.

REFERENCES

Gibson, E. J. Learning to read. *Science,* 1965, *148,* 1066–1072.

Seibel, R. Organization in human verbal learning: The study sheet paradigm and experiments one & two. Paper read at Psychonomic Society meeting, October, 1965.

Some Comments on Strategy and Tactics in Research on Instructional Materials

ARTHUR A. LUMSDAINE

University of Washington

I would like to address my remarks to some general questions of perspective and strategy, rather than specifically to the particular papers that have been presented here.

First, I would like to say something about our realm of discourse — that is, the relevant domain for a conference such as this one. Rothkopf identified some reasons at the outset for the importance of giving particular attention to written (or printed) materials. I would like to suggest that these characteristics — in particular, the documentary characteristics of written materials (i.e., their reproducibility) — are shared by other materials such as audio-visual or audio-recorded materials. I would prefer to have us talk about recorded or documentary instruction generally, rather than confining our attention solely to the written or printed verbal species of this genre of instruction.

There is, to be sure, one feature not stressed by Rothkopf that peculiarly characterizes written instruction and gives it some special amenability to the kinds of analyses that we have seen illustrated here. This is the fact that printed material is digital, at least for cultures that use alphabets. This feature may considerably constrain the number of stimulus dimensions to be dealt with, and thus facilitate the kinds of analyses that we have heard about. Having done a good deal of work with cinematic and other pictorial presentations, which are less readily digitalized, I can appreciate the advantage of this feature. However, this distinction starts to disappear when we begin dealing with techniques, such as Mathews has described, in which substantially pictorial material is generated from and stored as digital information.

In any case, I think that much of the general rationale underlying this conference — that is, the argument that written instructional materials are a peculiarly strategic focus for attempting to apply scientific findings — does apply to other forms of recorded or documentary materials. This may be illustrated by the existence of a great many parallels between the kinds of problems and the kinds of findings that have emerged from research on audio-visual media and the kinds of problems and findings that have been dealt with in this conference. (For general reviews see Lumsdaine, 1961, chap. 31; Lumsdaine, 1963; Lumsdaine and May, 1965.)

Several studies that have been mentioned in the conference illustrate such parallels. In some instances it was clear either from what was said during the conference or from extrasession conversations that these parallels were known, but in other instances it was quite clear that they were not. In some instances, the parallels were perhaps only klang associations that may have had no real relevance, but in other instances they did seem quite relevant. At least, cross comparisons of the two groups of studies are likely to be provocative in their implications, even where earlier studies have dealt with teaching of procedures, such as manual assembly tasks, rather than with purely verbal tasks.

For example, the studies on "inserted question" that Rothkopf mentions find parallels in some earlier studies by Maccoby, Michael, and Levine (see Lumsdaine, 1961, chap. 19) and also in some earlier work that May and I did back in the late 1940s at Yale and published some years later (May and Lumsdaine, 1958). There the medium was film, but the same variables of inserted questions were employed. In some instances, the results were similar to what Rothkopf suggested, but in other cases the results were quite different. The interesting question, of course, is, Why are the results different? Can these be associated with intrinsic differences among the media? Is there something intrinsic about the character of an audio-visual, or audio-paced, presentation in which each short segment is gone the moment after it is presented and cannot be looked at again easily? Or, as seems more likely, are the differences in effects (e.g., of prior inserted questions versus later inserted questions) due to other factors not inherently associated with the media?

May and I (1958, chap. 7) did obtain considerable differences in selective attention based on prior questions, which Rothkopf did not. On the other hand, Maccoby, Michael, and Levine found it was very hard to get effects of inserted questions following the passage on anything other than the material to which the questions directly related, which was indeed the nonmaterial effect that Rothkopf seems to have been interested in. (In order to get such effects, what had to be done was to degenerate the interest level of material to make it somewhat boring; some of Rothkopf's results may have been related to the fact that his instructional sequences were quite long, while those in the earlier studies were shorter.)

I would also like to comment briefly on the difference in orientation that is characteristic of what we may call an "engineering," or "technological," approach, and a "basic science" approach to research on instructional materials. This is bound up with the distinction between studying the learning process in "passive" terms—that is, studying how people *do* learn from written or other materials—versus studying the orientation of how they *ought* to learn—that is, studying learning with a direct concern for how one can take responsibility for seeing that learning takes place efficiently. The latter viewpoint means manipulating the conditions of learning to try to optimize, in some sense, the learning that takes place.

Some of the studies reported in this symposium do not seem to be conceived with this kind of purpose; they seem to be inquiries into what *affects* learning rather than how to *effect* it. I do not say this in deprecation—there is a great deal of merit in each approach—but I do wish to point out the distinction. I believe that it is important to look at the kinds of variables that are manipulated in experiments not only from the standpoint of the behavior that learners spontaneously exhibit, but also with the conscious aim of trying to improve the effectiveness of that behavior through manipulation of instructional materials to that end.

Furthermore, I do not think that an engineering effort—that is, an attempt to construct more effective materials to do a practical job of instruction—is likely to come about simply as a derivative from the results of scientific studies that are not practically oriented. On the contrary, I think that some of the scientific questions that need to be answered arise from dilemmas that confront individuals who try to program instruction at the practical level. This happens when they reach decision points at which they do not know what to do, and to which existing research does not provide an adequate guide (cf., Lumsdaine, 1962, pp. 134–151).

Two questions provide a kind of strategic "razor" that can be applied usefully to the kinds of research we are concerned with here. These questions, applicable to each of the results or conclusions of a study, are: (1) do we really know it? and (2) if we really do know it, what can we do with it?

The second of the two questions involves the practical question of how much effect you will have if you apply what your research has revealed. Perhaps we should step back more often from our fascination with our theories, our manipulations, and our data and ask the question, Suppose we did pin this down, what would we be able to do with it then? rather than only concerning ourselves with what nature is like, and then later on trying to find out some way to apply what we have learned.

Initially, it might be good strategy to select for first attention in experiments those independent variables that would seem likely to account for most variance in respect to various classes of dependent variables. In addition, we need to assess results in terms of the magnitude of potency of effects produced, not just in terms of "significance" in the sense of reliability. I shall return to this point later.

The answer to the first question posed above would seem to be primarily a matter of determining the limits of generalizability of what we think we have found out. The relevant limits apply to both the independent and the dependent variables. With dependent variables, the question is: Will we get the same results if we use different measures? As an important particular example, will we get the same results if we measure retention after a period of time as compared with what we get with just an immediate measure? A number of studies have suggested rather strongly that we are likely to find quite marked differences in results (qualitative differences, not just that the findings are attenuated as we get more error due to forgetting) when retention is measured after some post-training delay (see Lumsdaine and May, 1965, p. 503). The "same" dependent variable measured after a period of time may be a quite different variable than when measured immediately after learning. Yet, presumably for practical reasons of convenience, study after study has failed to take the trouble to use delayed retention measures. I would like to suggest that we go as far as we can in trying to get retention measures for *all* studies of learning from verbal material.

Similarly, several studies, as well as general considerations of the sort that Glaser has mentioned to the symposium, suggest that results are likely to differ rather markedly as a function of characteristics of the individual learner. Since in almost every study it is possible to get at least some relevant measure of the intellectual ability of each subject, I would like to suggest that the results routinely be analyzed as a function of such measures to see whether there are interactions between the experimental variables and intellectual ability. Thus, we may obtain patterns of results for higher and lower intelligence. I am not suggesting that I.Q. differentiation is the best one in all instances, but at least some such differential analysis should be made, which has not always been done in past studies.

In trying to compare across studies conducted in different areas, I have found numerous studies in which interesting differential findings were obtained as a function of ability, after which the investigators did another study dealing with similar variables, but with no report of possible interactions with ability. Further, in some cases the data that a subsequent investigator might look at to see if there is an anticipated kind of difference as a function of individual differences do not even exist; or, at least, the data have not been reported in a form that permits the analysis to be made. This suggests the general desirability of making it a matter of routine to preserve the basic data in such form that additional analyses can be performed later as a function of relevant characteristics of the learner. (The AERA–APA–DAVI Joint Committee on Programmed Instruction [1966] has recommended this step for all evaluative studies of instructional programs.)

Two other questions of general strategy deserve to be noted here, at least briefly, because they come up rather frequently. One of these is the problem of what conclusion to draw when something is found in one investigator's experiment but not in another's, in which the conditions are somewhat different. Perhaps more resources than usual should be devoted to providing a potential link with previous experiments by having common conditions. That is, we need to try more often to base our conclusions on intraexperimental rather than interexperimental comparisons. Otherwise, the differential conclusion ascribed to any one respect in which the two experiments differed is confounded because the experiments also differed in other respects. The other general issue was illustrated in the difference in preference between what Barbara Musgrave was advocating and what Goss and Newman said they preferred. As I understood it, Musgrave said she would rather jump ahead and introduce two or more factors at once that might have a sizable cumulative effect on learning. The alternative point of view seems to be more cautious: let's not go that far quite that fast. There seems to me no reason why one cannot do both. That is, one can change both of two (or more) characteristics, one at a time, in a fourfold design, so that one gets both the comparison between the simplest and the doubly elaborated treatment, which also reveals the single effects. I would prefer this strategy to either of the two that have been advocated.

Finally, I would like to emphasize my complete concurrence with Musgrave's interest, which was also displayed by several other people, on the importance of definition of objectives. This is important in the context that has been raised by Newman and others, but also in terms of the focusing of attention on trying to determine *what* you ought to teach as distinct from *how* you ought to teach it. I suspect that if we wanted to improve education, we could do a great deal more, in terms of total proportion of variance amounted for, by improving *what* we teach, rather than by variations in the relative efficiency of just *how* we teach a particular thing. I mean this both at the specific level of what substeps you have to get through (that is, the analysis of a particular learning task in terms of subgoals), and also at the more remote level, i.e., the general composition of the curriculum. The latter is not, as it stands, an experimental problem. Thus, it is not surprising that not very many experimental psychologists have devoted their attention to it. Yet there is reason for concern that perhaps we may be devoting too much attention to what may be relatively minor refinements in how to present material (i.e., minor in terms of their total impact) and not enough attention to the question of what people really need to learn. The answer to the latter can, I think, be regarded basically as a problem of transfer of training, provided that one can define at least some ultimate, or at least penultimate, criteria to which transfer can be referred.

This raises the problem of validity, which has come up in connection with several of the papers. For example, I was intrigued with the kinds of word association measures that Verplanck [1] discussed. One thing that disturbed me, however, was that in terms of speaking of the validity of these measures, he had to fall back·on the old, threadbare grade-point average. Of course, the difficulty in getting meaningful statements about validity relates to the difficulty of defining specifically the kinds of behaviors that we are really interested in teaching. (It is sometimes said that the difference between education and training is that in training you know what you are trying to teach.)

The difficulty of defining objectives differs greatly for various educational situations. At least one instance in which something closer to validation might be obtained for such measures as Verplanck has proposed would be to concentrate initially on subject matters where there is clearly less of an opinion component (e.g., courses in statistical methods or research design). Here it is quite clear that at least one of the desired outcomes is to get people to be able to solve certain kinds of problems. This outcome has a very high degree of face validity as an objective. In this case one could readily investigate the predictive validity of associational measures, such as Verplanck's, against that criterion.

A point that came up several times during the symposium, and may deserve some special attention, is the distinction between those variables that are indicative of how much the person learns *if* he is exposed to material, as contrasted with how persistent he will be in studying, or how much "Zeigarnik-effect" he shows. In short, does he really tend to go on to completing the task?

It seems to me that we should be very much interested in both of these as objectives, and that some of the controversy about which independent variables may be effective may be resolvable when looked at in terms of such differences in classes of dependent variables. One example during this conference was the concern expressed about the relevance of laboratory studies of partial reinforcement. It seems rather clear that this independent variable is likely to be much more relevant to the continuation of study (e.g., continuing to turn pages) than to the learning of substantive content when one *is* exposed.

In short, different classes of independent variables (semantic, syntactic, etc.) need to be distinguished explicitly from other classes of independent variables with reference to the kinds of dependent variables to which they are relevant. Further, more attention is needed generally for the second ("motivational") class of dependent variables, which have not been measured very often in experimental situations to identify the independent variables that influence them.

With respect to the problems of generalizability on the side of the independent variable, I have been impressed previously, and have been reinforced considerably by what I have heard here, with the hazards of being overconfident about the unequivocality of given independent variables in instructional studies. We find it convenient to label procedures with a given term, and then do experiments, which in some instances obtain positive results, in others negative results. For example, there is a variety of confusing results on the role of overt practice as contrasted with more implicit forms of behavior. Holland (1965) has reported that what is nominally the "same" variable (overt response) works in quite a different way, depending on how it is implemented.

The skeptical conclusion that emerges from such considerations and findings is that a particular "variable," as employed by one experimenter in one program, is often a quite different thing from the same "variable" as manipulated by an experimenter in another field. In the traditional literature of experimental psychology, in the fine print section not too long after the beginning of the article, a rather full, not always full enough, specification of procedure is given. If one relies on such an operational definition of what the independent variable is, then the hazard is greatly minimized. But it seems to be the practice in dealing with practical instructional problems (in studies of programmed instruction, etc.) to incur the "naming fallacy" of using a verbal label to characterize a nonoperationally defined "variable," which is really an aggregate of variables that sometimes operate one way and sometimes another way. It is not what the variable is called that really matters but the way it is implemented. Sometimes the diversity of results associated with a particular "variable" almost reaches the point where one wonders if one can expect to generalize much beyond the confines of a particular program and a particular investigator's manipulation of that particular variable.

I think the most constructive approach is to try to define independent variables better, and also to test empirically the generalizability of the independent variables whose effects are being studied. The approach suggested here is, in effect, that of considering as the "subject" in the experiment the experimenter or the programmer, not the learner. Independent variables will then be defined in terms of instructions to programmers or editors or teachers as to what they are to do about a particular procedure. Generalizability will be tested by having a number of experimenters or programmers independently try to implement these instructions. In this case the proper number of degrees of freedom in the analysis is not the number of learners, but the number of programmers. At least one or two studies are under way in which this is being done.

Many, perhaps most, independent instructional variables cannot yet be characterized in sufficiently analytic terms to make safe generalizations beyond the boundaries of the original experiment. Indeed, one may question whether the results of many of the experiments published thus far really will mean very much until this kind of explicit demonstration of generalizability is made. To do so obviously increases the expense of the experiments. Therefore, a strategy is needed to try to distinguish those kinds of variables that appear to have sufficient intrinsic stability so that an explicit demonstration of generalizability, though ideally desirable, will not be necessary.

I would like to reinforce two other notions before I conclude. One is the need to consider a wider range of dependent variables. As the prime example of this, we need to incorporate into more studies both the level of achievement attained by the student when exposure to material is insured, and also the extent to which the student voluntarily continues with the material — the motivational variable. That is, we need to measure the extent to which what is learned is influenced by how far the student persists in study when not compelled, and how much attention he pays, rather than how much he learns when his exposure is enforced externally. This calls for the kind of experimental situation the student can "tune out" or "cut out" at any point he wants to. I suspect that some of the current contradictions in results reported and predictions made in this conference may be resolved when this differentiation is made.

The final point that I would like to make concerns a difference between the more traditionally oriented verbal-learning studies and the studies with a more applied orientation. There is considerable variation within, as well as between, each of these two classes of studies in the extent to which the strategy of investigation pays conscious attention to selecting for initial study those variables which the experimenter guesses, or has some reason to believe, will account for the most variance in the dependent variables. This is simply the strategy of trying to get at the most important factors first. We have had examples of this within both classes of papers; but there also seems to be a tendency, which is not *necessarily* bad, to become bemused in the more traditional laboratory investigation with a particular independent variable that seems of theoretical interest but does not really account for a very large share of variance. I would like to suggest that, in selecting independent variables for investigation, perhaps a little more conscious attention can be given to the strategy of sequence in which one investigates different independent variables, with particular attention given to how big a difference they seem likely to make.

The problem here is related to the fact that we are the victims of a fashion in statistical logic that is primarily conceived around the null-hypothesis-testing paradigm. This asks how significant variables are (essentially meaning how reliable is the evidence that there is some nonchance difference), but does not as such provide, at least as usually employed, any explicit accounting of the proportion of dependent-variable variance accounted for by a given independent variable. It is true that we do say occasionally when we get one, "Here is a whopping difference," and occasionally we encounter phrases like "small but significant," but there is no very good and widely applied form of analysis that deals directly with the importance (size) of the effects resulting from each factor being manipulated. I think that this lack, until remedied, constitutes a real obstacle to the translation of laboratory research into usefully applicable results, and therefore represents a problem that urgently needs to be resolved in order that the basic purposes of this conference may be ultimately realized.

NOTE

1. The reference is to a talk to the symposium by Dr. William S. Verplanck (University of Tennessee). The talk described work on the use of word association measures as indices of academic success. This material is being proposed for publication elsewhere.

REFERENCES

Cochran, D. L. The effect of practice schedules and perceptual variables on learning from a filmed demonstration. Unpublished doctoral dissertation, Univ. of California, Los Angeles, 1966.

Fairbanks, G., Guttman, N., and Miron, M. S. Effects of time compression of connected speech. *J. Speech and Hearing Disorders*, 1957, *22*, 10–19.

Holland, J. G. Response contingencies in teaching-machine programs. *J. Progr. Instr.*, 1963, *3*, 1–8.

Joint Committee on Programmed Instruction, American Educational Research Association, American Psychological Association, and NEA Department of Audiovisual Instruction. *Recommendations for reporting the effectiveness of programmed instruction materials.* Washington, D.C.: National Education Association, 1966.

Lumsdaine, A. A. Some theoretical and practical problems in programmed instruction. In J. E. Coulson (Ed.), *Programmed Learning and Computer Based Instruction.* New York: Wiley, 1962.

———. Instruments and media of instruction. In N. L. Gage (Ed.), *Handbook of research on teaching.* Chicago: Rand-McNally, 1963.

Lumsdaine, A. A. (Ed.). *Student response in programmed instruction.* Washington, D.C.: National Academy of Sciences, 1961.

Lumsdaine, A. A., and May, M. A. Mass communication and educational media. *Annu. Rev. Psychol.*, 1965, *16*, 475–534.

May, M. A., and Lumsdaine, A. A. *Learning from films.* New Haven: Yale Univ. Press, 1958.